DEAR READER

In this captivating collection, we invite you to explore a realm where art and music entwine, giving life to a vibrant tapestry inspired by the landscape of Taylor's lyrics. From her debut album to "Midnights," each page aims to capture the essence of a song, offering a unique perspective and visual interpretation.

Welcome to a world where every song tells a story, and every story is a testament to the enduring power of Taylor Swift's music.

TABLE OF CONTENTS

TABLE OF CONTENTS

Taylor Swift

Released: October 24th, 2006

"Youthful, Heartfelt, Innocent, Fresh, Authentic"

Tim McGraw

First single released on her debut album
Released: June 19, 2006
Recorded at Quad Studios In Nashville, TN

Did You Know?

In the lyrics, Swift wants her boyfriend to remember all the times they danced to her favorite Tim McGraw song. The song in question, she told CMT, is "Can't Tell Me Nothin'" from McGraw's 2004 album, *Live Like You Were Dying*.

McGraw noted of the song, "It was awesome. I didn't know if I should take it as a compliment, or if I should feel old."

Liz Rose collaborated with Swift in crafting multiple songs for the album, among them this track and "Teardrops on My Guitar."

When Swift headlined at the Nissan Stadium in Nashville during her 2018 Reputation tour, she performed this with help from Tim McGraw and Faith Hill.

Charts & Awards

- Debuted at #60 on the U.S. Billboard Hot Country Songs chart
- Spent 26 weeks on the chart before reaching a peak of #6
- Peaked at #40 on the Hot 100 chart

- Won BMI Country Award for "Award Winning Songs" In 2007
- Won CMT Music Award for "Breakthrough Video of the Year" In 2007

In Taylor's Words

"I wrote Tim McGraw in my freshman year of high school. I got the idea in math class. I was just sitting there, and I started humming this melody. I kind of related it to this situation I was in. I was dating a guy who was about to go off to college. I knew we were going to break up. So I started thinking about all the things that I knew would remind him of me. Surprisingly, the first thing that came to mind was that my favorite country artist is Tim McGraw."

Picture to Burn

Fourth single released on her debut album
Released as a single: February 4th, 2008
Recorded at The Castle Studios In Nashville, TN

Charts & Awards

- Peaked at #3 on the U.S. Billboard Hot Country Songs chart
- Spent 20 weeks on the chart before reaching its peak
- Peaked at #28 on the Hot 100 chart
- Won SESAC Nashville Music Award for "Country Performance Activity Award" In 2008
- Won BMI Country Awards for "Publisher of the Year" and "Award Winning Songs" In 2009

Did You Know?

The song is written in the key of G major, set in common time. The chord progression throughout the entire song, except the bridge, is G-Am-C-D.

The video game Band Hero features this song, along with "Love Story" and "You Belong with Me."

Trey Fanjoy, who had previously collaborated with Swift on music videos, took the directorial reins for "Picture to Burn." Swift noted that they aimed to create a video with an edgy and comical flair, departing from the tone of their earlier joint projects.

Swift performed this as the final song of her main set on all venues of her first headlining concert tour, the *Fearless Tour* (2009-2010).

In Taylor's Words

"I always try to tell the audience that I really do try to be a nice person... but if you break my heart, hurt my feelings, or are really mean to me, I'm going to write a song about you. This song is the perfect example."

Teardrops on my Guitar

Second single released on her debut album
Released as a single: February 13th, 2007
Recorded at The Sound Cottage In Nashville, TN

Did You Know?

This was iTunes #1 selling country single in 2007.

The song was performed as the second surprise song in Nashville, Tennessee, on May 5, 2023, on the on-going *Eras Tour*.

Following its debut as a single, Drew Hardwick, the inspiration behind the song, made efforts to reach out to Swift through voicemails. Despite this, Swift felt too uneasy to return the calls.

Recording for the music video took place on January 9, 2007, at Hume-Fogg High School, where the drama room underwent a transformation to recreate a bedroom setting for the performance scenes.

Charts & Awards

- Spent 27 weeks on the chart before reaching its peak at #13
- Peaked within the top 10 of four airplay charts—Hot Country Songs, Mainstream Top 40, Adult Pop Songs, and Adult Contemporary
- Nominated for MTV Video Music Awards for "Best New Artist" in 2008
- Won SESAC Nashville Music Awards for "Recurrent Country Performance Activity Awards" in 2008

In Taylor's Words

"This is a song that I wrote about a guy who went to school with me, and I was that 'friend,' you know, that girl who's your friend. And, you know, he had this awesome girlfriend who he would tell me about every single day. And, you know, I was that girl that he would go to and be like, 'what should I get her for Valentine's Day? I have to make this Valentine's Day so awesome! It's her birthday, what should I do? What would the perfect gift for a girl be?' And of course I'd give him, like, the most awesome ideas, awesome plans, like, I would want them! And, you know, it didn't end up, like, in the end of the chick-flick where they get together in the end. It didn't happen like that."

A Place in This World

Fourth track on her debut album
Released: October 24th, 2007
Recorded at The Castle Studios In Nashville, TN

Charts & Awards

- "A Place In This World" does not have a charting history on the Billboard charts
- To date, this song has been streamed online 35,528,541 times

Did You Know?

At the age of thirteen, Swift penned "A Place in This World" in November 2003.

Taylor performed this song during the *Reputation Stadium Tour* as a surprise song.

Initially, Taylor contemplated naming her debut album "A Place in This World" but eventually opted to name it after herself.

This song is written In the musical key A with a tempo of 115 beats per minute.

In Taylor's Words

"It was tough trying to find out how I was going to get where I wanted to go. I knew where I wanted to be, but I just didn't know how to get there. I'm really happy this song is on the album, because I feel like I finally figured it out."

Cold As You

Fifth track on her debut album
Released: October 24th, 2006
Recorded at Darkhouse Recording in Franklin, TN

Charts & Awards

- "Cold as You" does not have a charting history on the Billboard charts
- To date, this song has been streamed online 36,757,928 times

Did You Know?

This song is written In the musical key F with a tempo of 176 beats per minute.

On April 28, 2023, during The Eras Tour in Atlanta, Georgia, Swift delivered a surprise performance of "Cold as You" as the first song.

Within the lyric booklet of her debut album, she discreetly embedded a hidden message in every song. The hidden message within this specific track is: "It's time to let go."

"Cold As You" was the starting point for Taylor's consistent theme of featuring emotionally vulnerable ballads as the fifth track on each of her albums.

In Taylor's Words

"I wrote this song with Liz, and I think the lyrics to this song are some of the best we've ever written. It's about that moment where you realize someone isn't at all who you thought they were, and that you've been trying to make excuses for someone who doesn't deserve them. And that some people are just never going to love you. We were halfway through writing this when I started singing 'And now that I'm sitting here thinking it through, I've never been anywhere cold as you'."

The Outside

Sixth track on her debut album
Released: October 24th, 2006
Recorded at Darkhouse Recording in Franklin, TN

Did You Know?

Taylor penned the lyrics to this song when she was just 12 years old about her experience not fitting in with other girls at school.

Within the lyric booklet of her debut album, she discreetly embedded a hidden message in every song. The hidden message within this specific track is: "You are not alone."

This song is written In the musical key F with a tempo of 113 beats per minute.

Taylor amusingly noted in her journal entries that she finished the track on Valentine's Day because she had "nothing better to do".

Charts & Awards

- "The Outside" does not have a charting history on the Billboard charts
- To date, this song has been streamed online 25,242,018 times

In Taylor's Words

"A lot of times back then when I was 12 or 13, I would write songs about relationships, when I wasn't in relationships, because I would look at other people and try to observe what they were going through. But in the case of "The Outside," I was writing exactly what I saw. I was writing from pain. And I've always felt so lucky, because I've never needed an escape like drinking or drugs or anything like that to escape from the bad days. Music has always been that escape for me."

Tied Together With a Smile

Seventh track on her debut album
Released: October 24th, 2006
Recorded at Darkhouse Recording in Franklin, TN

Charts & Awards

- "Tied Together With a Smile" does not have a charting history on the Billboard charts
- To date, this song has been streamed online 28,455,469 times

Did You Know?

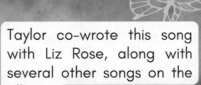

Taylor co-wrote this song with Liz Rose, along with several other songs on the album.

Within the lyric booklet of her debut album, she discreetly embedded a hidden message in every song. The hidden message within this specific track is: "You are loved."

This song is written In the musical key D with a tempo of 146 beats per minute.

In Taylor's Words

"I wrote 'Tied Together With A Smile' about one of my friends, who is this beauty queen, pageant princess — a gorgeous, popular girl in high school. Every guy wanted to be with her, every girl wanted to be her. I wrote that song the day I found out she had an eating disorder. There are a couple songs on the album like that, that are just watching other people and making observations. But most of the songs on the album are about actual people that have been in my life."

Stay Beautiful

Eigth track on her debut album
Released: October 24th, 2006
Recorded at The Castle Studios In Nashville, TN

Did You Know?

Taylor worked with producer Nathan Chapman to produce her entire debut album.

This song is written In the musical key G sharp with a tempo of 132 beats per minute.

Within the lyric booklet of her debut album, she discreetly embedded a hidden message in every song. The hidden message within this specific track is: "Shake n bake." Taylor has never explained its meaning.

Charts & Awards

- "Stay Beautiful" does not have a charting history on the Billboard charts
- To date, this song has been streamed online 30,157,022 times

In Taylor's Words

"After hearing my songs, a lot of people ask me, 'How many boyfriends have you HAD?' And I always tell them that more of my songs come from observation than actual experience. In other words, you don't have to date someone to write a song about them. This is a song I wrote about a guy I never dated! Wow, right? Haha. This song is about a guy I thought was cute, and never really talked to him much. But something about him inspired this song, just watching him."

Should've Said No

Fifth single released on her debut album
Released as a single: May 18th, 2008
Recorded at The Castle Studios In Nashville, TN

Did You Know?

She sang the song as the opening act to *Rascal Flatts*' 2008 tour.

She crafted the song a mere two days before the album's mastering and publication, and, in a collaborative effort with producer Nathan Chapman, they worked through the night to finalize the track.

Swift delivered a live performance of "Should've Said No" at the 43rd Academy of Country Music Awards, and this rendition was recorded and subsequently released as the official music video.

Charts & Awards

- Peaked at #1 on the U.S. Billboard Hot Country Songs chart
- Peaked at #33 on the Hot 100 chart
- Certified platinum by the Recording Industry Association of America in 2009

- Won at BMI Country Awards for "BMI Award" in 2009

In Taylor's Words

"Just being a human being, I've realized that before every big problem you create for yourself, before every huge mess you have to clean up, there was a crucial moment where you could've just said no. This is a song I wrote about a guy who never should have cheated on me."

Mary's Song (Oh My My My)

Tenth track on her debut album
Released: October 24th, 2006
Recorded at The Castle Studios In Nashville, TN

Did You Know?

Taylor has performed "Mary's Song (Oh My My My)" a total of 22 times. During her early career as a tour opening act for prominent country music stars, she often featured the song in her setlist to promote her debut album. Nevertheless, she hasn't performed the song since 2008.

Within the lyric booklet of her debut album, she discreetly embedded a hidden message in every song. The hidden message within this specific track is: "Sometimes love is forever."

At the age of 16, Swift demonstrated a remarkable ability to convey the depth and complexity of a lifelong partnership through her songwriting. The lyrics are brimming with emotion and vivid imagery, allowing listeners to feel as though they are experiencing the moments with Mary and Billy firsthand.

This song is written In the musical key D with a tempo of 75 beats per minute.

Charts & Awards

- "Mary's Song" does not have a charting history on the Billboard charts
- To date, this song has been streamed online 38,782,980 times

In Taylor's Words

"I wrote this song about a couple who lived next door to us. They'd been married forever and they came over one night for dinner, and were just so cute. They were talking about how they fell in love and got married, and how they met when they were just little kids. I thought it was so sweet, because you can go to the grocery store and read the tabloids, and see who's breaking up and cheating on each other (or just listen to some of my songs, haha). But it was really comforting to know that all I had to do was go home and look next door to see a perfect example of forever."

Our Song

Third single released on her debut album
Released as a single: September 9th, 2007
Recorded at The Castle Studios In Nashville, TN

Did You Know?

This song marked the moment when Swift, at the age of seventeen, became the youngest individual to independently write and perform a Hot Country Songs number one hit.

The music video for "Our Song" showcases a variety of outfits that are distinctly tied to mid-2000s fashion, including elements like pink lip gloss, layered tank tops paired with Soffe shorts, and black elbow-length arm warmers.

During the Country Music Association Awards on November 7, 2007, Swift delivered a performance of the song and was honored with the Horizon Award, recognizing her as the best new artist of the year.

Charts & Awards

- Peaked at #1 on the U.S. Billboard Hot Country Songs chart
- Peaked at #16 on the Hot 100 chart
- Certified four times platinum by the Recording Industry Association of America in 2014

- Won at BMI Country Awards for "BMI Award" in 2008
- Won at CMT Music Awards for "Female Video of the Year" and "Video of the Year" In 2008

In Taylor's Words

I wrote this song in my freshman year of high school, for my ninth grade talent show. So I was sitting there thinking, "I've gotta write a song that's gonna relate to everyone in the talent show, and it's gotta be upbeat." And at that time, I was dating a guy, and we didn't have a song. So I went ahead and wrote us one, and I played it at the talent show at the end of the year. And months later, people would come up to me, and they're like, "I loved that song that you played -- 'Our Song.'" And then they'd start singing lines of it back to me. And they'd only heard it once, so I thought, "There must be something here!"

I'm Only Me When I'm With You

Twelfth track on the deluxe copy of her debut album
Released: November 6th, 2007
Recorded at The Castle Studios In Nashville, TN

Did You Know?

This song was co-written and produced by Taylor alongside Robert Ellis Orrall and Angelo Petraglia.

It is speculated that this song is about Taylor's friend Abigail Anderson.

Released on March 3, 2008, the music video is a montage of home videos featuring Taylor with her family, Abigail, and various friends.

This song is written In the musical key G sharp with a tempo of 144 beats per minute.

"I'm Only Me When I'm With You" is certified Platinum by the RIAA.

Charts & Awards

- "I'm Only Me When I'm With You" does not have a charting history on the Billboard charts
- To date, this song has been streamed online 43,996,223 times

In Taylor's Words

"The 'I'm Only Me When I'm With You' video was something I edited on my laptop. And it was just footage I had from being on the road, when I was like 16 or 17. We were all travelling on one bus. Like the whole band, me, my mom. It was a huge moment when we upgraded to two buses, and we had a girl's bus and a guy's bus. For a long time, it was just like, people cram together on this bus. It was hilarious, and fun, and a lot of those moments are captured in this video, which was just stuff that I had filmed on my camera. So, it's funny to go back and look at it. I never feel like I wasn't allowed to be a teenager just because I was in this business. Like, I definitely still got to have that."

Invisible

Thirteenth track on the deluxe copy of her debut album
Released: November 6th, 2007
Recorded at The Tracking Room in Nashville, TN

Did You Know?

Among her debut record's tracks, "Invisible" stands out as one of Taylor's favorites, even though it eventually became a bonus track.

Taylor has performed "Invisible" a total of thirteen times, frequently including it in her performances to promote her debut album.

She treated the audience to an acoustic rendition of "Invisible" as a surprise song during her "Reputation Stadium Tour" in Tampa, Florida, on August 14, 2018.

"Invisible" is certified Gold by the RIAA.

Charts & Awards

- "Invisible" does not have a charting history on the Billboard charts
- To date, this song has been streamed online 30,277,014 times

In Taylor's Words

"Then there's the song "Invisible," which is about the son of my parents' friends. They were always at my house and their son was my age, and he would always tell me about other girls he liked. I felt, well, invisible. Obviously. So I wrote that song about it, and it was a bonus track on my first album."

A Perfectly Good Heart

Fourteenth track on the deluxe copy of her debut album
Released: November 6th, 2007
Recorded at Abtrax Recording in Nashville, TN

Did You Know?

Taylor wrote this track when she was just fourteen years old.

She co-wrote the track with Brett James and Troy Verges.

Taylor has performed "A Perfectly Good Heart" almost 40 times.

Charts & Awards

- "A Perfectly Good Heart" does not have a charting history on the Billboard charts
- To date, this song has been streamed online 21,890,683 times

In Taylor's Words

"I thought it would be really important to put this on the album because, you know, it's just really innocent. It's about getting your heart broken for the first time and not understanding why somebody would wanna do that. It's before the mind games come in to play, before your second or third relationship, where you don't know anything but trusting people. And this song is about getting that trust betrayed."

FEARLESS

(TAYLOR'S VERSION)

RELEASED: NOVEMBER 11th, 2008
RECLAIMED: APRIL 9th, 2021

"Vulnerable, Romantic, Empowering, Nostalgic, Timeless"

FEARLESS

DID YOU KNOW?

She co-wrote the song with her frequent songwriting partner at the time, Liz Rose, but reached out to songwriter Hillary Lindsey, best known for her work on Carrie Underwood's hit "Jesus, Take The Wheel," to join in and help bring the composition to completion.

Crafted in the key of F major, Swift's vocals cover a range of two octaves, extending from F3 to C5. The song follows the chord progression of F-C-G-B♭.

On November 10, 2008, Taylor made her debut televised performance of "Fearless" on the Late Show with David Letterman.

Fifth single released from her second album
Released as a single: January 3rd, 2010
Reclaimed: April 9th, 2021
Recorded: Blackbird Studios in Nashville, TN

CHARTS & AWARDS

- Debuted at #71 and peaked at #9 on the Billboard Hot 100 Chart
- Debuted at #14 on the Billboard Hot Country Chart
- Certified platinum by the RIAA
- Won at the BMI Awards for "Award-Winning Songs" and "Publisher of the Year" In 2010

IN TAYLOR'S WORDS

"This is a song about the fearlessness of falling in love. No matter how many break up songs you write, no matter how many times you get hurt, you will always fall in love again. When I wrote 'Fearless,' I wasn't dating anyone. I wasn't even in the beginning stages of dating anybody. I really was all by myself out on tour and I got this idea for a song about the best first date. I think sometimes when you're writing love songs, you don't write them about what you're going through at the moment, you write about what you wish you had. So, this song is about the best first date I haven't had yet."

FIFTEEN

DID YOU KNOW?

Swift partnered with electronics retailer Best Buy for a program called @15, to donate forty concert tickets and a guitar autographed by Swift to local teen-oriented charity groups, such as chapters of Boys & Girls Clubs of America and Big Brothers Big Sisters

At the 51st Annual Grammy Awards, Taylor Swift debuted the song "Fifteen" in a duet with singer Miley Cyrus.

Directed by Roman White, the music video for the song was helmed by the same director of "You Belong With Me." Both Abigail and Taylor make appearances in the video, depicting the two friends navigating through various situations of teenage life.

Fourth single released from her second album
Released as a single: August 30, 2009
Reclaimed: April 9th, 2021
Recorded: Blackbird Studios in Nashville, TN

CHARTS & AWARDS

- Debuted at #79 and peaked at #23 on the Billboard Hot 100 Chart
- Peaked at #14 on the Billboard Hot Country Chart
- Certified platinum x2 by the RIAA
- Nominated for "Best Female Video" at the MTV Video Music Awards in 2010
- Won "Choice Country Song" at the Teen Choice Awards in 2010

IN TAYLOR'S WORDS

"I wrote this around the story line of my best friend from high school, Abigail. I started everything with the line, 'Abigail gave everything she had to a boy who changed his mind' and wrote everything else from that point, almost backwards. I just decided I really wanted to tell that story about our first year of high school because I felt in my freshman year, I grew up more than any year in my life so far. The thing about high school is, you don't know anything. You don't know anything, but you think you know everything."

LOVE STORY

Initially, the song received a lukewarm response from both her record company and parents. However, she persisted in championing it, feeling as if as she had something to prove.

In the creation of the "Love Story" music video, Taylor envisioned a period piece inspired by the Medieval, Renaissance, and Regency periods. Her goal was to craft a timeless narrative that could unfold seamlessly in the 1700s, 1800s, or even 2008.

"Love Story" was the concluding performance on Taylor's second concert tour, the "Speak Now World Tour" (2011-2012). In these performances, Taylor floated over the crowd while donning a captivating gold princess gown.

First single released from her second album
Released as a single: September 15, 2008
Reclaimed: April 9th, 2021
Recorded: Blackbird Studios in Nashville, TN

CHARTS & AWARDS

- Peaked at #4 on the Billboard Hot 100 Chart
- Peaked at #1 on the Billboard Hot Country Chart
- Certified platinum by the RIAA
- Nominated for "Video of the Year" at the Academy of Country Music Awards in 2009
- Nominated for "Choice Love Song" at the Teen Choice Awards In 2009
- Won "Video of the Year" at the CMT Music Awards in 2009
- Won "Song of the Year" at the BMI Country Awards in 2009

IN TAYLOR'S WORDS

"This is a song I wrote when I was dating a guy who wasn't exactly the popular choice. His situation was a little complicated, but I didn't care. I started this song with the line, 'This love is difficult, but it's real.' When I wrote the ending to this song, I felt like it was the ending every girl wants to go with her love story. It's the ending that I want. You want a guy who doesn't care what anyone thinks, what anyone says."

HEY STEPHEN

DID YOU KNOW?

Fourth track of her second album
Released as a single: October 21, 2008
Reclaimed: April 9th, 2021
Recorded: Prime Recording in Nashville, TN

The finger snaps at the end of the upright-bass-driven groove were provided by Martina McBride's children. Taylor enlisted the kids' participation during the recording session, held at the studio of John McBride, Martina McBride's husband.

She sang "Hey Stephen" as a surprise song on *The Eras Tour* show on May 14, 2023, in Philadelphia.

The source of inspiration for the song was Stephen Barker Liles, a member of *Love and Theft*, with whom she shared a cordial relationship. Following the release of "Fearless", Swift sent him a text about the song and notes she enjoyed incorporating a personal confession into the album.

CHARTS & AWARDS

- Peaked at #94 on the Billboard Hot 100 Chart
- (Taylor's Version) Peaked at #28 on the Billboard Hot Country Chart In 2021
- Certified Gold by RIAA

- To date, the original version has been streamed 47,363,486 times
- (Taylor's Version) has been streamed 75,022,432 times

IN TAYLOR'S WORDS

"It's about someone who I've always been friends with and always kind of had a thing for... and he doesn't know. It's always fun for me to put something on the album that is personal. Something I know I'm going to have to deal with when the record comes out."

For her debut televised rendition of "White Horse" at the 2008 American Music Awards on November 23, 2008, Taylor graced the stage in a white evening gown, seated on a floral-patterned couch.

In a post that has since been removed from her label's website, Taylor confessed that she initially had no intention of including this song on the album. She had planned to save it for her third album, "Speak Now," as she believed she had already adequately conveyed the emotional depth on the current record.

Directed by Trey Fanjoy, the music video for the song showcases Swift revisiting memories with her ex-boyfriend. It unfolds the narrative of her discovering his infidelity after ending their relationship over a phone call.

WHITE HORSE

Second single of her second album
Released as a single: December 8th, 2008
Reclaimed: April 9th, 2021
Recorded: Blackbird Studio in Nashville, TN

CHARTS & AWARDS

- Peaked at #13 on the Billboard Hot 100 Chart
- (Taylor's Version) Peaked at #29 on the Billboard Hot Country Chart In 2021
- Certified Double Platinum by RIAA
- At the 52nd Grammy Awards, this single won "Best Country Song" and "Best Female Country Vocal Performance"
- (Taylor's Version) has been streamed 106,389,439 times

IN TAYLOR'S WORDS

"When we're little girls, our parents read us storybooks. And we think that Prince Charming's gonna come along, is gonna have a white cape on, is going to put us on a pedestal. And the bad guy wears black and we always know who that guy is. But what we don't realize is that, in reality, the bad guy is wearing jeans. And he's cute. And he's charming, makes you laugh, and you believe him. You think he's the good guy. Then, you realize he's not."

YOU BELONG WITH ME

DID YOU KNOW?

Inspired by a conversation she accidentally overheard between a member of her touring band and his girlfriend, Swift teamed up with Liz Rose to compose the song. The lyrics vividly portray a narrator's unrequited love for a boy who remains unnoticed by his girlfriend.

At the end of the chorus, there is a three-note drop covering a brief distance (B-A#), followed by a larger drop (A#-D#). Musicologists Nate Sloan and Charlie Harding have coined this three-note melodic motif as the "T-Drop," a recurring element in many of Swift's subsequent songs.

It ranked first on *Teen Vogue*'s 2020 list of the "91 Best Songs About Unrequited Love".

She took the stage to perform the song at the 2009 MTV Video Music Awards on September 13, 2009—the very day when Kanye West famously interrupted her award acceptance speech.

Third single of her second album
Released as a single: April 20, 2009
Reclaimed: April 9th, 2021
Recorded: Blackbird Studio in Nashville, TN

CHARTS & AWARDS

- Peaked at #2 on the Billboard Hot 100 Chart
- (Taylor's Version) Peaked at #16 on the Billboard Hot Country Chart In 2021
- Certified Platinum x7 by RIAA
- Nominated for "Video of the Year" at the CMT Music Awards
- Nominated for "Record of the Year", "Song of the Year", and "Best Female Pop Vocal" at the 52nd Grammy Awards in 2010
- Won "Best Female Video" at the MTV Video Music Awards In 2009
- Won "Song of the Year" at the BMI Country Awards in 2009
- (Taylor's Version) has been streamed 492,903,609 times

IN TAYLOR'S WORDS

"This song is basically about wanting someone who is with this girl who doesn't appreciate him at all. Basically like 'girl-next-door-itis.' You like this guy who you have for your whole life, and you know him better than she does but somehow the popular girl gets the guy every time."

BREATHE

DID YOU KNOW?

Taylor delivered the first live performance of "Breathe" almost a decade after its release on August 18, 2018, in Miami Gardens, Florida, as part of the *Reputation Stadium Tour*.

It is speculated that the mentioned best friend in the song is Emily Poe, who formerly served as a fiddle player in Taylor's band but departed when she commenced law school.

This ballad has a tempo of 72 beats per minute. It is written in the key of D flat major, and with vocals that span one octave (G3 to B4).

After falling in love with Colbie Caillait's Album, Swift reached out to her management, inquiring about the possibility of collaborating with Caillat. They confirmed her availability, coinciding with an upcoming concert in Nashville, Tennessee.

Featuring Colbie Caillat
Seventh track of her second album
Released: October 21, 2008
Reclaimed: April 9th, 2021
Recorded: Blackbird Studio in Nashville, TN

CHARTS & AWARDS

- Peaked at #87 on the Billboard Hot 100 Chart
- (Taylor's Version) Peaked at #34 on the Billboard Hot Country Chart In 2021
- Certified Gold by RIAA
- Nominated for "Best Pop Collaboration with Vocals" at the 52nd Grammy Awards In 2010

IN TAYLOR'S WORDS

"It was total therapy because I came in and I was like, 'Look, one of my best friends, I'm gonna have to not see anymore and is not gonna be part of what I do. It's the hardest thing to go through. It's crazy listening to the song because you would think it's about a relationship, and it's really about losing a friend, and having a fallout."

TELL ME WHY

Eighth track of her second album
Released: October 21, 2008
Reclaimed: April 9th, 2021
Recorded: Blackbird Studio in Nashville, TN

DID YOU KNOW?

Taylor played the song as a surprise during *The RED Tour* In 2013. She did not play the song again live for 10 years until *The Eras Tour* In 2023.

This ballad has a tempo of 100 beats per minute. It is written in the key of G.

Taylor included a hidden message for each song within the lyric booklet of each album until 2014. The hidden message in this specific song is: "Guess I was fooled by your smile."

CHARTS & AWARDS

- (Taylor's Version) Peaked at #41 on the Billboard Hot Country Chart In 2021
- To date, the original version has been streamed 30,191,566 times
- (Taylor's Version) has been streamed 48,262,248 times

IN TAYLOR'S WORDS

"I'd been talking to a guy I've never 'officially' dated. Sometimes it's the hardest thing when you have all these dreams of dating them, and you're getting close, but it doesn't work out. He would say things that would make me go, 'Did you just say that?' It bothered me so much because he would say one thing and do another, do one thing and say another. Because he didn't know what he wanted, he would just play all these mind games."

DID YOU KNOW?

This song has a tempo of 134 beats per minute. It is written in the key of F sharp.

Penned by Taylor in April 2007 and co-produced with Nathan Chapman, this song drew inspiration from an ex-boyfriend who turned out to be exactly opposite of Taylor's impressions.

A remix version was released for an episode of CSI: Crime Scene Investigation, featuring Swift in a guest appearance.

Taylor included a hidden message for each song within the lyric booklet of each album until 2014. The hidden message in this specific song is: " She can have you."

YOU'RE NOT SORRY

Ninth track of her second album
Released: October 21, 2008
Reclaimed: April 9th, 2021
Recorded: Blackbird Studio in Nashville, TN

CHARTS & AWARDS

- Peaked at #11 on the Billboard Hot 100
- (Taylor's Version) Peaked at #40 on the Billboard Hot Country Chart In 2021
- Certified Platinum by RIAA
- To date, the original version has been streamed 44,651,799 times
- (Taylor's Version) has been streamed 60,066,941 times

IN TAYLOR'S WORDS

"It is about this guy who turned out to not be who I thought he was. He came across as Prince Charming. Well, it turned out Prince Charming had a lot of secrets that he didn't tell me about. And one by one, I would figure them out. I would find out who he really was. I wrote this when I was at the breaking point of, 'You know what? Don't even think that you can keep on hurting me.' It was to a point where I had to walk away."

THE WAY I LOVED YOU

DID YOU KNOW?

Tenth track of her second album
Released: November 11th, 2008
Reclaimed: April 9th, 2021
Recorded: Blackbird Studio in Nashville, TN

This song has a tempo of 161 beats per minute. It is written in the key of F.

In the process of writing for Fearless in 2007, Taylor spontaneously reached out to country singer-songwriter John Rich and requested his collaboration on "The Way I Loved You."

Taylor included a hidden message for each song within the lyric booklet of each album until 2014. The hidden message in this specific song is: "We can't go back."

CHARTS & AWARDS

- Peaked at #72 on the Billboard Hot 100
- (Taylor's Version) Peaked at #24 on the Billboard Hot Country Chart In 2021
- To date, the original version has been streamed 66,846,742 times
- (Taylor's Version) has been streamed 345,800,841 times

IN TAYLOR'S WORDS

"It was always one of my goals to write with John. I had heard so many things about him. I just wanted to see what it was like to get into a room with him because I know I'm a very opinionated writer and I knew he was a very opinionated writer. So I knew this was either going to be the best thing in the world or was just going to be a complete train wreck."

FOREVER & ALWAYS

Eleventh track of her second album
Released: November 11th, 2008
Reclaimed: April 9th, 2021
Recorded: Blackbird Studio in Nashville, TN

DID YOU KNOW?

This song has a tempo of 128 beats per minute. It is written in the key of A sharp.

Taylor confirms that "Forever & Always" was inspired by her breakup with singer Joe Jonas. on The Ellen DeGeneres Show, she revealed him as "the boy who broke up with me over the phone in 25 seconds when I was 18".

Taylor first performed "Forever & Always" during her concert for the 2009 Dick Clark's New Year's Rockin' Eve, as part of a medley with "Picture to Burn", "Love Story", and "Change", on December 31, 2008.

Taylor included a hidden message for each song within the lyric booklet of each album until 2014. The hidden message in this specific song is: "If you play these games we're both going to lose."

CHARTS & AWARDS

- Peaked at #34 on the Billboard Hot 100
- (Taylor's Version) Peaked at #12 on the Billboard Hot Country Chart In 2021
- To date, the original version has been streamed 51,756,574 times
- (Taylor's Version) has been streamed 92,193,917 times

IN TAYLOR'S WORDS

"It's about watching somebody fade away in a relationship. They said they were going to be with you forever, that they loved you, and then something changed in the relationship and you don't know what it is, but you're watching them slowly drift. That emotion of rejection, for me, usually starts out sad and then gets mad. This song starts with this pretty melody that's easy to sing along with, then in the end I'm basically screaming it because I'm so mad. I'm really proud of that."

THE BEST DAY

Twelfth track of her second album
Released: November 11th, 2008
Reclaimed: April 9th, 2021
Recorded: Blackbird Studio in Nashville, TN

DID YOU KNOW?

This song has a tempo of 125 beats per minute. It is written in the key of C sharp.

Taylor debuted "The Best Day" at the initial two concerts of her *Fearless Tour* in Evansville, Indiana (April 2009). However, she had to remove the poignant song from the setlist because her mother would burst into tears backstage every time she heard it.

Taylor first performed "Forever & Always" during her concert for the 2009 Dick Clark's New Year's Rockin' Eve, as part of a medley with "Picture to Burn", "Love Story", and "Change", on December 31, 2008.

Taylor included a hidden message for each song within the lyric booklet of each album until 2014. The hidden message in this specific song is: "God bless Andrea Swift."

CHARTS & AWARDS

- Peaked at #56 on the Billboard Hot Country Songs Chart
- (Taylor's Version) Peaked at #45 on the Billboard Hot Country Chart In 2021
- Won "Best Family Feature" at the 2021 CMT Awards
- Certified Gold by RIAA
- (Taylor's Version) has been streamed 43,664,617 times

IN TAYLOR'S WORDS

"I wrote this song on the road and didn't tell my mom about it. I decided that I was going to keep it a secret and give it to her as a surprise for Christmas. I wrote it in the summer and then recorded it secretly with the band in the studio. After it was done, I synched the song up to all these home videos of her, and my family. She didn't even realize it was me singing until halfway through the song! She didn't have any idea that I could possibly write and record a song without her knowing about it. When she finally got it, she just started bawling her eyes out."

CHANGE

The song was originally named "Champions Tonight" and was later changed to "Change".

"Change" reflects Taylor's dreams and ambitions within the music industry, despite being under contract with the smallest record label in Nashville at the time.

After starting the song, Taylor allowed the track to rest, anticipating a pivotal moment in her life to serve as its conclusion. This moment arrived in 2007 when she secured the "Horizon Award" at the CMAs.

Thirteenth track of her second album
Released: August 8th, 2008
Reclaimed: April 9th, 2021
Recorded: Blackbird Studio in Nashville, TN

CHARTS & AWARDS

It was included on the *AT&T* Team USA Soundtrack for the 2008 Summer Olympics. All proceeds from the song were donated to Team USA.

- Peaked at #10 on the Billboard Hot 100 Chart
- Certified Gold by RIAA
- To date, the original version has been streamed 25,921,013 times
- (Taylor's Version) has been streamed 37,692,037 times

Taylor made her debut televised performance of "Change" at the 2010 Academy of Country Music Awards, accompanied by a teenage choir. Taylor held the final note for 15 seconds and then crowd-surfed.

IN TAYLOR'S WORDS

"At one point, I began to understand that it would be harder for me on a smaller record label to get to the places and accomplish the things that artists were accomplishing on bigger record labels. I realized that I wouldn't get favors pulled for me because there weren't any other artists on the label to pull favors from. It was going to be an uphill climb and all that I had to encourage me was the hope that someday things would change. That things would be different. After so many times of just saying that to myself over and over, I finally wrote it down in a song."

JUMP THEN FALL

DID YOU KNOW?

First bonus track on "Fearless Platinum Edition"
Released: October 26th, 2009
Reclaimed: April 9th, 2021
Recorded: Blackbird Studio in Nashville, TN

Taylor played this song for the first time at her first-ever stadium show in 2010 during the "Fearless Tour" at Gillette Stadium In Foxborough, MA.

It found its place on the soundtrack of the film *Valentine's Day*, a movie in which Taylor has a starring role.

This song has a tempo of 125 beats per minute. It is written in the key of C sharp.

The lyrics of the song convey a comforting message from Taylor to a boy she admires. She assures him she'll stay, expressing her commitment to stand by him through challenging times.

CHARTS & AWARDS

- Peaked at #10 on the Billboard Hot 100 Chart
- Certified Gold by RIAA
- To date, the original version has been streamed 24,531,017 times
- (Taylor's Version) has been streamed 46,322,596 times

IN TAYLOR'S WORDS

"It's probably the happiest, bounciest, most fun song to drive down the street listening to. It's one of my favorites on the Platinum Edition. It's just really fun and happy and takes me back to a good place."

UNTOUCHABLE

Second bonus track on "Fearless Platinum Edition"
Released: October 26th, 2009
Reclaimed: April 9th, 2021
Recorded: Blackbird Studio in Nashville, TN

DID YOU KNOW?

Taylor first performed "Untouchable" at her show for "Live From Clear Channel Stripped" in 2008, and later again at Saturday Night Live in 2009

Following this, Taylor didn't sing the song again for 12 years. On November 25, 2023, she played it on piano as a surprise song, in São Paulo on *The Eras Tour*.

Originally composed by the rock band "Luna Halo", Taylor received a co-writing credit for her version as she made significant alterations to the melody and verses.

This song has a tempo of 200 beats per minute. It is written in the key of F.

CHARTS & AWARDS

- Peaked at #19 on the Billboard Hot 100 Chart
- To date, the original version has been streamed 21,670,614, times
- (Taylor's Version) has been streamed 56,501,564 times

COME IN WITH THE RAIN

DID YOU KNOW?

In addition to "Should've Said No," "White Horse," "You're Not Sorry," and "The Other Side Of The Door", There is speculation that "Come In With The Rain" was inspired by Taylor's high school romance with Sam Armstrong.

This song has a tempo of 144 beats per minute. It is written in the key of D.

Taylor released journal entries alongside her seventh studio album, "Lover", which revealed doodles featuring lyrics from "Come In With The Rain," dated October 12th, 2006.

Taylor included a hidden message for each song within the lyric booklet of each album until 2014. The hidden message in this specific song is: "Won't admit that I wish you;d come back."

Third bonus track on "Fearless Platinum Edition"
Released: October 26th, 2009
Reclaimed: April 9th, 2021
Recorded: Blackbird Studio in Nashville, TN

CHARTS & AWARDS

- Peaked at #30 on the Billboard Hot 100 Chart
- To date, the original version has been streamed 16,066,868 times
- (Taylor's Version) has been streamed 34,203,090 times

IN TAYLOR'S WORDS

"The six new songs on the Fearless [Platinum Edition] are songs that I either recorded and wrote really recently, wrote maybe a year ago and almost put on Fearless but decided not to for one reason or another, or are songs that I wrote when I was 14/15 and re-recorded recently. It's a good mixture of songs from different time periods throughout my life. When I make an album, I always have a general theme for it. And when I hear songs, or go back and listen to old ones, there are some that I know fit in with the theme."

SUPERSTAR

Fourth bonus track on "Fearless Platinum Edition"
Released: October 26th, 2009
Reclaimed: April 9th, 2021
Recorded: Blackbird Studio in Nashville, TN

DID YOU KNOW?

At some point in 2005, Taylor released a digital EP called "Majorly Indie Demos" that Included the demos of "SuperStar" and "We Were Happy" were on it.

This song has a tempo of 172 beats per minute. It is written in the key of D.

"SuperStar" revolves around Taylor's admiration for her celebrity crush. Despite being aware that she's just one among many fans, she still envisions a scenario where he reciprocates the same feelings.

Taylor included a hidden message for each song within the lyric booklet of each album until 2014. The hidden message in this specific song is: "I'll never tell."

CHARTS & AWARDS

- Peaked at #26 on the Billboard Hot 100 Chart
- To date, the original version has been streamed 13,241,119 times
- (Taylor's Version) has been streamed 30,782,659 times

IN TAYLOR'S WORDS

"The six new songs on the Fearless [Platinum Edition] are songs that I either recorded and wrote really recently, wrote maybe a year ago and almost put on Fearless but decided not to for one reason or another, or are songs that I wrote when I was 14/15 and re-recorded recently. It's a good mixture of songs from different time periods throughout my life. When I make an album, I always have a general theme for it. And when I hear songs, or go back and listen to old ones, there are some that I know fit in with the theme."

THE OTHER SIDE OF THE DOOR

DID YOU KNOW?

In addition to "Should've Said No," "White Horse," "You're Not Sorry," and "Come in with the Rain", There is speculation that "The Other Side of the Door" was inspired by Taylor's high school romance with Sam Armstrong.

This song has a tempo of 164 beats per minute. It is written in the key of E.

Taylor debuted "The Other Side Of The Door" 14 years after its release during her sixth headlining concert tour, *The Eras Tour*, making it the first surprise song in her Atlanta show on April 28, 2023.

Taylor included a hidden message for each song within the lyric booklet of each album until 2014. The hidden message in this specific song is: "What I was really thinking when I slammed the door."

Fifth bonus track on "Fearless Platinum Edition"
Released: October 26th, 2009
Reclaimed: April 9th, 2021
Recorded: Blackbird Studio in Nashville, TN

CHARTS & AWARDS

- Peaked at #23 on the Billboard Hot 100 Chart
- To date, the original version has been streamed 14,318,820 times
- (Taylor's Version) has been streamed 59,693,114 times

IN TAYLOR'S WORDS

"'The Other Side Of The Door' is one of my favorites listening to because it talks about when you're in a fight with someone you're in a relationship with and you slam the door and you're like [acts dramatic], 'Leave me alone, I never wanna talk to you again, I hate you!' But what you really mean is, 'Please go buy me flowers and beg that I forgive you and stand at the door and don't leave for three days.' It's all about the dramatics of relationships where you're like [acts dramatic], 'I hate you so much, I never wanna talk to you again', and you mean the opposite. So that's a fun one that I'm really excited about getting out there."

TODAY WAS A FAIRYTALE

Twentieth track on "Fearless (Taylor's Version)"
Released: January 19th, 2010
Reclaimed: April 9th, 2021
Recorded: Prime Recording in Nashville, TN

DID YOU KNOW?

In addition to "Should've Said No," "White Horse," "You're Not Sorry," and "Come in with the Rain", There is speculation that "The Other Side of the Door" was inspired by Taylor's high school romance with Sam Armstrong.

This song has a tempo of 158 beats per minute. It is written in the key of G. It follows the chord progression G-C-Em-D.

"This song was originally written for a movie Taylor acted in, *Valentine's Day* that premiered in 2009.

Swift performed a medley, which included the song, at the 52nd Grammy Awards.

CHARTS & AWARDS

- Peaked at #2 on the Billboard Hot 100 Chart
- Certified Platinum by RIAA
- To date, the original version has been streamed 14,318,820 times
- (Taylor's Version) has been streamed 59,693,114 times

IN TAYLOR'S WORDS

"I wrote that song last summer, and when this movie opportunity came about, I reached back into my pocket and thought, 'I think this is perfect for the soundtrack. I hope it's perfect for the soundtrack.'

YOU ALL OVER ME

DID YOU KNOW?

In 2005, Taylor initially co-wrote "You All Over Me" with Scooter Carusoe, and a leaked online demo recording of the song surfaced in 2017.

She later produced this song with Aaron Dessner in 2021.

This song has a tempo of 143 beats per minute. It is written in the key of D.

"You All Over Me" was first performed live on June 3, 2023, in Chicago during one of Taylor's "The Eras Tour" shows, featuring surprise guest Maren Morris.

Featuring Maren Morris
First Vault Track on "Fearless (Taylor's Version)"
Released: March 26th, 2021
Recorded: Kitty Committee in London, UK

CHARTS & AWARDS

- Peaked at #6 on the Billboard Hot Country Songs Chart
- It was the second consecutive single from "Fearless (Taylor's Version)" to land inside top-10 on that chart
- To date, it has been streamed 99,375,312 times

IN TAYLOR'S WORDS

"You All Over Me' is a song that I wrote with a writer that goes by the name Scooter Carusoe - his name is Travis Hill. This was one of the songs that I remember us painstakingly going over the lyrics and trying to come up with all these different symbolic, imagery references to how it could feel after you have your heart broken. Just to feel like you've been ruined by the whole thing. And I think that's one of the hardest things about heartbreak: feeling like it's damaged you. And now you carry that damage with you. So I was really proud of this song back then, I'm still proud of it now. And I think it actually makes more sense that a 31 year old person be singing it. So all's well that ends well. And I was really excited because Maren Morris was gracious enough to sing backup vocals on it and she's one of my favorite artists."

MR. PERFECTLY FINE

DID YOU KNOW?

Originally written in 2009 for the platinum edition of her second studio album, the song is speculated to be about Joe Jonas.

This song has a tempo of 136 beats per minute. It is written in the key of B.

"Mr. Perfectly Fine" was first performed live on June 16, 2023, in Pittsburgh during one of Taylor's "The Eras Tour" shows.

Written exclusively by Taylor in 2009, the song was recorded between November 2020 and January 2021, with Taylor and Jack Antonoff handling the production. Mikey and Evan from Jack's band Bleachers also contributed to some of the backing instruments.

Second Vault Track on "Fearless (Taylor's Version)"

Released: April 7th, 2021

Recorded: Kitty Committee in London, UK

CHARTS & AWARDS

- Peaked at #2 on the Billboard Hot Country Songs Chart
- Won "Top Ten International Gold Song" at the RTHK International Pop Awards
- To date, it has been streamed 317,683,711 times

IN TAYLOR'S WORDS

"'Mr. Perfectly Fine' is a song that I wrote alone. It was definitely an early indicator of me creeping towards a pop sensibility. I've always listened to every type of music and even though 'Fearless' is a country album there were always these pop melodies creeping in. But I love this song, I love the bridge, I think the lyrics are just wonderfully scathing and full of the teen angst that you would hope to hear on an album that I wrote when I was 17 or 18, or on that cusp."

WE WERE HAPPY

Featuring Keith Urban
Third Vault Track on "Fearless (Taylor's Version)"
Released: April 9th, 2021
Recorded: Kitty Committee in London, UK

DID YOU KNOW?

Originally penned by Taylor and Liz Rose in 2008, the song was produced by Taylor and Aaron Dessner in 2021, with Australian country singer Keith Urban contributing uncredited backing vocals.

This song has a tempo of 106 beats per minute. It is written in the key of C.

This song delves into her feelings of guilt stemming from falling out of love with a boy and the shattered dreams of the future they once envisioned together.

CHARTS & AWARDS

- Peaked at number 15 on the Bubbling Under Hot 100 chart
- To date, it has been streamed 57,574,483, times

IN TAYLOR'S WORDS

"I'm really honored that Keith Urban is a part of this project, duetting on 'That's When' and singing harmonies on 'We Were Happy'. I was his opening act during the Fearless album era and his music has inspired me endlessly."

THATS WHEN

Featuring Keith Urban
Fourth Vault Track on "Fearless (Taylor's Version)"
Released: April 9th, 2021
Recorded: Kitty Committee in London, UK

DID YOU KNOW?

A quote from Taylor on Keith Urban: "I remember during the *Fearless* era, Keith was a really wonderful figure in my life. He was somebody I opened up for on tour. I was a huge fan, I listened to his music constantly. He was just constantly a positive part of my life when I was 18. And so now we have this incredible duet, featuring Keith. "

This song has a tempo of 90 beats per minute. It is written in the key of F.

Swift originally co-wrote "That's When" with Brett and Brad Warren, the members of the country music duo The Warren Brothers, when she was 14 years old.

CHARTS & AWARDS

- Peaked at number 30 on the Billboard Hot Country Songs Chart
- To date, it has been streamed 67,154,470 times

IN TAYLOR'S WORDS

"In 'That's When' I changed the perspectives because it wasn't a duet originally. It was about a girl, and the person she loves comes to her, and says, 'I need some space away from the relationship'. And she's like, 'Fine, whenever you wanna come back you can.' And over time I just wanted to change the story into me singing about needing space from the relationship, even though I love the person. And that person being gracious enough to be like, 'Take your time, whatever you need'. Because I just had not really explored that angle before, of needing your independence and somebody granting it to you."

DON'T YOU

Fifth Vault Track on "Fearless (Taylor's Version)"
Released: April 9th, 2021
Recorded: Kitty Committee in London, UK

DID YOU KNOW?

The song portrays Taylor running into an ex, bringing back memories of their past and wondering why the other person doesn't feel the same hurt that she still does.

This song has a tempo of 102 beats per minute. It is written in the key of D sharp.

Swift collaborated with Jack Antonoff to co-produce the version she recorded for "Fearless (Taylor's Version)", with Antonoff also providing background vocals and playing electric guitar, keyboards, and drums.

There is speculation that the song revolves around Joe Jonas and the aftermath of their breakup, particularly when he started dating actress Camilla Belle shortly after their split, which occurred after meeting on the set of the Jonas Brothers' "Lovebug" video.

CHARTS & AWARDS

- Peaked at number 42 on the Billboard Hot Country Songs Chart
- To date, it has been streamed 59,422,373 times

IN TAYLOR'S WORDS

"'Don't You' is a song that I wrote with Tommy Lee James, who is a fantastic writer. We wrote it about the idea of seeing someone that you used to have a thing for and seeing them out in public for the first time after you've heard that they've moved on. Your life is kind of in shambles, and they have moved on, and are really happy. It's almost like even them being nice to you hurts you because you're in such a state of pain and you haven't moved on yet. So that was a really fun song to write because that's just a wellspring of emotion to draw from. Jack Antonoff produced it and I think he did a really, really beautiful job of highlighting the melody and letting it be really airy, sort of like a dreamscape."

BYE BYE BABY

DID YOU KNOW?

Sixth Vault Track on "Fearless (Taylor's Version)"
Released: April 9th, 2021
Recorded: Kitty Committee in London, UK

Originally titled "The One Thing," this song underwent changes before its official release in 2021, likely due to its resemblance to Michelle Branch's "Goodbye To You," which may have contributed to its removal from the initial album version.

This song has a tempo of 80 beats per minute. It is written in the key of G.

The song portrays Taylor driving away after a breakup that her boyfriend initiated; she still harbors feelings for him, but all that remains is his sympathy, leaving her in disbelief as the relationship unexpectedly comes to an end.

CHARTS & AWARDS

- Peaked at number 49 on the Billboard Hot Country Songs Chart
- To date, it has been streamed 46,936,618 times

Speak Now

TAYLOR'S VERSION

RELEASED: OCTOBER 25, 2010
RECLAIMED: JULY 27, 2023

Confessional, Resilient, Dreamy, Honest

Mine

FIRST SINGLE ON HER THIRD ALBUM

RELEASED AS A SINGLE: AUGUST 4TH, 2010

RECLAIMED: JULY 7TH, 2023

RECORDED AT BLACKBIRD STUDIOS IN NASHVILLE, TN

CHARTS & AWARDS

- DEBUTED AND PEAKED AT #3 ON THE BILLBOARD HOT 100 CHARTS
- PEAKED AT #2 ON THE HOT COUNTRY SONGS CHARTS
- CERTIFIED TRIPLE PLATINUM BY RIAA
- WON "VIDEO OF THE YEAR" AT CMT MUSIC AWARDS IN 2011
- NOMINATED FOR FAVORITE SONG AT NICKELODEON KIDS' CHOICE AWARDS IN 2011
- NOMINATED FOR "CHOICE LOVE SONG" AT THE TEEN CHOICE AWARDS IN 2011
- NOMINATED FOR "TOP COUNTRY SONG" AT THE BILLBOARD MUSIC AWARDS IN 2011

DID YOU KNOW?

ORIGINALLY SLATED FOR AUGUST 16, 2010, "MINE" FACED AN EARLY RELEASE ON AUGUST 4, 2010, DUE TO AN UNAUTHORIZED MP3 LEAK, PROMPTING BIG MACHINE RECORDS TO EXPEDITE ITS DEBUT ON COUNTRY RADIO AND ITUNES.

THE SONG WAS PERFORMED AS THE SURPRISE SONG ON TAYLOR'S "REPUTATION STADIUM TOUR" IN JUNE 2018 FOR HER SHOW IN LOUISVILLE, KY.

"MINE," ONE OF SPEAK NOW'S FOURTEEN SOLO-WRITTEN TRACKS, SAW COLLABORATION IN PRODUCTION WITH NATHAN CHAPMAN, SWIFT'S CONSISTENT CO-PRODUCER ACROSS HER STUDIO ALBUMS AT THAT POINT.

IN TAYLOR'S WORDS

"'MINE' IS A SONG ABOUT SOMEBODY WHO'S BEEN HURT BY LOVE AND HAS SEEN IT FAIL OVER AND OVER AGAIN. AND ISN'T LOOKING FOR LOVE, BUT FINDS IT. AND NOW SHE HAS TO WORK THROUGH THE FACT THAT SHE'S SEEN ALL OF THESE PEOPLE GET THEIR HEARTS BROKEN AND SHE HAS TO REALIZE, 'THIS TIME IT'S WORTH FIGHTING FOR. AND MAYBE IF WE JUST HOLD ON TO THIS AND WORK THROUGH THE PROBLEMS THAT LOVE INEVITABLY BRINGS ON, IT COULD BE WORTH IT.' AND I DO THINK THAT ABOUT LOVE. THAT IF YOU FIND THE RIGHT PERSON IT COULD BE WORTH FIGHTING FOR."

Sparks Fly

FIFTH SINGLE ON HER THIRD ALBUM

RELEASED AS A SINGLE: JULY 18TH, 2011

RECLAIMED: JULY 7TH, 2023

RECORDED AT BLACKBIRD STUDIOS IN NASHVILLE, TN

CHARTS & AWARDS

- PEAKED AT #17 ON THE BILLBOARD HOT 100 CHARTS
- PEAKED AT #1 ON THE HOT COUNTRY SONGS CHARTS
- CERTIFIED PLATINUM BY RIAA
- WON "VIDEO OF THE YEAR" AT CMT MUSIC AWARDS IN 2011
- NOMINATED FOR "FAVORITE SONG" AT NICKELODEON KIDS' CHOICE AWARDS IN 2012
- NOMINATED FOR "CHOICE COUNTRY SONG" AT THE TEEN CHOICE AWARDS IN 2012
- TO DATE, THE ORIGINAL VERSION HAS BEEN STREAMED 173,217,222
- (TAYLOR'S VERSION) HAS BEEN STREAMED 81,318,901 TIMES

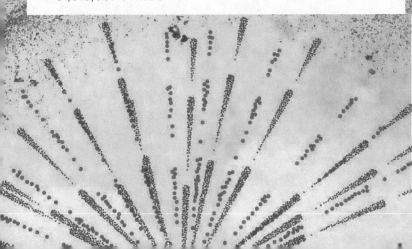

DID YOU KNOW?

ORIGINALLY WRITTEN BY TAYLOR PRIOR TO HER SELF-TITLED DEBUT IN 2006, THE SONG EARNED A SPOT ON HER THIRD ALBUM IN RESPONSE TO FAN REQUESTS.

TAYLOR'S LIVE PERFORMANCE, RECORDED DURING A 2007 CONCERT AND LATER CIRCULATED ON THE INTERNET, TRANSFORMED THE TRACK INTO A FAN FAVORITE.

THE TRACK APPEARED IN A PROMOTIONAL TRAILER FOR THE CW SERIES "HART OF DIXIE" AND WAS ALSO PART OF THE LINEUP FOR THE 2012 "MACY'S 4TH OF JULY FIREWORKS SHOW."

DEBUTING ON HER OFFICIAL WEBSITE ON AUGUST 2011, THE MUSIC VIDEO SEAMLESSLY WEAVES TOGETHER CLIPS FROM TAYLOR'S "SPEAK NOW WORLD TOUR," INCLUDING PERFORMANCES OF "SPEAK NOW," "BACK TO DECEMBER," "BETTER THAN REVENGE," AND "MEAN," ALONG WITH EXCLUSIVE FOOTAGE.

IN TAYLOR'S WORDS

"THE SONG 'SPARKS FLY' IS ABOUT FALLING FOR SOMEONE THAT YOU MAYBE SHOULDN'T FALL FOR, BUT YOU CAN'T STOP YOURSELF BECAUSE THERE'S SUCH A CONNECTION, THERE'S SUCH CHEMISTRY. THIS IS A SONG THAT I WROTE A FEW YEARS AGO AND HAD BEEN WORKING ON IT EVER SINCE IN THE LAST TWO YEARS AND JUST HONING IN ON LITTLE LYRICS AND CHANGING THEM, SO IT'S REALLY BEEN AWESOME TO SEE IT CHANGE OVER THE YEARS."

Back to December

SECOND SINGLE ON HER THIRD ALBUM

RELEASED AS A SINGLE: NOVEMBER 15TH, 2010

RECLAIMED: JULY 7TH, 2023

RECORDED AT BLACKBIRD STUDIOS IN NASHVILLE, TN

CHARTS & AWARDS

- DEBUTED AND PEAKED AT #6 ON THE BILLBOARD HOT 100 CHARTS
- PEAKED AT #2 ON THE HOT COUNTRY SONGS CHARTS
- CERTIFIED DOUBLE PLATINUM BY RIAA
- WON "VIDEO OF THE YEAR" AT CMT MUSIC AWARDS IN 2011
- NOMINATED FOR "FEMALE VIDEO OF THE YEAR" AT THE AMERICAN COUNTRY AWARDS IN 2011
- NOMINATED FOR "CHOICE BREAK-UP SONG" AT THE TEEN CHOICE AWARDS IN 2011

DID YOU KNOW?

FANS THEORIZED THAT THE SONG WAS TAYLOR SWIFT'S APOLOGY TO HER EX-BOYFRIEND TAYLOR LAUTNER, A SENTIMENT LATER CORROBORATED BY LAUTNER.

THE MUSIC VIDEO FOR THIS SONG WAS FILMED IN LATE DECEMBER 2010 BEFORE CHRISTMAS DAY. THE DIRECTOR HAD A CLEAR VISION FOR THE VIDEO'S LOOK AND FEEL: HE TOLD MTV NEWS THAT HE WANTED THE VIDEO TO BE SIMPLE YET METAPHORICAL FOR TAYLOR'S FEELINGS.

FILMED IN LATE DECEMBER 2010 BEFORE CHRISTMAS DAY, THE MUSIC VIDEO FOR THIS SONG WAS GUIDED BY THE DIRECTOR'S VISION, AIMING FOR SIMPLICITY YET METAPHORICALLY CAPTURING TAYLOR'S EMOTIONS.

TAYLOR FIRST PERFORMED "BACK TO DECEMBER" IN PARIS AT A SHOWCASE AT THE SALLE WAGRAM THEATER, ON OCTOBER 18, 2010.

IN TAYLOR'S WORDS

"BACK TO DECEMBER' IS A SONG THAT ADDRESSES A FIRST FOR ME, IN THAT I'VE NEVER APOLOGIZED TO SOMEONE IN A SONG BEFORE. THIS IS ABOUT A PERSON WHO WAS INCREDIBLE TO ME — JUST PERFECT IN A RELATIONSHIP, AND I WAS REALLY CARELESS WITH HIM. SO, THIS IS A SONG FULL OF WORDS THAT I WOULD SAY TO HIM THAT HE DESERVES TO HEAR."

Speak Now

PROMOTIONAL SINGLE ON HER THIRD ALBUM

RELEASED AS A SINGLE: OCTOBER 5TH, 2010

RECLAIMED: JULY 7TH, 2023

RECORDED AT BLACKBIRD STUDIOS IN NASHVILLE, TN

CHARTS & AWARDS

- DEBUTED AND PEAKED AT #8 ON THE BILLBOARD HOT 100 CHARTS
- PEAKED AT #58 ON THE HOT COUNTRY SONGS CHARTS
- CERTIFIED GOLD BY RIAA
- TO DATE, THE ORIGINAL VERSION HAS BEEN STREAMED 173,217,222
- (TAYLOR'S VERSION) HAS BEEN STREAMED 81,318,901 TIMES

DID YOU KNOW?

HAYLEY WILLIAMS OF "PARAMORE" IS SPECULATED TO BE THE INSPIRATION, WHO COINCIDENTALLY ATTENDED THE WEDDING OF HER EX-BOYFRIEND AND EX-BANDMATE JOSH FARRO IN APRIL 2010.

ON SEPTEMBER 22, 2018, TAYLOR PERFORMED THIS AS THE ACOUSTIC SURPRISE TRACK DURING THE NEW ORLEANS SHOW OF THE "REPUTATION STADIUM TOUR," AND AGAIN ON APRIL 13, 2023, AS PART OF "THE ERAS TOUR" IN TAMPA.

THE TEMPO OF THIS SONG IS 119 BEATS PER MINUTE AND IN THE MUSICAL KEY OF G. FOLLOWING THE G—D—AM—C CHORD PROGRESSION, THE SONG INCORPORATES THE '50S ROCK PROGRESSION.

IN TAYLOR'S WORDS

"ONE OF MY FRIENDS, THE GUY SHE HAD BEEN IN LOVE WITH SINCE CHILDHOOD WAS MARRYING THIS OTHER GIRL. AND MY FIRST INCLINATION WAS TO SAY, 'WELL, ARE YOU GONNA SPEAK NOW?' AND THEN I STARTED THINKING ABOUT WHAT I WOULD DO IF I WAS STILL IN LOVE WITH SOMEONE WHO WAS MARRYING SOMEONE WHO THEY SHOULDN'T BE MARRYING. AND SO I WROTE THIS SONG ABOUT EXACTLY WHAT MY GAME PLAN WOULD BE."

Dear John

FIFTH TRACK ON HER THIRD ALBUM

RELEASED: OCTOBER 25TH, 2010

RECLAIMED: JULY 7TH, 2023

RECORDED AT BLACKBIRD STUDIOS IN NASHVILLE, TN

CHARTS & AWARDS

- DEBUTED AND PEAKED AT #54 ON THE BILLBOARD HOT 100 CHART
- PEAKED AT #4 ON THE COUNTRY DIGITAL SONGS CHART
- (TAYLOR'S VERSION) PEAKED AT #26 ON THE BILLBOARD HOT 100 CHART
- TO DATE, THE ORIGINAL VERSION HAS BEEN STREAMED 136,862,039
- (TAYLOR'S VERSION) HAS BEEN STREAMED 73,171,056 TIMES

Speak Now

DID YOU KNOW?

ONE OF TAYLOR'S EX BOYFRIENDS, JOHN MAYER, IS THE SUBJECT OF THE SONG. MAYER, NOTORIOUS FOR OPENLY DISCUSSING HIS RELATIONSHIPS WITH VARIOUS PROMINENT WOMEN IN THE MEDIA, COMPLAINED IN A ROLLING STONE INTERVIEW ABOUT TAYLOR COMPOSING THE SONG ABOUT HIM.

SINCE 2012, TAYLOR DIDN'T PERFORM THE SONG FOR ELEVEN YEARS BECAUSE THE MEMORIES FROM THAT RELATIONSHIP STILL HURT TOO MUCH. SHE EVENTUALLY CHOSE IT AS THE FIRST SURPRISE SONG FOR HER CONCERT IN MINNEAPOLIS ON JUNE 24, 2023 AS APART OF "THE ERAS TOUR."

IN THE COURSE OF HER "SPEAK NOW WORLD TOUR," AS THE SONG REACHED ITS CONCLUSION, ONSTAGE FIREWORKS BURST FORTH TO COMPLEMENT THE LYRICS.

IN TAYLOR'S WORDS

"THE SONG 'DEAR JOHN' IS SORT OF LIKE THE LAST EMAIL YOU WOULD EVER SEND TO SOMEONE THAT YOU USED TO BE IN A RELATIONSHIP WITH. USUALLY, PEOPLE WRITE THIS VENTING LAST EMAIL TO SOMEONE AND THEY SAY EVERYTHING THAT THEY WANT TO SAY TO THAT PERSON, AND THEN THEY USUALLY DON'T SEND IT. I GUESS BY PUTTING THIS SONG ON THE ALBUM I AM PUSHING SEND."

Mean

THIRD SINGLE ON HER THIRD ALBUM

RELEASED AS A SINGLE: MARCH 13, 2011

RECLAIMED: JULY 7TH, 2023

RECORDED AT BLACKBIRD STUDIOS IN NASHVILLE, TN

CHARTS & AWARDS

- DEBUTED AND PEAKED AT #11 ON THE BILLBOARD HOT 100 CHART
- PEAKED AT #2 ON THE HOT DIGITAL SONGS CHART
- (TAYLOR'S VERSION) PEAKED AT #39 ON THE BILLBOARD HOT 100 CHART
- WON "BEST COUNTRY SOLO PERFORMANCE" AND "BEST COUNTRY SONG" AT THE 54TH GRAMMY AWARDS
- TO DATE, THE ORIGINAL VERSION HAS BEEN STREAMED 218,434,433
- (TAYLOR'S VERSION) HAS BEEN STREAMED 66,250,835 TIMES

DID YOU KNOW?

ALONE IN THE KITCHEN OF HER NOW-SOLD LA COTTAGE, TAYLOR PENNED THE SONG DIRECTED AT A CRITIC WHO HAD DENOUNCED HER PERFORMANCE WITH STEVIE NICKS AT THE 52ND GRAMMY AWARDS.

SERVING AS A TESTAMENT TO ITS UPLIFTING MESSAGE, "MEAN" WAS EMPLOYED FOR THE "FREE FALLING TO END BULLYING" CAMPAIGN IN COLLABORATION WITH THE ANDERSON CENTER FOR AUTISM.

THE MUSIC VIDEO FOR "MEAN" WAS DIRECTED BY DECLAN WHITEBLOOM. SWIFT AND HER BAND SHOTS ARE INTERSPERSED WITH SEQUENCES DEPICTING INDIVIDUALS WHO HAVE EXPERIENCED BULLYING, INCLUDING APPEARANCES BY ACTRESSES JOEY KING AND PRESLEY CASH IN THE VIDEO.

IN TAYLOR'S WORDS

"WHEN YOU DO WHAT I DO, YOU PUT YOURSELF OUT THERE FOR A LOT OF PEOPLE TO SAY WHATEVER THEY WANT ABOUT IT. I GET THAT NOT EVERYONE IS GONNA LIKE EVERYTHING THAT YOU DO. AND I GET THAT NO MATTER WHAT YOU'RE GOING TO GET CRITICIZED FOR SOMETHING. THERE ARE A MILLION DIFFERENT OPINIONS FROM A MILLION DIFFERENT PEOPLE. BUT I ALSO GET THAT THERE ARE DIFFERENT WAYS TO CRITICIZE SOMEONE. THERE'S CONSTRUCTIVE CRITICISM, THERE'S PROFESSIONAL CRITICISM, AND THEN THERE'S JUST BEING MEAN. AND THERE'S A LINE THAT YOU CROSS WHEN YOU JUST START TO ATTACK EVERYTHING ABOUT A PERSON. AND THERE'S ONE GUY, MAN, WHO JUST CROSSED THE LINE, OVER AND OVER AGAIN. JUST BEING MEAN AND SAYING THINGS THAT WOULD RUIN MY DAY. THIS HAPPENS NO MATTER WHAT YOU DO, NO MATTER HOW OLD YOU ARE, NOT MATTER WHAT YOUR JOB IS."

The Story of Us

FOURTH SINGLE ON HER THIRD ALBUM

RELEASED AS A SINGLE: APRIL 19TH, 2011

RECLAIMED: JULY 7TH, 2023

RECORDED AT BLACKBIRD STUDIOS IN NASHVILLE, TN

CHARTS & AWARDS

- DEBUTED AND PEAKED AT #41 ON THE BILLBOARD HOT 100 CHART
- PEAKED AT #2 ON THE COUNTRY DIGITAL SONGS CHART
- CERTIFIED PLATINUM BY RIAA
- (TAYLOR'S VERSION) PEAKED AT #42 ON THE BILLBOARD HOT 100 CHART
- TO DATE, THE ORIGINAL VERSION HAS BEEN STREAMED 147,293,965
- (TAYLOR'S VERSION) HAS BEEN STREAMED 65,634,791 TIMES

DID YOU KNOW?

ON SEPTEMBER 8, 2018, SHE SURPRISED THE AUDIENCE BY PERFORMING THE SONG DURING THE KANSAS CITY LEG OF THE "REPUTATION STADIUM TOUR."

DIRECTED BY NOBLE JONES, THE MUSIC VIDEO FOR THE SONG WAS FILMED AT VANDERBILT UNIVERSITY, WHERE TAYLOR'S BROTHER AUSTIN WAS A STUDENT; SOME OF HIS FRIENDS ARE INCLUDED IN THE VIDEO.

THIS WAS THE LAST SONG SWIFT WROTE FOR "SPEAK NOW". WHEN SHE FINISHED IT, SHE SAID SHE KNEW THE ALBUM WAS COMPLETE.

HE TEMPO OF THIS SONG IS 140 BEATS PER MINUTE AND IT IS WRITTEN IN THE MUSICAL KEY OF G.

IN TAYLOR'S WORDS

"'THE STORY OF US' IS ABOUT RUNNING INTO SOMEONE I HAD BEEN IN A RELATIONSHIP WITH AT AN AWARDS SHOW, AND WE WERE SEATED A FEW SEATS AWAY FROM EACH OTHER. I JUST WANTED TO SAY TO HIM, 'IS THIS KILLING YOU? BECAUSE IT'S KILLING ME.' BUT I DIDN'T. I COULDN'T. BECAUSE WE BOTH HAD THESE SILENT SHIELDS UP. I WENT HOME AND I SAT THERE AT THE KITCHEN TABLE AND I SAID TO MY MOM, 'I FELT LIKE I WAS STANDING ALONE IN A CROWDED ROOM.' THEN I GOT UP AND RAN INTO MY BEDROOM, AS SHE'S SEEN ME DO MANY TIMES. AND SHE PROBABLY ASSUMED I HAD COME UP WITH A LINE IN THE SONG. AND I HAD. AND THAT WAS ACTUALLY THE LAST SONG I WROTE ON THE ALBUM, AND AFTER I FINISHED THAT ONE, I KNEW I WAS DONE."

Never Grow Up

EIGHTH TRACK ON HER THIRD ALBUM

RELEASED: OCTOBER 25TH, 2010

RECLAIMED: JULY 7TH, 2023

RECORDED AT BLACKBIRD STUDIOS IN NASHVILLE, TN

CHARTS & AWARDS

- PEAKED AT #84 ON THE BILLBOARD HOT 100 CHART
- CERTIFIED GOLD BY RIAA
- (TAYLOR'S VERSION) PEAKED AT #58 ON THE BILLBOARD HOT 100 CHART
- TO DATE, THE ORIGINAL VERSION HAS BEEN STREAMED 81,587,248
- (TAYLOR'S VERSION) HAS BEEN STREAMED 40,317,251 TIMES

DID YOU KNOW?

NEVER GROW UP" WAS USED IN A HEARTWARMING WALMART CHRISTMAS COMMERCIAL IN 2012. THE VISUALS CAPTURE THE JOY OF CHILDREN AND PARENTS ON CHRISTMAS MORNING.

""NEVER GROW UP" WAS THE FIRST SURPRISE SONG FOR HER SHOW ON JULY 7, 2023, IN KANSAS CITY WHILE ON "THE ERAS TOUR".

TAYLOR HAS ONLY PUBLICLY PERFORMED THE SONG A HANDFUL OF TIMES, AS IT MAKES HER QUITE EMOTIONAL.

HE TEMPO OF THIS SONG IS 125 BEATS PER MINUTE AND IT IS WRITTEN IN THE MUSICAL KEY OF D.

IN TAYLOR'S WORDS

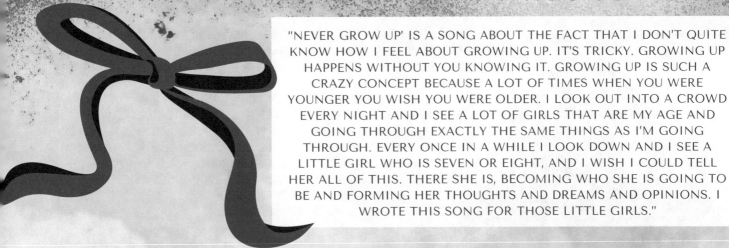

"NEVER GROW UP' IS A SONG ABOUT THE FACT THAT I DON'T QUITE KNOW HOW I FEEL ABOUT GROWING UP. IT'S TRICKY. GROWING UP HAPPENS WITHOUT YOU KNOWING IT. GROWING UP IS SUCH A CRAZY CONCEPT BECAUSE A LOT OF TIMES WHEN YOU WERE YOUNGER YOU WISH YOU WERE OLDER. I LOOK OUT INTO A CROWD EVERY NIGHT AND I SEE A LOT OF GIRLS THAT ARE MY AGE AND GOING THROUGH EXACTLY THE SAME THINGS AS I'M GOING THROUGH. EVERY ONCE IN A WHILE I LOOK DOWN AND I SEE A LITTLE GIRL WHO IS SEVEN OR EIGHT, AND I WISH I COULD TELL HER ALL OF THIS. THERE SHE IS, BECOMING WHO SHE IS GOING TO BE AND FORMING HER THOUGHTS AND DREAMS AND OPINIONS. I WROTE THIS SONG FOR THOSE LITTLE GIRLS."

Enchanted

NINTH TRACK ON HER THIRD ALBUM

RELEASED: OCTOBER 25TH, 2010

RECLAIMED: JULY 7TH, 2023

RECORDED AT BLACKBIRD STUDIOS IN NASHVILLE, TN

CHARTS & AWARDS

- PEAKED AT #75 ON THE BILLBOARD HOT 100 CHART
- CERTIFIED PLATINUM BY RIAA
- (TAYLOR'S VERSION) PEAKED AT #19 ON THE BILLBOARD HOT 100 CHART
- TO DATE, THE ORIGINAL VERSION HAS BEEN STREAMED 721,616,569
- (TAYLOR'S VERSION) HAS BEEN STREAMED 165,443,281 TIMES

DID YOU KNOW?

TAYLOR EXPRESSED THAT THE BRIDGE IN "ENCHANTED" IS HER FAVORITE PART AS IT MIRRORS HER STREAM OF CONSCIOUSNESS DURING THE WRITING PROCESS.

THE ADAM REFERRED TO IS ADAM YOUNG, THE IMAGINATIVE FORCE BEHIND OWL CITY. THEY CONNECTED ONLINE AND VIA PHONE BEFORE THEIR INITIAL IN-PERSON MEETING AT A PARTY.

ADAM POSTED HIS OWN VERSION OF THE SONG IN RESPONSE TO TAYLOR, CONFIRMING HE FELT THE SAME.

TAYOR HAS HIDDEN WORDS IN HER LYRIC BOOKLET IN EVERY ALBUM UNTIL 2014. THE SPECIFIC HIDDEN MESSAGE FOR THIS SONG IS: ADAM

IN TAYLOR'S WORDS

I WROTE "ENCHANTED" ABOUT A GUY WHO I WAS ENCHANTED TO MEET, OBVIOUSLY. HE WAS SOMEBODY THAT I HAD TALKED TO A COUPLE OF TIMES ON EMAIL, AND THEN I WAS IN NEW YORK AND WENT TO MEET HIM. I REMEMBER JUST THE WHOLE WAY HOME THINKING, "I HOPE HE'S NOT IN LOVE WITH SOMEBODY." IT WAS JUST WONDERFUL, THAT FEELING. LIKE, "OH MY GOSH. WHO'S HE WITH? DOES HE LIKE ME? DOES HE LIKE SOMEBODY ELSE? WHAT DOES IT MEAN?" I GOT HOME AND HE HAD EMAILED ME AND SAID SOMETHING LIKE, "SORRY I WAS SO QUIET. I WAS JUST WONDERSTRUCK MEETING YOU." AND SO I INCORPORATED THE WORD WONDERSTRUCK, INTO THE SONG AS A, "HEY, THIS ONE'S SORTA FOR YOU."

Better Than Revenge

TENTH TRACK ON HER THIRD ALBUM

RELEASED: OCTOBER 25TH, 2010

RECLAIMED: JULY 7TH, 2023

RECORDED AT BLACKBIRD STUDIOS IN NASHVILLE, TN

CHARTS & AWARDS

- PEAKED AT #56 ON THE BILLBOARD HOT 100 CHART
- CERTIFIED GOLD BY RIAA
- (TAYLOR'S VERSION) PEAKED AT #28 ON THE BILLBOARD HOT 100 CHART
- TO DATE, THE ORIGINAL VERSION HAS BEEN STREAMED 180,905,708
- (TAYLOR'S VERSION) HAS BEEN STREAMED 86,738,426 TIMES

DID YOU KNOW?

AS TAYLOR ACHIEVED GREATER SUCCESS WITH HER SUBSEQUENT POP ALBUMS, THE MEDIA SCRUTINIZED THE CONTENTIOUS LYRICS OF "BETTER THAN REVENGE," CASTING DOUBT ON HER FEMINIST STANCE. EVOLVING WITH MATURITY, TAYLOR REVISED THE SONG'S LYRICS, ELIMINATING WORDS THAT COULD DEMEAN OTHER WOMEN.

TAYLOR FEATURED "BETTER THAN REVENGE" IN THE SET LIST OF HER "SPEAK NOW WORLD TOUR" (2011–2012). IN SUBSEQUENT YEARS, SHE HESITATED TO PERFORM THE SONG, CITING CONCERNS ABOUT ITS MISOGYNISTIC MESSAGE.

TAYLOR PERFORMED "BETTER THAN REVENGE" ELEVEN YEARS LATER AS THE SURPRISE SONG ON "THE ERAS TOUR" IN BUENOS AIRES, ARGENTINA.

TAYOR HAS HIDDEN WORDS IN HER LYRIC BOOKLET IN EVERY ALBUM UNTIL 2014. THE SPECIFIC HIDDEN MESSAGE FOR THIS SONG IS: YOU THOUGHT I WOULD FORGET.

IN TAYLOR'S WORDS

"I WAS 18 WHEN I WROTE 'BETTER THAN REVENGE'. THAT'S THE AGE YOU ARE WHEN YOU THINK SOMEONE CAN ACTUALLY TAKE YOUR BOYFRIEND. THEN YOU GROW UP AND REALIZE NO ONE CAN TAKE SOMEONE FROM YOU IF THEY DON'T WANT TO LEAVE."

Innocent

ELEVENTH TRACK ON HER THIRD ALBUM

RELEASED: SEPTEMBER 12TH, 2010

RECLAIMED: JULY 7TH, 2023

RECORDED AT BLACKBIRD STUDIOS IN NASHVILLE, TN

CHARTS & AWARDS

- PEAKED AT #27 ON THE BILLBOARD HOT 100 CHART
- (TAYLOR'S VERSION) PEAKED AT #63 ON THE BILLBOARD HOT 100 CHART
- TO DATE, THE ORIGINAL VERSION HAS BEEN STREAMED 34,409,659
- (TAYLOR'S VERSION) HAS BEEN STREAMED 50,393,359 TIMES

DID YOU KNOW?

IN THE AFTERMATH OF KANYE WEST'S INTERRUPTION OF HER ACCEPTANCE SPEECH AT THE 2009 MTV VIDEO MUSIC AWARDS, TAYLOR WROTE THE SONG AS AN EXPRESSION OF EMPATHY TOWARD HIM IN THE FACE OF THE PUBLIC BACKLASH HE EXPERIENCED.

SWIFT PREMIERED "INNOCENT" IN A LIVE PERFORMANCE AT THE 2010 MTV VIDEO MUSIC AWARDS ON SEPTEMBER 12, 2010, AIMING TO MOVE BEYOND THE PAST INCIDENT.

ON NOVEMBER 24TH 2023, SWIFT SANG "INNOCENT" AS A SURPRISE SONG DURING A CONCERT IN SAO PAULO, AS PART OF "THE ERAS TOUR".

TAYOR HAS HIDDEN WORDS IN HER LYRIC BOOKLET IN EVERY ALBUM UNTIL 2014. THE SPECIFIC HIDDEN MESSAGE FOR THIS SONG IS: LIFE IS FULL OF LITTLE INTERRUPTIONS.

IN TAYLOR'S WORDS

"THE SONG 'INNOCENT' IS ABOUT SOMETHING THAT REALLY INTENSELY AFFECTED ME EMOTIONALLY. IT TOOK A WHILE TO WRITE THAT SONG. THAT WAS A HUGE, INTENSE THING IN MY LIFE THAT RESONATED FOR A LONG TIME. IT WAS BROUGHT UP TO ME IN GROCERY STORES, AND EVERYWHERE I WENT, AND IN A LOT OF TIMES IN MY LIFE WHEN I DON'T KNOW HOW I FEEL ABOUT SOMETHING, I SAY NOTHING. AND THAT'S WHAT I DID UNTIL I COULD COME TO THE CONCLUSION THAT I CAME TO IN ORDER TO WRITE 'INNOCENT.' EVEN THEN, I DIDN'T TALK ABOUT IT, AND I STILL DON'T REALLY."

Haunted

TWELFTH TRACK ON HER THIRD ALBUM

RELEASED: OCTOBER 25TH, 2010

RECLAIMED: JULY 7TH, 2023

RECORDED AT BLACKBIRD STUDIOS IN NASHVILLE, TN

CHARTS & AWARDS

- PEAKED AT #63 ON THE BILLBOARD HOT 100 CHART
- (TAYLOR'S VERSION) PEAKED AT #50 ON THE BILLBOARD HOT 100 CHART
- CERTIFIED GOLD BY RIAA
- TO DATE, THE ORIGINAL VERSION HAS BEEN STREAMED 98,379,507
- (TAYLOR'S VERSION) HAS BEEN STREAMED 52,907,469 TIMES

DID YOU KNOW?

DURING THE "SPEAK NOW WORLD TOUR," TAYLOR DELIVERED A THEATRICAL RENDITION OF THIS SONG, INCORPORATING AERIAL BACKUP DANCERS SUSPENDED FROM BELLS.

AT ITS ESSENCE, THE SONG EXUDES PROFOUND SADNESS, DESPERATION, AND CONFUSION AS TAYLOR SINGS ABOUT CLINGING TO THE REMNANTS OF A CONCLUDED RELATIONSHIP.

TAYOR HAS HIDDEN WORDS IN HER LYRIC BOOKLET IN EVERY ALBUM UNTIL 2014. THE SPECIFIC HIDDEN MESSAGE FOR THIS SONG IS: STILL TO THIS DAY.

QUOTE FROM TAYLOR ON THE COMPOSITION OF THE TRACK: "I WANTED THE MUSIC AND THE ORCHESTRATION TO REFLECT THE INTENSITY OF THE EMOTION THE SONG IS ABOUT, SO WE RECORDED STRINGS WITH PAUL BUCKMASTER AT CAPITOL STUDIOS IN LOS ANGELES."

IN TAYLOR'S WORDS

"'HAUNTED' IS ABOUT THE MOMENT THAT YOU REALIZE THE PERSON YOU'RE IN LOVE WITH IS DRIFTING AND FADING FAST. AND YOU DON'T KNOW WHAT TO DO, BUT IN THAT PERIOD OF TIME, IN THAT PHASE OF LOVE, WHERE IT'S FADING OUT, TIME MOVES SO SLOWLY. EVERYTHING HINGES ON WHAT THAT LAST TEXT MESSAGE SAID, AND YOU'RE REALIZING THAT HE'S KIND OF FALLING OUT OF LOVE. THAT'S A REALLY HEARTBREAKING AND TRAGIC THING TO GO THROUGH BECAUSE THE WHOLE TIME YOU'RE TRYING TO TELL YOURSELF IT'S NOT HAPPENING. I WENT THROUGH THIS, AND I ENDED UP WAKING UP IN THE MIDDLE OF THE NIGHT WRITING THIS SONG ABOUT IT."

Last Kiss

THIRTEENTH TRACK ON HER THIRD ALBUM

RELEASED: OCTOBER 25TH, 2010

RECLAIMED: JULY 7TH, 2023

RECORDED AT BLACKBIRD STUDIOS IN NASHVILLE, TN

CHARTS & AWARDS

- PEAKED AT #71 ON THE BILLBOARD HOT 100 CHART
- (TAYLOR'S VERSION) PEAKED AT #57 ON THE BILLBOARD HOT 100 CHART
- TO DATE, THE ORIGINAL VERSION HAS BEEN STREAMED 52,167,180
- (TAYLOR'S VERSION) HAS BEEN STREAMED 52,907,469 TIMES

DID YOU KNOW?

"LAST KISS" IS TAYLOR'S THIRD LONGEST SONG FOLLOWED BY "DEAR JOHN" AND ALL TOO WELL (10 MINUTE VERSION)".

TAYOR HAS HIDDEN WORDS IN HER LYRIC BOOKLET IN EVERY ALBUM UNTIL 2014. THE SPECIFIC HIDDEN MESSAGE FOR THIS SONG IS: FOREVER AND ALWAYS.

BOTH "FOREVER & ALWAYS" AND "LAST KISS" CENTER ON JOE JONAS, WITH THE FORMER DELVING INTO THE ANGRY AND CONFUSED EMOTIONS TAYLOR EXPERIENCED UPON HIS DEPARTURE, WHILE THE LATTER CAPTURES A MELANCHOLIC AND NOSTALGIC SADNESS THAT ENSUES.

THE TRACK OPENS WITH A 27-SECOND INTRODUCTION, POTENTIALLY MIRRORING THE BRIEF 27-SECOND PHONE CALL THAT MARKED THE END OF TAYLOR SWIFT'S RELATIONSHIP WITH JOE JONAS.

IN TAYLOR'S WORDS

"THE SONG 'LAST KISS' IS SORT OF LIKE A LETTER TO SOMEBODY. YOU SAY ALL OF THESE DESPERATE, HOPELESS FEELINGS THAT YOU HAVE AFTER A BREAKUP. GOING THROUGH A BREAKUP YOU FEEL ALL OF THESE DIFFERENT THINGS. YOU FEEL ANGER, AND YOU FEEL CONFUSION, AND FRUSTRATION. AND THEN THERE IS THE ABSOLUTE SADNESS. THE SADNESS OF LOSING THIS PERSON, LOSING ALL THE MEMORIES AND THE HOPES YOU HAD FOR THE FUTURE. THERE ARE JUST TIMES WHEN YOU HAVE THIS MOMENT OF TRUTH WHERE YOU JUST ADMIT TO YOURSELF THAT YOU MISS ALL THESE THINGS. WHEN I WAS IN ONE OF THOSE MOMENTS I WROTE THIS SONG."

Long Live

FOURTEENTH TRACK ON HER THIRD ALBUM

RELEASED: OCTOBER 25TH, 2010

RECLAIMED: JULY 7TH, 2023

RECORDED AT BLACKBIRD STUDIOS IN NASHVILLE, TN

CHARTS & AWARDS

- PEAKED AT #85 ON THE BILLBOARD HOT 100 CHART
- (TAYLOR'S VERSION) PEAKED AT #53 ON THE BILLBOARD HOT 100 CHART
- TO DATE, THE ORIGINAL VERSION HAS BEEN STREAMED 95,627,738
- (TAYLOR'S VERSION) HAS BEEN STREAMED 78,069,840 TIMES

DID YOU KNOW?

AS PART OF HER SETLIST FOR THE "SPEAK NOW WORLD TOUR," TAYLOR FEATURED THE SONG IN EVERY PERFORMANCE AS THE FINAL SONG BEFORE THE ENCORE.

"LONG LIVE" TOOK ITS INSPIRATION FROM A BACKSTAGE MOMENT SHARED BY TAYLOR AND HER BAND ON THE ULTIMATE DATE OF THE "FEARLESS TOUR" AT GILLETTE STADIUM IN 2010.

THE LINE REFERENCING THE "BAND OF THIEVES" PERTAINS TO THE MOMENT AT THE 2009 CMA AWARDS WHEN TAYLOR, DESPITE HER BAND BEING UNDERDRESSED, INVITED THEM ON STAGE AFTER WINNING THE "ENTERTAINER OF THE YEAR" AWARD.

ROLLING STONE DESCRIBED THE SONG AS "THE BEST BON JOVI SONG BON JOVI NEVER WROTE."

IN TAYLOR'S WORDS

"THIS SONG IS ABOUT MY BAND, AND MY PRODUCER, AND ALL THE PEOPLE WHO HAVE HELPED US BUILD THIS BRICK BY BRICK. THE FANS, THE PEOPLE WHO I FEEL THAT WE ARE ALL IN THIS TOGETHER, THIS SONG TALKS ABOUT THE TRIUMPHANT MOMENTS THAT WE'VE HAD IN THE LAST TWO YEARS. WE'VE HAD TIMES WHERE WE JUST JUMP UP AND DOWN, AND DANCE LIKE WE DON'T CARE HOW WE'RE DANCING, AND JUST SCREAM AT THE TOP OF OUR LUNGS, 'HOW IS THIS HAPPENING?' AND I FEEL VERY LUCKY TO EVEN HAVE HAD ONE OF THOSE MOMENTS, NONETHELESS ALL THE ONES THAT I GOT TO HAVE. 'LONG LIVE' IS ABOUT HOW I FEEL REFLECTING ON IT. THIS SONG FOR ME IS LIKE LOOKING AT A PHOTO ALBUM OF ALL THE AWARD SHOWS, AND ALL THE STADIUM SHOWS, AND ALL THE HANDS IN THE AIR IN THE CROWD. IT'S SORT OF THE FIRST LOVE SONG THAT I'VE WRITTEN TO MY TEAM."

Ours

SIXTH SINGLE ON HER THIRD ALBUM

RELEASED: OCTOBER 25TH, 2010

RECLAIMED: JULY 7TH, 2023

RECORDED AT BLACKBIRD STUDIOS IN NASHVILLE, TN

CHARTS & AWARDS

- PEAKED AT #13 ON THE BILLBOARD HOT 100 CHART
- (TAYLOR'S VERSION) PEAKED AT #68 ON THE BILLBOARD HOT 100 CHART
- CERTIFIED PLATINUM BY RIAA
- NOMINATED FOR "FEMALE SINGLE OF THE YEAR" AND FEMALE VIDEO OF THE YEAR" AT THE AMERICAN COUNTRY AWARDS IN 2012
- NOMINATED FOR "FEMALE VIDEO OF THE YEAR AT THE CTM AWARDS IN 2012
- TO DATE, THE ORIGINAL VERSION HAS BEEN STREAMED 69,426,278
- (TAYLOR'S VERSION) HAS BEEN STREAMED 37,717,375 TIMES

DID YOU KNOW?

TAYLOR PLAYED "OURS" AS THE SURPRISE ACOUSTIC SONG IN ARLINGTON, TEXAS ON MARCH 31ST, 2023 DURING "THE ERAS TOUR"

IN THE MUSIC VIDEO OF "OURS," TAYLOR APPEARS AS AN OFFICE WORKER NAVIGATING A CHALLENGING DAY BY SEEKING SOLACE IN DIFFERENT VIDEOS OF HER BOYFRIEND, PORTRAYED BY ZACH GILFORD. GILFORD GAINED RECOGNITION FOR HIS PORTRAYAL OF MATT SARACEN IN THE NBC TELEVISION DRAMA SERIES "FRIDAY NIGHT LIGHTS."

SWIFT FIRST PERFORMED THE SONG LIVE ON NOVEMBER 9, 2011 AT THE COUNTRY MUSIC ASSOCIATION AWARDS ON.

THIS SONG IS WRITTEN IN THE MUSICAL KEY OF C WITH A TEMPO OF 160 BEATS PER MINUTE.

IN TAYLOR'S WORDS

"I'M EXCITED ABOUT TELLING THE BEGINNINGS OF STORIES, LIKE THE STORY OF THIS SONG CALLED 'OURS,' WHERE I WROTE IT ABOUT THIS GUY NOBODY THOUGHT I SHOULD BE WITH. SO I WROTE THIS SONG SPECIFICALLY JUST TO PLAY IT FOR HIM, JUST TO SHOW HIM, 'I DON'T CARE WHAT ANYONE SAYS. I DON'T CARE THAT YOU HAVE TATTOOS. I DON'T CARE THAT YOU HAVE A GAP BETWEEN YOUR TEETH. I LOVE YOU FOR WHO YOU ARE.' AND THAT SONG ENDED UP ACTUALLY MAKING IT ON SPEAK NOW AND BECOMING A NO. 1 SONG."

If This Was A Movie

SIXTEENTH TRACK ON HER THIRD ALBUM
RELEASED: OCTOBER 25TH, 2010
RECLAIMED: JULY 7TH, 2023
RECORDED AT BLACKBIRD STUDIOS IN NASHVILLE, TN

CHARTS & AWARDS

- PEAKED AT #10 ON THE BILLBOARD HOT 100 CHART
- TO DATE, THE ORIGINAL VERSION HAS BEEN STREAMED 42,133,005
- (TAYLOR'S VERSION) HAS BEEN STREAMED 51,559,291 TIMES

DID YOU KNOW?

TAYLOR TEAMED UP WITH MARTIN JOHNSON, THE LEAD SINGER OF BOYS LIKE GIRLS, TO PEN "IF THIS WAS A MOVIE." THIS MARKS HER ONLY CO-AUTHORED TRACK ON THE "SPEAK NOW" ALBUM.

ALMOST 13 YEARS AFTER ITS RELEASE, TAYLOR PERFORMED "IF THIS WAS A MOVIE" FOR THE FIRST TIME ON JUNE 23, 2023 IN MINNEAPOLIS, MN DURING "THE ERAS TOUR".

ORIGINALLY A DELUXE TRACK ON SPEAK NOW, "IF THIS WAS A MOVIE" IS NOW INCLUDED IN THE EP "THE MORE FEARLESS (TAYLOR'S VERSION) CHAPTER (2023)", WITH SPECULATION SUGGESTING THAT ITS STATUS AS THE ONLY CO-WRITTEN TRACK ON SPEAK NOW MAY BE THE REASON FOR ITS PROMOTION AND INCLUSION AS A "FEARLESS (TAYLOR'S VERSION) SONG".

Superman

PROMOTIONAL SINGLE ON HER THIRD ALBUM

RELEASED: OCTOBER 25TH, 2010

RECLAIMED: JULY 7TH, 2023

RECORDED AT BLACKBIRD STUDIOS IN NASHVILLE, TN

CHARTS & AWARDS

- PEAKED AT #13 ON THE BILLBOARD HOT 100 CHART
- (TAYLOR'S VERSION) PEAKED AT #74 ON THE BILLBOARD HOT 100 CHART
- TO DATE, THE ORIGINAL VERSION HAS BEEN STREAMED 24,845,642
- (TAYLOR'S VERSION) HAS BEEN STREAMED 29,208,358 TIMES

DID YOU KNOW?

TAYLOR PLAYED "OURS" AS THE SURPRISE ACOUSTIC SONG IN ARLINGTON, TEXAS ON MARCH 31ST, 2023 DURING "THE ERAS TOUR"

IN THE LYRICS, SHE NARRATES THE STORY OF A BOY WHO PARTED WAYS WITH HER, BUT HOPING FOR HIS EVENTUAL RETURN AT THE RIGHT MOMENT. IT IS SPECULATED TO BE REFERRING TO HER RELATIONSHIP WITH JOHN MAYER.

THIS SONG IS WRITTEN IN THE MUSICAL KEY OF G WITH A TEMPO OF 132 BEATS PER MINUTE.

ON SEPTEMBER 24, 2011, DURING HER "SPEAK NOW WORLD TOUR" IN KANSAS CITY, TAYLOR PRESENTED AN ACOUSTIC PERFORMANCE OF THE SONG "SUPERMAN."

IN TAYLOR'S WORDS

"THIS IS ABOUT, WELL, A GUY, AS USUAL. THIS WAS A GUY THAT I WAS SORT OF ENAMORED WITH. THIS SONG GOT ITS TITLE BY SOMETHING THAT I JUST SAID RANDOMLY IN CONVERSATION. [WHEN] HE WALKED OUT OF THE ROOM, I TURNED TO ONE OF MY FRIENDS AND SAID, 'IT'S LIKE WATCHING SUPERMAN FLY AWAY.'"

Electric Touch

FIRST VAULT TRACK ON SPEAK NOW (TAYLOR'S VERSION)

FEATURING FALL OUT BOY

RELEASED: JULY 7TH, 2023

RECORDED AT LONG POND STUDIOS IN HUDSON VALLEY, NY

CHARTS & AWARDS

- PEAKED AT #35 ON THE BILLBOARD HOT 100 CHART
- PEAKED AT #16 ON THE US HOT COUNTRY SONGS CHART
- TO DATE, IT HAS BEEN STREAMED 61,315,343 TIMES

DID YOU KNOW?

TAYLOR HAS LONG CONSIDERED FALL OUT BOY ONE OF HER FAVORITE BANDS, AND IN 2013, THEY COLLABORATED ON SEVERAL PERFORMANCES OF THE BAND'S SONG "MY SONGS KNOW WHAT YOU DID IN THE DARK," APPEARING TOGETHER DURING TAYLOR'S "THE RED TOUR" AND AT THE 2013 VICTORIA'S SECRET FASHION SHOW.

"ELECTRIC TOUCH" EXPRESSES A YEARNING FOR HOPE, VULNERABILITY, AND THE UNPREDICTABILITY OF NEW LOVE WHILE ALSO DREAMING OF THE REWARDS OF EMBRACING NEW ROMANCE.

THIS SONG IS WRITTEN IN THE MUSICAL KEY OF G WITH A TEMPO OF 131 BEATS PER MINUTE.

IN TAYLOR'S WORDS

"I'M VERY EXCITED TO SHOW YOU THE BACK COVER OF SPEAK NOW (MY VERSION) INCLUDING THE VAULT TRACKS AND COLLABORATIONS WITH HAYLEY WILLIAMS FROM PARAMORE AND FALL OUT BOY. SINCE SPEAK NOW WAS ALL ABOUT MY SONGWRITING, I DECIDED TO GO TO THE ARTISTS WHO I FEEL INFLUENCED ME MOST POWERFULLY AS A LYRICIST AT THAT TIME AND ASK THEM TO SING ON THE ALBUM. THEY'RE SO COOL AND GENEROUS FOR AGREEING TO SUPPORT MY VERSION OF SPEAK NOW."

When Emma Falls In Love

SECOND VAULT TRACK ON SPEAK NOW (TAYLOR'S VERSION)

RELEASED: JULY 7TH, 2023

RECORDED AT LONG POND STUDIOS IN HUDSON VALLEY, NY

CHARTS & AWARDS

- PEAKED AT #34 ON THE BILLBOARD HOT 100 CHART
- PEAKED AT #15 ON THE US HOT COUNTRY SONGS CHART
- TO DATE, IT HAS BEEN STREAMED 59724426 TIMES

DID YOU KNOW?

TAYLOR SAID ABOUT THE SONG, "I WROTE THIS ABOUT ONE OF MY BEST FRIENDS!" IT IS SPECULATED THAT IT IS WRITTEN ABOUT ACTRESS EMMA STONE AS THE TWO HAVE HISTORICALLY BEEN VERY CLOSE FRIENDS.

THE FIRST PERFORMANCE OF "WHEN EMMA FALLS IN LOVE" WAS ON JULY 7TH, 2023 IN KANSAS CITY DURING "THE ERAS TOUR."

THIS SONG IS WRITTEN IN THE MUSICAL KEY OF D WITH A TEMPO OF 78 BEATS PER MINUTE.

THE SONG WAS PRODUCED WITH AARON DESSNER WHO WAS A KEY PRODUCER IN THE "FOLKLORE" AND "EVERMORE" ALBUMS. HE ALSO PLAYED ACOUSTIC GUITAR, BASS GUITAR, ELECTRIC GUITAR AND PIANO ON THE TRACK.

I Can See You

THIRD VAULT TRACK ON SPEAK NOW (TAYLOR'S VERSION)

RELEASED: JULY 7TH, 2023

RECORDED AT LONG POND STUDIOS IN HUDSON VALLEY, NY

CHARTS & AWARDS

- PEAKED AT #5 ON THE BILLBOARD HOT 100 CHART
- PEAKED AT #15 ON THE US HOT COUNTRY SONGS CHART
- TO DATE, IT HAS BEEN STREAMED 181,997,454 TIMES

IN TAYLOR'S WORDS

"I'VE BEEN COUNTING DOWN FOR MONTHS AND FINALLY THE 'I CAN SEE YOU' VIDEO IS OUT. I WROTE THIS VIDEO TREATMENT OVER A YEAR AGO AND REALLY WANTED TO PLAY OUT SYMBOLICALLY HOW IT'S FELT FOR ME TO HAVE THE FANS HELPING ME RECLAIM MY MUSIC. I HAD MY HEART SET ON JOEY KING, TAYLOR LAUTNER AND PRESLEY CASH STARRING IN IT. JOEY AND PRESLEY HAD BEEN IN THE VIDEO FOR 'MEAN' WHEN THEY WERE 9 AND 13 AND THEY ARE BACK!"

DID YOU KNOW?

AFTER THIS SONG CHARTED TO NUMBER FIVE, IT MARKED HER AS THE FIRST ARTIST SINCE THE BEATLES IN 1964 TO HAVE SONGS FROM THREE DISTINCT ALBUMS SIMULTANEOUSLY CHARTING IN THE TOP TEN.

DURING THE ERAS TOUR PERFORMANCE IN KANSAS CITY, MISSOURI ON JULY 7, 2023, TAYLOR SWIFT UNVEILED THE MUSIC VIDEO FOR "I CAN SEE YOU," FEATURING ON-STAGE APPEARANCES BY CO-STARS JOEY KING, TAYLOR LAUTNER, AND PRESLEY CASH.

IN APRIL 2023, THE FILMING FOR THE MUSIC VIDEO TOOK PLACE IN LIVERPOOL, ENGLAND, ENCOMPASSING VARIOUS LOCATIONS INCLUDING THE CUNARD BUILDING, THE TOBACCO WAREHOUSE, AND THE NATIONAL WESTMINSTER BANK.

THIS SONG IS WRITTEN IN THE MUSICAL KEY OF F SHARP WITH A TEMPO OF 123 BEATS PER MINUTE.

Castles Crumbling

FOURTH VAULT TRACK ON SPEAK NOW (TAYLOR'S VERSION)

FEATURING HAYLEY WILLIAMS

RELEASED: JULY 7TH, 2023

RECORDED AT LONG POND STUDIOS IN HUDSON VALLEY, NY

CHARTS & AWARDS

- PEAKED AT #35 ON THE BILLBOARD HOT 100 CHART
- PEAKED AT #16 ON THE US HOT COUNTRY SONGS CHART
- TO DATE, IT HAS BEEN STREAMED 60,477,089 TIMES

DID YOU KNOW?

A QUOTE FROM HAYLEY ON THE ALBUM: "TAYLOR WAS THE FIRST INDUSTRY FRIEND I EVER MADE AND HUNG OUT WITH OUTSIDE OF WORK THINGS. WHEN SPEAK NOW DROPPED, I BOUGHT MY FRIEND'S RECORD (AS YOU DO!) AND LISTENED TO THE WHOLE THING IN MY FIRST CAR, SITTING STILL IN THE DRIVEWAY. IT'S MY FAVORITE TAYLOR SWIFT ALBUM FOR SO MANY REASONS."

HAYLEY ALSO APPEARED AS A GUEST STAR ALONGSIDE TAYLOR ON HER "SPEAK NOW WORLD TOUR" IN 2011 AND ALSO FEATURED IN THE MUSIC VIDEO FOR TAYLOR'S 2015 SINGLE, "BAD BLOOD."

THIS SONG IS A GENTLE, ENCHANTING BALLAD WHERE TAYLOR REFLECTS ON THE CONSEQUENCES OF HER INITIAL YEAR EXPERIENCING TRUE SUPERSTARDOM.

IN TAYLOR'S WORDS

"I'M VERY EXCITED TO SHOW YOU THE BACK COVER OF SPEAK NOW (MY VERSION) INCLUDING THE VAULT TRACKS AND COLLABORATIONS WITH HAYLEY WILLIAMS FROM PARAMORE AND FALL OUT BOY. SINCE SPEAK NOW WAS ALL ABOUT MY SONGWRITING, I DECIDED TO GO TO THE ARTISTS WHO I FEEL INFLUENCED ME MOST POWERFULLY AS A LYRICIST AT THAT TIME AND ASK THEM TO SING ON THE ALBUM. THEY'RE SO COOL AND GENEROUS FOR AGREEING TO SUPPORT MY VERSION OF SPEAK NOW."

Foolish One

FIFTH VAULT TRACK ON SPEAK NOW (TAYLOR'S VERSION)
RELEASED: JULY 7TH, 2023
RECORDED AT LONG POND STUDIOS IN HUDSON VALLEY, NY

DID YOU KNOW?

CHARTS & AWARDS

- PEAKED AT #40 ON THE BILLBOARD HOT 100 CHART
- TO DATE, IT HAS BEEN STREAMED 62,965,726 TIMES

IN THE VERSES, TAYLOR CAPTURES THE TUMULTUOUS DYNAMICS OF THE RELATIONSHIP, ARTICULATING HER ONGOING STRUGGLE WITH A CYCLE OF HOPE AND DISAPPOINTMENT AS SHE YEARNS FOR ATTENTION AND CONFESSES HER ELUSIVE LONGING FOR LOVE.

THE SONG WAS ORIGINALLY REGISTERED AS AN ORIGINAL MUSICAL WORK IN 2009, BUT WAS RELEASED 14 YEARS LATER PUBLICLY.

THIS SONG IS WRITTEN IN THE MUSICAL KEY OF G AND HAS A TEMPO OF 97 BEATS PER MINUTE.

Timeless

SIXTH VAULT TRACK ON SPEAK NOW (TAYLOR'S VERSION)

RELEASED: JULY 7TH, 2023

RECORDED AT LONG POND STUDIOS IN HUDSON VALLEY, NY

CHARTS & AWARDS

- PEAKED AT #48 ON THE BILLBOARD HOT 100 CHART
- TO DATE, IT HAS BEEN STREAMED 62,965,726 TIMES

DID YOU KNOW?

ORIGINALLY WRITTEN IN 2009, THE SONG IS AN ENDURING LOVE STORY OF AN ELDERLY COUPLE, PRESUMABLY INSPIRED BY HER GRANDPARENTS MARJORIE AND ROBERT FINLAY; TAYLOR DESCRIBES PASSION AND THE UNSHAKABLE SENSE OF DESTINY THAT DEFINES THEIR RELATIONSHIP.

THE LYRIC VIDEO FOR THIS SONG UNDERLINES THIS INSPIRATION WITH PHOTOS OF HER GRANDPARENTS THROUGHOUT THEIR LIVES.

THIS SONG IS WRITTEN IN THE MUSICAL KEY OF D SHARP AND HAS A TEMPO OF 143 BEATS PER MINUTE.

THE FIRST PERFORMANCE OF THE SONG WAS ON JULY 14TH, 2023 IN DENVER DURING "THE ERAS TOUR".

RED (TAYLOR'S VERSION)

RELEASED: OCTOBER 12, 2012
RECLAIMED: NOVEMBER 12, 2021

"Passionate, Introspective, Evocative, Dynamic

STATE OF GRACE

First track on her fourth album
Released as a single: October 22nd, 2012
Reclaimed: November 12th, 2021
Recorded: Blackbird Studios in Nashville, TN

DID YOU KNOW?

Taylor delivered her first live performance of "State of Grace" on November 15, 2012, as part of the second season of the U.S. edition of "The X Factor."

Taylor has hidden messages in the lyric booklets for her albums until 2014. The specific hidden message for this track is: I love you doesn't count after goodbye.

Taylor describes "State of Grace" as both the introduction and conclusion of "RED." She considers it a warning about the dual nature of love – it can be both euphoric and heartbreaking.

CHARTS & AWARDS

- Peaked at #13 on the Billboard Hot 100 Chart
- (Taylor's Version) peaked at #18 on the Billboard Hot 100
- Certified Gold by RIAA
- To date, the original version has been streamed 59,615,161 times
- (Taylor's Version) has been streamed 106,315,124 times

IN TAYLOR'S WORDS

"I wrote this song about when you first fall in love with someone. The possibilities, kind of thinking about the different ways that it could go. It's a really big sound. To me, this sounds like the feeling of falling in love in an epic way."

RED

Fifth single on her fourth album
Released as a single: June 24th, 2013
Reclaimed: November 12th, 2021
Recorded: Blackbird Studios in Nashville, TN

DID YOU KNOW?

Taylor performed "Red" for the first time at the CMA Awards on November 6, 2013, the same night she received country music's highest honor - "The Pinnacle Award."

Taylor notes about this song: "I wrote this song about the fact that some things are just hard to forget because the emotions involved with them were so intense and, to me, intense emotion is red."

"Red" was Taylor's 13th song to reach the top 10 on the Billboard Hot 100 Chart. It was also Taylor's longest charting song at the time, spending 42 weeks on the chart.

CHARTS & AWARDS

- Peaked at #6 on the Billboard Hot 100 Chart
- (Taylor's Version) peaked at #25 on the Billboard Hot 100
- Certified Platinum by RIAA
- Nominated for "Female Video of the Year" at the CMT Music Awards in 2013
- To date, the original version has been streamed 242,349,156 times
- (Taylor's Version) has been streamed 236,821,135 times

IN TAYLOR'S WORDS

"I knew I hadn't jumped out of my comfort zone, which at the time was writing alone and working with Nathan. ['Red'] the song was a real turning point for RED, the album. When I wrote that song my mind started wandering to all the places we could go. If I were to think outside the box enough, go in with different people, I could learn from and have what they do rub off on me as well as have what I do rub off on them."

TREACHEROUS

Third track on her fourth album
Released as a single: June 24th, 2013
Reclaimed: November 12th, 2021
Recorded: Ballroom West In Los Angeles, CA

DID YOU KNOW?

Taylor first performed "Treacherous" during an online live video chat when she announced the RED album on August 13, 2012 from her mom's residence in Nashville.

Her Co-writer for the song, Dan Wilson, says of the track: "It's like deliberately putting yourself so close to someone that you will inevitably fall into their arms. Taking command of the situation by letting go of all command."

Her co-writer for this song, Dan Wilson, wrote the 1998 hit song "Closing Time" during his time in the rock band Semisonic.

CHARTS & AWARDS

- Peaked at #102 on the Billboard Charts
- (Taylor's Version) peaked at #54 on the Billboard Hot 100
- To date, the original version has been streamed 54,041,275 times
- (Taylor's Version) has been streamed 94,606,466 times

IN TAYLOR'S WORDS

"I wrote 'Treacherous' with Dan Wilson, and we came up with a way to say, you know, 'This is dangerous and I realize that I might get hurt if I go through with this, if I move forward with you. But...but I want to.' You know? It's like that kind of conflicted feeling of it being a risk every time you fall in love – especially with certain types of people. That was a song that I'm really proud of because it's got this bridge that sounds like a second chorus. It's got all these big vocals, and it's kind of the intensity of that moment when you're deciding to let yourself fall in love with someone."

DID YOU KNOW?

The music video was shot near Los Angeles and stars Reeve Carney as Taylor's love interest. Taylor's pink hairstyle and edgy fashion was what many consider to be the beginning of her shifting from the well known "good girl" Image.

The debut performance happened at the American Music Awards on November 18th, 2012.

With the release of "I Knew You Were Trouble", Taylor became the first artist in digital history to have 2 songs that debuted with over 400,000 copies.

I KNEW YOU WERE TROUBLE.

Third single on her fourth album
Released as a single: October 9th, 2012
Reclaimed: November 12th, 2021
Recorded: Conway Studios In Los Angeles, CA

CHARTS & AWARDS

- Peaked at #3 on the Billboard Hot 100 Chart
- (Taylor's Version) peaked at #54 on the Billboard Hot 100
- RIAA certified 10x Diamond
- Won Best Female Video at the MTV Video Music Awards In 2013
- Nominated for "Choice Single by a Female Artist" at the Teen Choice Awards In 2013
- To date, the original version has been streamed 756,612,124 times
- (Taylor's Version) has been streamed 268,635,334 times

IN TAYLOR'S WORDS

"[It's] about knowing the second you see someone like, 'Oh, this is going to be interesting. It's going to be dangerous, but look at me going in there anyway.' I think that for me, it was the first time I ever kind of noticed that in myself, like when you are curious about something you know might be bad for you, but you know that you are going to go for it anyway because if you don't, you'll have greater regrets about not seeing where that would go."

(OG version)

ALL TOO WELL

Fifth track on her fourth album
Released: October 22, 2012
Reclaimed: November 12th, 2021
Recorded: Pain In the Art Studios in Nashville, TN

On January 26, 2014, at the 56th Annual Grammy Awards in Los Angeles, Taylor performed "All Too Well," while her album RED was nominated for both "Album of the Year" and "Best Country Album."

"All Too Well" was the first song Taylor wrote on the "RED" album. Despite being a clear fan favorite, the song was never released as a single.

There is extensive speculation that "All Too Well" is inspired by Taylor's relationship with actor Jake Gyllenhaal, which occurred between October and December 2010.

Taylor has previously hidden messages in the lyric booklets of each song on her albums until 2014. This specific song's hidden message is: "Maple Lattes" which refers to a Thanksgiving date Taylor and Jake enjoyed maple lattes in cafe in Brooklyn, NY.

CHARTS & AWARDS

- Peaked at #80 on the Billboard Hot 100 Chart
- (Taylor's Version) peaked at #1 on the Billboard Hot 100
- Certified RIAA Platinum
- To date, the original version has been streamed 237,613,138 times
- (Taylor's Version) has been streamed 218,141,356 times

IN TAYLOR'S WORDS

"It was a day when I was a broken human, walking into rehearsal, just feeling terrible about what was going on in my personal life. I remember we had just hired David Cook, who is now my band leader. I think it was his first day meeting me and I ended up just playing four chords over and over again. The band started kicking in, like Amos Heller on bass. People just started playing along with me. I think they could tell I was really going through it. And I just started singing, and riffing, and sort of ad-libbing this song that, basically, was 'All Too Well.' "

DID YOU KNOW?

Taylor entered the "RED" album era desiring to switch up musical styles. Collaborating with producer Max Martin, 'Billboard' describes "22" as Taylor's "most blatantly 'pop' song" written to date.

The music video for the song was filmed In Malibu, CA and premiered on "Good Morning America" on March 13th, 2013.

The song was written In December of 2011 around the time of Taylor's 22nd birthday. It describes Taylor's feelings of imperfection, yet excitement of growing up and moving towards adulthood.

Taylor has previously hidden messages in the lyric booklets of each song on her albums until 2014. This specific song's hidden message is: "Ashley, Dianna, Claire, Selena" - the names of several of Taylor's close friends.

22

Third single on her fourth album
Released as a single: March 12th, 2013
Reclaimed: November 12th, 2021
Recorded: Conway Studios in Los Angeles, CA

CHARTS & AWARDS

- Peaked at #20 on the Billboard Hot 100 Chart
- (Taylor's Version) peaked at #52 on the Billboard Hot 100
- Certified RIAA Triple Platinum
- Nominated for "Best Song of the Year" at the Neox Fan Awards in 2013
- To date, the original version has been streamed 363,909,391 times
- (Taylor's Version) has been streamed 213,712,449 times

IN TAYLOR'S WORDS

"For me, being 22 has been my favorite year of my life. I like all the possibilities of how you're still learning, but you know enough. You still know nothing, but you know that you know nothing. You're old enough to start planning your life, but you're young enough to know there are so many unanswered questions. That brings about a carefree feeling that is sort of based on indecision and fear and a the same time letting lose. Being 22 has taught me so much."

I ALMOST DO

Seventh Track on her fourth album
Released: October 22nd, 2012
Reclaimed: November 12th, 2021
Recorded: Blackbird Studios in Nashville, TN

DID YOU KNOW?

Taylor did not Include this In the regular set list for "the RED tour" and did not perform the song for the 10 years following this album. On June 9th, 2023, Taylor revisited the song again played on piano during "The Eras Tour."

The song is also referring to Taylor's relationship with Jake Gyllenhaal and the instinct to reach back out despite a painful break-up. Taylor suffered a six month writing block following the conclusion of the relationship.

Taylor has previously hidden messages in the lyric booklets of each song on her albums until 2014. This specific song's hidden message is: "Wrote this instead of calling".

CHARTS & AWARDS

- Peaked at #50 on the Billboard Hot 100 Chart
- (Taylor's Version) peaked at #59 on the Billboard Hot 100
- To date, the original version has been streamed 60,805,468 times
- (Taylor's Version) has been streamed 79,048,123 times

IN TAYLOR'S WORDS

"'I Almost Do' is a song I wrote about the conflict that you feel when you want to take someone back, and you want to give it another try, but you know you can't. And you can't because you know it's hurt you so deeply that you know that you couldn't bear to go through that again. So you're sitting there, and wondering where they are, and hope that they think about you, and that you're almost picking up the phone call, but you just can't. I think I needed to write this song in order to not call that person, actually. I think that writing the song was what I did instead of picking up the phone."

DID YOU KNOW?

Taylor collaborated with Max Martin and Shellback on this song Inspired by hearing rumors that she may be getting back together with her ex-boyfriend. Taylor answered firmly dispelled these rumors as the lyrics to the track started to form.

The single spent 9 weeks as #1 on the Hot Country Songs Chart, breaking a record set In 1965 by Connie Smith.

At the time, "We Are Never Ever Getting Back Together" was Taylor's first song to reach #1 on the Billboard Hot 100 Chart.

In 2012, This song broke the Guinness World Record for "Fastest Selling Single In Digital History".

The first to be presented in 4K resolution, the music video was released in August 2012 and was recorded In one continous shot.

WE ARE NEVER EVER GETTING BACK TOGETHER

First single on her fourth album
Released: August 13th, 2012
Reclaimed: November 12th, 2021
Recorded: Conway Studios in Los Angeles, CA

CHARTS & AWARDS

- Debuted at #72 and Peaked two days later at #1 on the Billboard Hot 100 Chart
- (Taylor's Version) peaked at #55 on the Billboard Hot 100
- Certified RIAA 8x Platinium
- Nominated for "Record of the Year" at the 55th Annual Grammy Awards
- Won "Top Country Song" at the Billboard Music Awards In 2013
- Won "Choice Country Song" at the Teen Choice Awards In 2013
- Won "World's Best Song" at the World Music Awards In 2014
- To date, the original version has been streamed 626,496,246 times
- (Taylor's Version) has been streamed 253,904,888 times

IN TAYLOR'S WORDS

"It's a definitive portrait of how I felt when I finally stopped caring what my ex thought of me. He made me feel like I wasn't as good or as relevant as these hipster bands he listened to. So I made a song that I knew would absolutely drive him crazy when he heard it on the radio. Not only would it hopefully be played a lot, so that he'd have to hear it, but it's the opposite of the kind of music that he was trying to make me feel inferior to."

STAY STAY STAY

Ninth Track on her fourth album
Released: October 22nd, 2012
Reclaimed: November 12th, 2021
Recorded: Blackbird Studios in Nashville, TN

DID YOU KNOW?

Taylor co-wrote this song with Nathan Chapman, a long time collaborator. It follows the chord progession G-C-Em-D, a common pattern throughout Taylor's discography.

Taylor included this song on the first part of "the RED Tour" setlist along with performing a mash-up of the song with "Ho Hey" by the Lumineers.

Taylor has previously hidden messages in the lyric booklets of each song on her albums until 2014. This specific song's hidden message is: "Daydreaming about real love".

CHARTS & AWARDS

- Peaked at #91 on the Billboard Hot 100 Chart
- (Taylor's Version) peaked at #67 on the Billboard Hot 100
- To date, the original version has been streamed 55,982,398 times
- (Taylor's Version) has been streamed 76,682,422 times

IN TAYLOR'S WORDS

"The song 'Stay Stay Stay' is a song that I wrote based on what I've seen of real relationships, where it's not perfect, there are moments where you're just so sick of that person, you get into a stupid fight. It's still worth it to stay in it. There's something about it that you can't live without. In the bridge it says, 'I'd like to hang out with you for my whole life' and I think that's what probably the key to finding the one, you just want to hang out with them forever."

THE LAST TIME

Seventh Single on her fourth album
Released as a single: November 4th, 2013
Reclaimed: November 12th, 2021
Recorded: The Garage in Topanga Cyn, CA

DID YOU KNOW?

Known for his contribution to albums from Snow Patrol and U2, Jacknife Lee was the primary producer on the track. In addition, Gary Lightbody of the band Snow Patrol sings Swift.

The song's story Is of a cyclical relationship that can't break the pattern of heartbreak followed by forgiveness.

The song was performed by Taylor and Gary on "The X Factor" on November 13th, 2013, to kick off the release as a single in the United Kingdom.

Taylor has previously hidden messages in the lyric booklets of each song on her albums until 2014. This specific song's hidden message is: "LA on your break".

CHARTS & AWARDS

- Original version of the track did not chart on the Billboard Hot 100
- (Taylor's Version) peaked at #66 on the Billboard Hot 100
- To date, the original version has been streamed 65,004,880 times
- (Taylor's Version) has been streamed 93,148,807 times

IN TAYLOR'S WORDS

"The Last Time' is a song that I wrote with Gary Lightbody, of Snow Patrol. I've always wanted to work with Snow Patrol, they're my favourite band. This was a song that I wrote about something I had been going through. I picture a door and, on the outside of the door, standing outside in the cold, there's this guy who's left his girlfriend over and over again and comes back and asks for a second chance over and over and over again. On the other side of the door, you have this girl standing there with tears in her eyes, wondering how she could possibly turn him away when she loves him this much, but she can't get hurt again. It's both of these people swearing that this would be the last time."

HOLY GROUND

Eleventh track on her fourth album
Released: October 22nd, 2012
Reclaimed: November 12th, 2021
Recorded: Enormous Studios in Los Angeles, CA

DID YOU KNOW?

Similar to "Last Kiss", the song is speculated to be about her relationship with Joe Jonas. The hidden message In the lyric booklet for this song is: "When you came to the show in SD." This may hint at feeling that she has made amends with Joe after he attended her "Speak Now World Tour" in San Francisco.

As an acoustic surprise song, Taylor played "Holy Ground" during her "1989 World Tour" In Dublin, Ireland on June 30th, 2015.

Taylor worked with producer Jeff Bhasker on this track, following her previous intention to explore unique new styles of music In the "RED" album. Bhasker is known for his drum-heavy production on albums like "Some Nights" by the band Fun.

CHARTS & AWARDS

- Original version of the track did not chart on the Billboard Hot 100
- (Taylor's Version) peaked at #76 on the Billboard Hot 100
- To date, the original version has been streamed 53,166,874 times
- (Taylor's Version) has been streamed 73,141,332 times

IN TAYLOR'S WORDS

"The song 'Holy Ground' was a song that I wrote about the feeling I got after years had gone by and I finally appreciated a past relationship for what it was, rather than being bitter about what it didn't end up being. And I was sitting there, thinking about it after I'd just seen him and I was just like, 'You know what, that was good.' It was, it was good, having that in my life, and I wrote the song and I immediately heard Jeff Bhasker's production. I hadn't ever worked with Jeff, but he has done some amazing work."

DID YOU KNOW?

The song came to life in 2011 while Taylor was touring for the "Speak Now World Tour." Upon recording the track, Taylor used the very first take as she felt it perfectly captured her emotions and the essence of the track.

Taylor played "Sad Beautiful Tragic" live for the first time in 10 years during "The Eras Tour" in Arlington, Texas on March 31st, 2023.

Taylor revealed in September 2022, that in writing each of her songs, they fall Into 3 distinct categories: "Fountain Pen", "Quill Pen" or "Glitter Gel Pen". Taylor notes: "I came up with these categories based on what writing tool I imagine having in my hand when I scribbled it down, figuratively." This song Is thought to be categorized as a "Fountain Pen" song which include modern lyrics full of familiar references and vivid imagery.

SAD BEAUTIFUL TRAGIC

Twelfth track on her fourth album
Released: October 22nd, 2012
Reclaimed: November 12th, 2021
Recorded: Pain in the Art Studios in Nashville, TN

CHARTS & AWARDS

- Original version of the track did not chart on the Billboard Hot 100
- (Taylor's Version) peaked at #85 on the Billboard Hot 100
- To date, the original version has been streamed 38,906,072 times
- (Taylor's Version) has been streamed 81,054,478 times

IN TAYLOR'S WORDS

"'Sad Beautiful Tragic' is really close to my heart. I remember it was after a show and I was on the bus thinking about this relationship that ended months and months before. The feeling wasn't sadness and anger or those things anymore. It was wistful loss. And so I just got my guitar and I hit on the fact that I was thinking in terms of rhyming; I rhymed magic with tragic, changed a few things and ended it with what a sad beautiful tragic love affair. I wanted to tell the story in terms of a cloudy recollection of what went wrong. It's kind of the murky gray, looking back on something you can't change or get back."

THE LUCKY ONE

Thirteenth track on her fourth album
Released: October 22nd, 2012
Reclaimed: November 12th, 2021
Recorded: Enormous Studios In Los Angeles, CA

In addition to "Holy Ground" - Taylor worked with producer Jeff Bhasker on this track, following her previous intention to explore unique new styles of music In the "RED" album. Bhasker is known for his drum-heavy production on albums like "Some Nights" by the band Fun.

Taylor notes during her re-recording of (Taylor's Version): "It's about how horrible being famous is." It Is rumored to be Inspired by a real life artist, with some speculating Joni Mitchell or Kim Wilde.

Taylor performed the song as an acoustic set during her "Reputation Stadium Tour" In Atlanta, GA on August 11th, 2018.

The song follows the chord progression: D-B minor-G-D which Is distinctly different than Taylor's most popular chord progression: D-A-Em-G.

CHARTS & AWARDS

- Original version of the track did not chart on the Billboard Hot 100
- (Taylor's Version) peaked at #85 on the Billboard Hot 100
- To date, the original version has been streamed 42,921,548 times
- (Taylor's Version) has been streamed 66,428,386 times

IN TAYLOR'S WORDS

"It kind of talks about some of my fears through telling the story of other people that I was inspired by. More than their stories being told, I'm pretty much singing about what I'm scared of in that song, ending up kind of caught up in this whole thing, and lonely, and feeling misunderstood, and feeling like when people think you're lucky that you're really not. It kind of expresses my greatest fear of having this not end up being fun anymore, having it end up being a scary place. Some people get there, some people end up there. It's a story song and it's something I'm really proud of because it kind of goes to a place that I'm terrified of."

DID YOU KNOW?

In 2013, Ed Sheeran became the primary opening act for Taylor during her "RED Tour," where the duo showcased their nightly rendition of "Everything Has Changed."

The music video for "Everything Has Changed" was filmed at a middle school In Oak Park, CA. The video tells the story of a friendship between a young boy and girl, later revealed to be the children of Ed and Taylor.

Taylor and Ed became friends around the time of this collaboration for the "RED" album and remain close. Ed notes: "I have long, long, long conversations with Taylor about stuff just because I feel like she's one of the only people that actually truly understands where I'm at because she's solo artist, she's stadiums."

EVERYTHING HAS CHANGED

Featuring Ed Sheeran
Sixth single on her fourth album
Released as a single: July 14th, 2013
Reclaimed: November 12th, 2021
Recorded: Ruby Red Studios in Santa Monica, CA

CHARTS & AWARDS

- Peaked at #32 the Billboard Hot 100
- (Taylor's Version) peaked at #63 on the Billboard Hot 100
- Certified RIAA Double Platinum
- Won as an "Award Winning Song" at the BMI Awards
- Won "Best Musical Collaboration" at the Radio Disney Music Awards In 2014
- To date, the original version has been streamed 264,102,081 times
- (Taylor's Version) has been streamed 123,217,318 times

IN TAYLOR'S WORDS

"'Everything Has Changed' is a song that I wrote with Ed Sheeran, and I think this is the one that we wrote on a trampoline in my backyard — how cute is that? He is a friend that I will just cherish forever, and looking back to the phases that we were at in our lives back then...It was shortly after this that we went on tour together. We had so many hilarious times, and this was the song that started all of it. And now when I think about this song, I think about how we'd make faces at each other onstage, and try to make the other one crack up. For me, this song is just about all the memories, all the fun times, the friendship montage — that's what I see in my head when I think about this."

STARLIGHT

Fifteenth track on her fourth album
Released: October 22nd, 2012
Reclaimed: November 12th, 2021
Recorded: Blackbird Studios in Nashville, TN

DID YOU KNOW?

At the "Ripple of Hope Gala" hosted by the Kennedy family on December 3, 2012, in New York City, Taylor performed her debut performance of "Starlight."

Taylor showcased this song in advertisements for one of her signature perfumes named "Taylor by Taylor Swift: Made of Starlight" in 2014.

Taylor revealed in September 2022, that in writing each of her songs, they fall Into 3 distinct categories: "Fountain Pen", "Quill Pen" or "Glitter Gel Pen". Taylor notes: "I came up with these categories based on what writing tool I imagine having in my hand when I scribbled it down, figuratively." This song Is thought to be categorized as a "Glitter Gel Pen" song which include lyrics that are "frivolous, carefree, and bouncy".

CHARTS & AWARDS

- Original version of the track did not chart on the Billboard Hot 100
- (Taylor's Version) peaked at #90 on the Billboard Hot 100
- To date, the original version has been streamed 42,540,039 times
- (Taylor's Version) has been streamed 60,065,322 times

IN TAYLOR'S WORDS

"'Starlight' is a song I wrote after seeing a picture of Ethel and Bobby Kennedy when they were seventeen. I saw this picture about a year and a half ago, and I didn't know anything about what they were doing or what was going on in the picture, but I just thought, 'They look like they're having the best night.' And so I wrote this song about what the night might've been like. I ended up meeting Ethel and going and playing it for her, and she just loved it. It was such a fun moment when she was just in love with the song and so happy about it. It's just this adorable picture that to me, it brought forth all these potentials for how that night could've been."

BEGIN AGAIN

Second single on her fourth album
Released as a single: October 1st, 2012
Reclaimed: November 12th, 2021
Recorded: Blackbird Studios in Nashville, TN

DID YOU KNOW?

As the final song of the original "RED" album, the song expresses hopefulness for a new relationship despite some of the heavy, heartbreaking tracks that came prior.

Directed by Philip Andelman, Taylor shot the music video for "Begin Again" in Paris, France.

Taylor has previously hidden messages in the lyric booklets of each song on her albums until 2014. This specific song's hidden message is: "I wear heels now". This message refers to Swift's new found confidence after overcoming the scars of her past relationships.

CHARTS & AWARDS

- Peaked at #7 on the Billboard Hot 100
- (Taylor's Version) peaked at #77 on the Billboard Hot 100
- Certified Platinum by RIAA
- Nominated for "Best Country Song" at the 56th Annual Grammy Awards
- Nominated for "Best Female Video" at the CMT Awards in 2013
- To date, the original version has been streamed 42,540,039 times
- (Taylor's Version) has been streamed 121,735,936 times

IN TAYLOR'S WORDS

"It's a song about when you've gotten through a really bad relationship and you finally dust yourself off and go on that first date after a horrible break up. And the vulnerability that goes along with all of that. Even after a relationship explodes into a million pieces, and burns down, and you're standing in a pile of the ash of what it once was, thinking, 'Why did I have to meet this person? Why did this have to happen?' But then, when you make eye contact with someone across the room and it clicks and, bam, you're there. In love again."

DID YOU KNOW?

Similar to "All Too Well" and "We Are Never Ever Getting Back Together", the subject of the song is speculated to be Jake Gyllenhaal. The song describes Taylor's 21st birthday that ended in disappointment when he doesn't show up on an incredibly important day.

Eleven years after its release, Taylor debuted "The Moment I Knew" as the second surprise song during her show on June 4, 2023, on "The Eras Tour" in Chicago.

Taylor revealed in September 2022, that in writing each of her songs, they fall Into 3 distinct categories: "Fountain Pen", "Quill Pen" or "Glitter Gel Pen". Taylor notes: "I came up with these categories based on what writing tool I imagine having in my hand when I scribbled it down, figuratively." This song Is thought to be categorized as a "Fountain Pen" song which include modern lyrics full of familiar references and vivid imagery.

THE MOMENT I KNEW

Seventeenth track on her fourth album
Released: October 22nd, 2012
Reclaimed: November 12th, 2021
Recorded: Pain in the Art Studios in Nashville, TN

CHARTS & AWARDS

- Peaked at #64 on the Billboard Hot 100
- (Taylor's Version) peaked at #83 on the Billboard Hot 100
- To date, the original version has been streamed 31,439,059 times
- (Taylor's Version) has been streamed 60,566,917 times

IN TAYLOR'S WORDS

"'The Moment I Knew' was a really difficult song for my friends and family to listen to because it is about my 21st birthday party and it was...not a good party, as you can hear in the song. It was...you know, standing there, waiting for someone to show up who never did. So it was a song that I felt was really important to put out to hear. Because nobody likes that feeling of waiting for somebody who's never going to walk through the door."

COME BACK...BE HERE

Eighteenth track on her fourth album
Released: October 22nd, 2012
Reclaimed: November 12th, 2021
Recorded: Ballroom West Studios in Los Angeles, CA

DID YOU KNOW?

Taylor worked on this bonus track with co-writer Dan Wilson, who also helped pen the song "Treacherous".

Six years after its conception, Taylor performed the song live for the first time in Toronto on August 5, 2018, on her "reputation Stadium Tour".

The song follows the chord progression: D-A-B minor-G which Is distinctly different than Taylor's most popular chord progression: D-A-Em-G.

Although Taylor notes that distance is a common struggle in her relationships, this Is the only song in her discography that focuses on the subject.

CHARTS & AWARDS

- The original version did not chart on the Billboard Hot 100
- (Taylor's Version) peaked at #83 on the Billboard Hot 100
- To date, the original version has been streamed 41,379,666 times
- (Taylor's Version) has been streamed 93,865,420 times

IN TAYLOR'S WORDS

"'Come Back...Be Here' is a song that I wrote with Dan Wilson about somebody I just met. It's about the feeling of just meeting someone and having all these sparks and then they leave, they have to go somewhere else. It's about the anxiety and wondering, 'How am I gonna see you again? I want to. How's this gonna happen?' There's a lot of fear that's involved with falling in love, especially when you're dealing with distance."

GIRL AT HOME

Nineteenth track on her fourth album
Released: October 22nd, 2012
Reclaimed: November 12th, 2021
Recorded: Pain in the Art Studios in Nashville, TN

DID YOU KNOW?

Similar to her reflections on "Picture to Burn" and "Better than Revenge", Taylor recognizes that some of the lyrics in this track do not align with her current attitude towards feminism and female empowerment.

When re-recorded for "RED (Taylor's Version)", the track was transformed from a country-pop to an electronic feel. Swedish producer, Elvira Anderfjärd, collaborated with Taylor on the song.

Taylor revealed in September 2022, that in writing each of her songs, they fall Into 3 distinct categories: "Fountain Pen", "Quill Pen" or "Glitter Gel Pen". Taylor notes: "I came up with these categories based on what writing tool I imagine having in my hand when I scribbled it down, figuratively." This song Is thought to be categorized as a "Fountain Pen" song which include modern lyrics full of familiar references and vivid imagery.

CHARTS & AWARDS

- The original version did not chart on the Billboard Hot 100
- (Taylor's Version) did not chart on the Billboard Hot 100
- To date, the original version has been streamed 22,575,971 times
- (Taylor's Version) has been streamed 50,296,786 times

IN TAYLOR'S WORDS

"There's a song called 'Girl at Home,' which was about a guy who had a girlfriend, and I just felt like it was disgusting that he was flirting with other girls."

RONAN

Charity single released during the RED era
Released: September 8th, 2012
Reclaimed: November 12th, 2021
Recorded: Blackbird Studios in Nashville, TN

DID YOU KNOW?

Inspired by Maya Thompson's blog, Taylor penned "Ronan" in response to the heartbreaking story of Thompson's four-year-old son, who tragically succumbed to neuroblastoma in 2011.

In October 2011, Taylor and Maya met when Taylor extended an invitation for Maya to attend the concert during her "Speak Now World Tour" in Glendale. Taylor revealed during their meeting that she wrote a song for Ronan; she later performed the song on "Stand Up To Cancer" with all proceeds going to cancer research.

Maya notes of the song: "Taylor has anchored [Ronan] to this world so you will never be lost, and now she has ensured you will forever be safe in a new, permeant home."

CHARTS & AWARDS

- Peaked at #16 on the Billboard Hot 100
- (Taylor's Version) did not chart on the Billboard Hot 100
- Certified RIAA Gold
- To date, the original version has been streamed 6,290,921 times
- (Taylor's Version) has been streamed 37,448,941 times

IN TAYLOR'S WORDS

"I've recently completed the re-recording of my 4th album, RED. It's really exceeded my expectations in so many ways, and one of those ways is that I thought it would be appropriate to add 'Ronan' to this album. RED was an album of heartbreak and healing, of rage and rawness, of tragedy and trauma, and of the loss of an imagined future alongside someone. I wrote 'Ronan' while I was making RED and discovered your story as you so honestly and devastatingly told it. My genuine hope is that you'll agree with me that this song should be included on this album. As my co-writer and the rightful owner of this story in its entirety, your opinion and approval of this idea really matters to me, and I'll honor your wishes here."

BETTER MAN

First vault track on RED (Taylor's Version)
Released: November 12th, 2021
Recorded: Blackbird Studios in Nashville, TN

CHARTS & AWARDS

- The song originally released by Little Big Town reached #1 on the Billboard Hot Country Chart and Is certified Platinum by the RIAA
- (Taylor's Version) peaked at #51 on the Billboard Hot 100 Chart
- To date, the track has been streamed 121,266,272 times

IN TAYLOR'S WORDS

"When I would play writers nights, I didn't have the experience of a writer writing something and then it going out into the world and you hearing it from someone else's perspective until recently. Little Big Town gave me the opportunity to feel that way, to be at the Bluebird and play a song you've maybe heard on the radio. I will always be forever grateful to them for that."

NOTHING NEW

Featuring Phoebe Bridgers
Second vault track on RED (Taylor's Version)
Released: November 12th, 2021
Recorded: Sound City In Los Angeles, CA

DID YOU KNOW?

Taylor originally wrote the song in 2012, as she began to feel the pressure of what she felt was the need to stay relevant. It also provides commentary on how the music industry treats female musicians.

Taylor performed "Nothing New" live for the first time in Nashville on May 5, 2023, together with Phoebe Bridgers during "The Eras Tour".

Taylor on working with Phoebe on the duet: "Phoebe Bridgers is one of my favorite artists, I think she's just phenomenal and I was so touched and honored when she jumped at the chance to record this as a duet. And she had such an amazing take on the song when she heard it, and how it applies to women and what we are taught about novelty, and newness, and youth."

CHARTS & AWARDS

- Peaked at #43 on the Billboard Hot 100 Chart
- Total of 1 week on the Billboard Hot 100 Chart
- To date, the track has been streamed 182,961,296 times

IN TAYLOR'S WORDS

"The song 'Nothing New' is a song that I wrote when I was 22 and tour. I was on the New Zealand/Australia leg of a tour, I wrote a little bit in each of those places. It was during a phase of my career when I was on my fourth album, and even though I was only 22 I just felt like old news, I really did. I think that new artists don't realize that when they put out their first or second album that they're in this shiny, new phase where everything you do is interesting and exciting to people. And it's only when you get to the moment after your breakthrough where you realize that you're gonna have to figure out some other shade of yourself to show people. Because people are not responding the same way they did when you were brand new. "

BABE

Third vault track on RED (Taylor's Version)
Released: November 12th, 2021
Recorded: Electric Lady Studios in New York, NY

DID YOU KNOW?

Taylor collaborated with Patrick Monahan of the band Train to write this song in 2012. Similar to "Better Man", the song cut from "RED" and was then released by the duo Sugarland in 2018.

Similar to "All Too Well" and "We Are Never Ever Getting Back Together", the subject of the song is speculated to be Jake Gyllenhaal. The track is a message to an ex-lover about broken loyalty that lead to the end of the relationship.

The music video by Sugarland was nominated for "Video of the Year" at the 2018 CMA Awards and also at the 2019 ACM Awards.

CHARTS & AWARDS

- The version published by Sugarland peaked at #72 on the Billboard Hot 100 Chart
- Sugarland's original version was certified RIAA Gold
- (Taylor's Version) peaked at #69 on the Billboard Hot 100 Chart
- Total of 1 week on the Billboard Hot 100 Chart
- To date, the track has been streamed 6,290,921 times

IN TAYLOR'S WORDS

"It's a song that I wrote with Pat Monahan when I was making the RED album. I'm so happy that it gets its own life. I'm so happy that Sugarland wanted to record it, and has done such a good job with it, and I'm so stoked to be able to sing on it, too."

MESSAGE IN A BOTTLE

Fouth vault track on RED (Taylor's Version)
Released: November 12th, 2021
Recorded: Kitty Committee Studios in Belfast, UK

DID YOU KNOW?

Collaborating on the production of the song, Shellback and Elvira Anderfjärd took on multiple roles, with Shellback playing guitar, Anderfjärd performing on bass and drums, and both contributing to the keyboards.

"Message in a Bottle" is set in the key of G major with a tempo of 116 beats per minute.

During the initial week of Red (Taylor's Version)'s release, it emerged as the most requested song across iHeartRadio stations.

Taylor performed this song for the first time live during "The Eras Tour" In Seattle on July 23, 2023.

CHARTS & AWARDS

- Certified Gold by the RIAA
- Peaked at #45 on the Billboard Hot 100 Chart
- Total of 13 weeks on the Billboard Hot 100 Chart
- To date, the track has been streamed 168,437,967 times

IN TAYLOR'S WORDS

"'Message In A Bottle' is such a fun song! It is so catchy and the melody is really contagious. Max Martin, Shellback and I...that was the first song we ever wrote together. We went on to write songs like 'We Are Never Ever Getting Back Together,' 'I Knew You Were Trouble.' and '22' and we felt like those songs really represented what we were doing on RED. We kept saying that somewhere down the line we'd put out 'Message In A Bottle' because we loved it so much and this is the first opportunity that we have to show it to the world. We're all really excited about it!"

I BET YOU THINK ABOUT ME

Featuring Chris Stapleton
Fifth vault track on RED (Taylor's Version)
Released: November 12th, 2021
Recorded: Kitty Committee Studios in Belfast, UK

DID YOU KNOW?

Taylor originally co-wrote the song with Lori McKenna in June 2011 at Gillette Stadium in Foxborough, MA. The song Is one of the few in Taylor's catalog that feature a harmonica.

The music video for the track was directed by Blake Lively, one of Taylor's closest friends. The video shows Taylor crashing the wedding of her ex-partner, played by Miles Teller. The bride in the video is played by Teller's real life spouse - Keleigh Sperry Teller. In a notable cameo, co-producer Aaron Dessner assumes the role of a wedding band member, and Swift's brother, actor Austin Swift, is acknowledged as a producer in the credits for the music video.

CHARTS & AWARDS

- Certified Platinum by the RIAA
- Peaked at #22 on the Billboard Hot 100 Chart
- Total of 2 weeks on the Billboard Hot 100 Chart
- Nominated for "Video of the Year" at the Academy of Country Music Awards and the CMT Music Awards in 2022
- Won "Best Country/Americana Song" at the Gold Derby Music Awards
- Nominated for "Best Country Song" at the 66th Annual Grammy Awards
- To date, the track has been streamed 184,416,215 times

IN TAYLOR'S WORDS

"The song 'I Bet You Think About Me' is a song I wrote with Lori McKenna who is one of my favorite singer-songwriters ever. I'd always wanted to work with her. I wrote this with her when I was at her house when I was playing Foxborough Stadium on the 'Speak Now Tour.' We wanted this song to be a comedic, tongue-in-cheek, funny, not-caring-what-anyone-thinks-about-you sort of breakup song. Because there are a lot of different types of heartbreak songs on RED, some of them are very sincere, some of them very stoic and heartbreaking, and sad. We wanted this to be more like, 'I don't care about anything!' And we wanted to kind of make people laugh at it, we wanted it to be sort of a drinking song. I think that's what it ended up being."

FOREVER WINTER

Sixth vault track on RED (Taylor's Version)
Released: November 12th, 2021
Recorded: Kitty Committee Studios in Belfast, UK

DID YOU KNOW?

This song is widely rumored to be about Swift's old high school friend, Jeff Lang, who battled addiction and mental health issues, and tragically passed away two weeks after the release of her third studio album, "Speak Now".

At the BMI Country Awards 2010 in Nashville, Taylor said, "It's been a really emotional week. Yesterday, I sang at the funeral of one of my best friends. And he was 21 and I used to play my songs for him first. So, I would like to thank Jeff Lang."

The poignant song explores Taylor's concerns about a loved one grappling with a mental illness, likely depression, and her yearning to embody a source of warmth like a summer sun in their life during what felt like a cold and dark winter.

CHARTS & AWARDS

- Peaked at #79 on the Billboard Hot 100 Chart
- Total of 1 week on the Billboard Hot 100 Chart
- To date, the track has been streamed 79,399,575 times

IN TAYLOR'S WORDS

"The song 'Forever Winter' is about being in a moment in your life where you love someone, or someone is such a good friend of yours, or you feel really close to someone, and you realize all at once that they've been struggling for a very long time. And you feel so guilty that you didn't see it sooner, and you wish you would've checked in on them more. That person means so much to you, but you didn't necessarily pick up on the signs that maybe they weren't okay. So, that's 'Forever Winter'."

In early 2012, Taylor and Ed collaborated on writing "Run" during her visit to Seattle, Washington, where they held a songwriting session in a hotel room.

It was actually written prior to "Everything Has Changed" and marked their first ever song written together.

A quote from Ed on the track: «We wrote 'Run' and then we wrote 'Everything Has Changed' maybe like a week later. And I remember always thinking, 'Well, 'Run' is the one that's gonna make the album.' It was always my favorite. But 'Everything Has Changed' just ended up sounding better because we produced them differently or whatever. So 'Run' has just been there for years and years. I've never really wanted to nudge Taylor about it – because it's her song. But I've always been secretly hoping that one day she'd be like, 'Hey, this song was cool!' And so we recorded that and it's really great! I'm so happy it's seeing the light of day.»

The producer of this track along with the "Folklore" and "Evermore"albums, Aaron Dessner went on to produce Ed Sheeran's 2023 album - "Subtract".

RUN

Featuring Ed Sheeran
Seventh vault track on RED (Taylor's Version)
Released: November 12th, 2021
Recorded: Kitty Committee Studios in Belfast, UK

CHARTS & AWARDS

- Peaked at #47 on the Billboard Hot 100 Chart
- Total of 1 week on the Billboard Hot 100 Chart
- To date, the track has been streamed 124,965,021 times

IN TAYLOR'S WORDS

"It's a song about the escapism of falling in love and how you don't really care what anyone else says when you feel this way – you just wanna run away with someone. And all the little secrets that you establish with this person, this secret world you create together."

THE VERY FIRST NIGHT

Eighth vault track on RED (Taylor's Version)
Released: November 12th, 2021
Recorded: Kitty Committee Studios in Belfast, UK

DID YOU KNOW?

Taylor collaborated on the track with Espen Lind and Amund Bjørklund of the group "Espionage". They are responsible for other hits like "Irreplaceable" by Beyonce.

Taylor played the song live for the first time In Buenos Aires, Argentina during "The Eras Tour" on November 9, 2023.

Nostalgically reflecting on a previous relationship, Taylor writes about recalling details like the first date, expressing a longing to revisit that exhilarating, love-struck sensation from the start of the relationship.

CHARTS & AWARDS

- Peaked at #61 on the Billboard Hot 100 Chart
- Total of 1 week on the Billboard Hot 100 Chart
- To date, the track has been streamed 145,919,921 times

IN TAYLOR'S WORDS

"'The Very First Night' is a song that I made with a production group called Espionage, and they're so cool, so talented. This is actually the first time anybody gets to hear the work we did together because this didn't end up on the album, even though I loved it so much and told myself that someday it would come out. It's a song about a common theme on the RED album, which is reminiscing. Reminiscing about something that's over now, and reminiscing about the good times, and how powerful memories can be."

DID YOU KNOW?

This song represents the unedited, unabridged version of her fan favorite song - "All Too Well". She first performed the full length version during a band practice on the "Speak Now World Tour". Upon its release on "RED (Taylor's Version)" it became the longest song to ever reach #1 on the Billboard Hot 100 Chart.

Taylor made her filmmaking debut with the creation of a short film alongside the 10-minute version of the song. The film was premiered In New York City on November 12th, 2021. It was also shown at the Tribeca and Toronto Film Festivals.

Taylor performed the 10-minute version on "Saturday Night Live" on November 13th, 2021 and set the record for the longest performance ever aired on the show.

(10 MINUTE VERSION)
ALL TOO WELL

Ninth vault track on her fourth album
Released: October 22, 2012
Reclaimed: November 12th, 2021
Recorded: Kitty Committee Studios in Belfast, UK

CHARTS & AWARDS

- Peaked at #1 on the Billboard Hot 100 Chart
- Certified RIAA Triple Platinum
- Won "Video of the Year", "Best Longform Video", and "Best Direction" at the 2022 MTV Video Music Awards
- Won "Favorite Music Video" at the American Music Awards in 2022
- Won "Best Music Video" at the 66th Annual Grammy Awards
- Won "Best Lyrics" at the iHeartRadio Music Awards in 2022
- To date, the 10-minute version has been streamed 707,916,744 times

IN TAYLOR'S WORDS

"This is the original song I wrote. 'All Too Well' was never a single, never had a video, and the fans just turned it into The Song from this album. I used to get so sad when I'd sing it that I could barely get through the song and over time I realized the fans were just screaming the words back to me so loudly that it was very joyful for me to sing. So this song was originally ten minutes long. I just kept writing, I couldn't stop, but it had to fit on an album. So I had to cut out certain verses, parts of the bridge, lots of things I really loved. I left some of my favorite lines on the cutting room floor. I'm really happy people get to hear it, and I'm so proud of it. I think this was the version of the song that was meant to be heard."

1989

TAYLOR'S VERSION

RELEASED: OCTOBER 27, 2014
RECLAIMED: OCTOBER 27, 2023

"Evolutionary, Electrifying, Retro, Self-assured"

WELCOME TO NEW YORK

FIRST TRACK ON HER FIFTH ALBUM
RELEASED:OCTOBER 27, 2014
RELCAIMED: OCTOBER 27, 2023
RECORDED: CONWAY STUDIOS IN LOS ANGELES, CA

CHARTS & AWARDS

- PEAKED AT #48 ON THE BILLBOARD HOT 100 CHART
- (TAYLOR'S VERSION) PEAKED AT #14 ON THE BILLBOARD HOT 100 CHART
- CERTIFIED PLATINUM BY THE RIAA
- TO DATE, THE ORIGINAL VERSION HAS BEEN STREAMED 234,535,603 TIMES
- (TAYLOR'S VERSION) HAS BEEN STREAMED 56,010,953 TIMES

DID YOU KNOW?

TAYLOR DONATED ALL PROCEEDS FROM THE TRACK TO NEW YORK CITY PUBLIC SCHOOLS. IN RESPONSE, THE CITY'S OFFICIAL TOURISM AGENCY NAMED HER THE TOURISM AMBASSADOR FOR NYC.

AS TAYLOR EMBRACED HER FULL TRANSITION TO POP, SHE COLLABORATED WITH NEW PRODUCERS INCLUDING RYAN TEDDER ON THIS TRACK.

TO MARK THE RELEASE OF THE ALBUM, SWIFT HOSTED A CONCERT NAMED "1989 SECRET SESSIONS" IN MANHATTAN ON OCTOBER 27, 2014. SHE PLAYED THIS TRACK FOR THE FIRST TIME LIVE DURING THAT CONCERT.

IN TAYLOR'S WORDS

"I WANTED TO START 1989 WITH THIS SONG BECAUSE NEW YORK HAS BEEN AN IMPORTANT LANDSCAPE AND LOCATION FOR THE STORY OF MY LIFE IN THE LAST COUPLE OF YEARS. I DREAMT AND OBSESSED OVER MOVING TO NEW YORK, AND THEN I DID IT. THE INSPIRATION THAT I FOUND IN THAT CITY IS HARD TO DESCRIBE AND TO COMPARE TO ANY OTHER FORCE OF INSPIRATION I'VE EVER EXPERIENCED IN MY LIFE. IT'S AN ELECTRIC CITY."

BLANK SPACE

SECOND SINGLE ON HER FIFTH ALBUM
RELEASED AS S SINGLE: NOVEMBER 10, 2014
RECLAIMED: OCTOBER 27, 2023
RECORDED: CONWAY STUDIOS IN LOS ANGELES, CA

CHARTS & AWARDS

- PEAKED AT #1 ON THE BILLBOARD HOT 100 CHART
- (TAYLOR'S VERSION) PEAKED AT #12 ON THE BILLBOARD HOT 100 CHART
- CERTIFIED 10X PLATINUM BY THE RIAA
- WON "SONG OF THE YEAR" AT THE AMERICAN MUSIC AWARDS IN 2015
- WON "BEST FEMALE VIDEO" AT THE MTV VIDEO MUSIC AWARDS IN 2015
- 4 GRAMMY NOMINATIONS IN 2016
- TO DATE, THE ORIGINAL VERSION HAS BEEN STREAMED 1,636,426,686 TIMES
- (TAYLOR'S VERSION) HAS BEEN STREAMED 72,927,563 TIMES

DID YOU KNOW?

ON THIS TRACK, TAYLOR PAINTS A CHARACTER OF "A GIRL WHO'S CRAZY BUT SEDUCTIVE BUT GLAMOROUS BUT NUTS BUT MANIPULATIVE".

THE MUSIC VIDEO FOR "BLANK SPACE" WAS SHOT IN LONG ISLAND, NY AT OHEKA CASTLE AND WOOLWORTH ESTATE. WHILE FILMING IN FRONT OFA VINTAGE CAR, TAYLOR UNINTENTIONALLY DAMAGED THE CAR'S FRONT, RESULTING IN A $3,200 EXPENSE FOR REPAINTING.

ROLLING STONE NAMED "BLANK SPACE" AT NUMBER 67 ON ITS LIST OF 100 GREATEST MUSIC VIDEOS OF ALL TIME.

IN TAYLOR'S WORDS

"EVERY FEW YEARS, THE MEDIA FINDS SOMETHING THEY UNANIMOUSLY AGREE IS ANNOYING ABOUT ME. 2012-2013 THEY THOUGHT I WAS DATING TOO MUCH. BECAUSE I DATED TWO PEOPLE IN A YEAR AND A HALF. 'OH, A SERIAL DATER. SHE ONLY WRITES SONGS TO GET EMOTIONAL REVENGE ON GUYS. SHE'S A MAN-HATER, DON'T LET HER NEAR YOUR BOYFRIEND.' IT WAS KIND OF EXCESSIVE AND AT FIRST IT WAS HURTFUL, BUT THEN I FOUND A LITTLE BIT OF COMEDY IN IT. THIS CHARACTER IS SO INTERESTING, THOUGH. IF YOU READ THESE GOSSIP SITES, THEY DESCRIBE HOW I AM SO OPPOSITE TO MY ACTUAL LIFE: I'M CLINGY, AND I'M AWFUL, AND I THROW FITS, AND THERE'S DRAMA, AN EMOTIONALLY FRAGILE, UNPREDICTABLE MESS. I PAINTED A WHOLE PICTURE OF THIS CHARACTER. SHE LIVES IN A MANSION WITH MARBLE FLOORS, SHE WEARS DOLCE & GABBANA AROUND THE HOUSE, AND SHE WEARS ANIMAL PRINT UNIRONICALLY. SO I CREATED THIS WHOLE CHARACTER AND I HAD FUN DOING IT."

BOTH SINGERS RYAN ADAMS AND FATHER JOHN MISTY HAVE COVERED STRIPPED DOWN ACOUSTIC VERSIONS OF THE SONG.

COMPRISING LINES GATHERED BY SWIFT OVER THE YEARS, SHE ASSEMBLED THIS SONG "LIKE A CROSSWORD PUZZLE," STRATEGICALLY PLACING THE LINES WHERE THEY SEAMLESSLY FIT.

STYLE

THIRD SINGLE ON HER FIFTH ALBUM
RELEASED AS S SINGLE: FEBRUARY 10, 2015
RECLAIMED: OCTOBER 27, 2023
RECORDED: CONWAY STUDIOS IN LOS ANGELES, CA

CHARTS & AWARDS

- PEAKED AT #6 ON THE BILLBOARD HOT 100 CHART
- (TAYLOR'S VERSION) PEAKED AT #9 ON THE BILLBOARD HOT 100 CHART
- CERTIFIED 6X PLATINUM BY THE RIAA
- WON AS AN "AWARD WINNING SONG" AT THE BMI POP AWARDS IN 2016
- TO DATE, THE ORIGINAL VERSION HAS BEEN STREAMED 1,636,426,686 TIMES
- (TAYLOR'S VERSION) HAS BEEN STREAMED 72,927,563 TIMES

DID YOU KNOW?

WITH THE MUSIC ORIGINALLY WRITTEN BY PRODUCER ALI PAYAMI AND GUITARIST NIKLAS LJUNGFELT FOR THEMSELVES, THE ESSENCE OF THE TRACK WAS INSPIRED BY DAFT PUNK. TAYLOR HEARD IT PLAYED WHILE WORKING AT MAX MARTIN'S STUDIO.

THE SONG WAS FIRST REVEALED TO THE PUBLIC WHEN IT WAS INCLUDED IN A TARGET COMMERCIAL.

SHE SHOWCASED THE SONG ALONGSIDE "BLANK SPACE" AT THE 2014 "VICTORIA'S SECRET FASHION SHOW" IN LONDON ON DECEMBER 2.

THE MUSIC VIDEO FOR THE SONG, DIRECTED BY FILMMAKER KYLE NEWMAN, DEBUTED ON FEBRUARY 13, 2015.

IN TAYLOR'S WORDS

"I LOVED COMPARING THESE TIMELESS VISUALS WITH A FEELING THAT NEVER GOES OUT OF STYLE. IT'S BASICALLY ONE OF THOSE RELATIONSHIPS THAT'S ALWAYS A BIT OFF. THE TWO PEOPLE ARE TRYING TO FORGET EACH OTHER. SO, IT'S LIKE, 'ALL RIGHT, I HEARD YOU WENT OFF WITH HER, AND WELL, I'VE DONE THAT, TOO.' MY PREVIOUS ALBUMS HAVE ALSO BEEN SORT OF LIKE, 'I WAS RIGHT, YOU WERE WRONG, YOU DID THIS, IT MADE ME FEEL LIKE THIS' - A RIGHTEOUS SENSE OF RIGHT AND WRONG IN A RELATIONSHIP. WHAT HAPPENS WHEN YOU GROW UP IS YOU REALIZE THE RULES IN A RELATIONSHIP ARE VERY BLURRED AND THAT IT GETS VERY COMPLICATED VERY QUICKLY, AND THERE'S NOT A CASE OF WHO WAS RIGHT OR WHO WAS WRONG."

OUT OF THE WOODS

SIXTH SINGLE ON HER FIFTH ALBUM
RELEASED AS S SINGLE: JANUARY 1, 2016
RECLAIMED: OCTOBER 27, 2023
RECORDED: JUNGLE CITY STUDIOS IN NEW YORK, NY

CHARTS & AWARDS

- PEAKED AT #18 ON THE BILLBOARD HOT 100 CHART
- (TAYLOR'S VERSION) PEAKED AT #16 ON THE BILLBOARD HOT 100 CHART
- CERTIFIED PLATINUM BY THE RIAA
- TO DATE, THE ORIGINAL VERSION HAS BEEN STREAMED 310,403,302 TIMES
- (TAYLOR'S VERSION) HAS BEEN STREAMED 62,591,502 TIMES

IN TAYLOR'S WORDS

"IT KIND OF CONJURED UP ALL THESE FEELINGS OF ANXIETY I HAD IN A RELATIONSHIP WHERE EVERYBODY WAS WATCHING. EVERYBODY WAS COMMENTING ON IT. YOU'RE CONSTANTLY JUST FEELING LIKE, 'ARE WE OUT OF THE WOODS YET? WHAT'S THE NEXT THING GONNA BE? WHAT'S THE NEXT HURDLE WE'RE GONNA HAVE TO JUMP OVER?' IT WAS INTERESTING TO WRITE ABOUT A RELATIONSHIP WHERE YOU'RE JUST HONESTLY LIKE, 'THIS IS PROBABLY NOT GONNA LAST, BUT HOW LONG IS IT GONNA LAST?' THOSE FRAGILE RELATIONSHIPS... IT DOESN'T MEAN THEY'RE NOT SUPPOSED TO HAPPEN. THE WHOLE TIME WE WERE HAVING HAPPY MEMORIES, OR CRAZY MEMORIES, OR RIDICULOUSLY ANXIOUS TIMES, IN MY HEAD IT WAS JUST LIKE, 'ARE WE OKAY YET? ARE WE THERE YET? ARE WE OUT OF THIS YET?'"

DID YOU KNOW?

"OUT OF THE WOODS" WAS ONE OF TWO SONGS PRODUCED BY JACK ANTONOFF ON "1989" AND HE NOTES THE SONG WAS INSPIRED BY THE BAND MY MORNING JACKET. THIS WOULD MARK THE BEGINNING OF MANY FUTURE COLLABORATIONS FOR THE PAIR.

THE MUSIC VIDEO WAS FILMED IN NEW ZEALAND AND CAUSED SOME CONTROVERSY RELATED TO THEIR ALLEGED PRESENCE IN A RESTRICTED AREA OF BETHELLS BEACH. TAYLOR DID NOT USE A STUNT DOUBLE FOR ANY OF THE SHOTS, CRAWLING THROUGH MUD AND RUNNING THROUGH HEAVY SNOW.

ON SEPTEMBER 30, 2015, AT THE GRAMMY MUSEUM IN LOS ANGELES, SWIFT DELIVERED A PARED-DOWN RENDITION OF "OUT OF THE WOODS" ON THE PIANO.

ALL YOU HAD TO DO WAS STAY

FIFTH TRACK ON HER FIFTH ALBUM
RELEASED: OCTOBER 27, 2014
RECLAIMED: OCTOBER 27, 2023
RECORDED: CONWAY STUDIOS IN LOS ANGELES, CA

CHARTS & AWARDS

- THE ORIGINAL VERSION DID NOT MAKE THE BILLBOARD HOT 100 CHART
- (TAYLOR'S VERSION) PEAKED AT #20 ON THE BILLBOARD HOT 100 CHART
- CERTIFIED PLATINUM BY THE RIAA
- TO DATE, THE ORIGINAL VERSION HAS BEEN STREAMED 212,509,183 TIMES
- (TAYLOR'S VERSION) HAS BEEN STREAMED 49,764,717 TIMES

DID YOU KNOW?

TAYLOR NOTES THE IDEA FOR THIS SONG CAME TO HER IN A DREAM AND THAT IT WAS ONE OF THE FIRST TRACKS SHE WROTE FOR "1989".

TAYLOR REVEALED IN SEPTEMBER 2022, THAT IN WRITING EACH OF HER SONGS, THEY FALL INTO 3 DISTINCT CATEGORIES: "FOUNTAIN PEN", "QUILL PEN" OR "GLITTER GEL PEN". TAYLOR NOTES: "I CAME UP WITH THESE CATEGORIES BASED ON WHAT WRITING TOOL I IMAGINE HAVING IN MY HAND WHEN I SCRIBBLED IT DOWN, FIGURATIVELY." THIS SONG IS THOUGHT TO BE CATEGORIZED AS A "FOUNTAIN PEN" SONG WHICH INCLUDE MODERN LYRICS FULL OF FAMILIAR REFERENCES AND VIVID IMAGERY.

IN TAYLOR'S WORDS

"THERE'S A SONG ON MY ALBUM CALLED 'ALL YOU HAD TO DO WAS STAY.' I WAS HAVING THIS DREAM, THAT WAS ACTUALLY ONE OF THOSE EMBARRASSING DREAMS, WHERE YOU'RE MORTIFIED IN THE DREAM, YOU'RE LIKE HUMILIATED. IN THE DREAM, MY EX HAD COME TO THE DOOR TO BEG FOR ME TO TALK TO HIM OR WHATEVER, AND I OPENED UP THE DOOR AND I WENT TO GO SAY, 'HI,' OR 'WHAT ARE YOU DOING HERE?' OR SOMETHING — SOMETHING NORMAL — BUT ALL THAT CAME OUT WAS THIS HIGH-PITCHED SINGING THAT SAID, 'STAY!' IT WAS ALMOST OPERATIC. SO I WROTE THIS SONG, AND I USED THAT SOUND IN THE SONG. WEIRD, RIGHT? I WOKE UP FROM THE DREAM, SAYING THE WEIRD PART INTO MY PHONE, FIGURING I HAD TO INCLUDE IT IN SOMETHING BECAUSE IT WAS JUST TOO STRANGE NOT TO. IN POP, IT'S FUN TO PLAY AROUND WITH LITTLE WEIRD NOISES LIKE THAT."

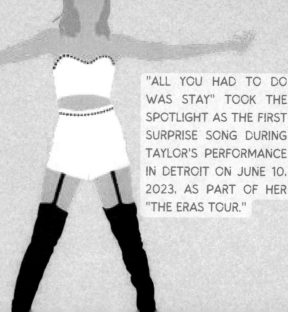

"ALL YOU HAD TO DO WAS STAY" TOOK THE SPOTLIGHT AS THE FIRST SURPRISE SONG DURING TAYLOR'S PERFORMANCE IN DETROIT ON JUNE 10, 2023, AS PART OF HER "THE ERAS TOUR."

SHAKE It OFF

FIRST SINGLE ON HER FIFTH ALBUM
RELEASED: AUGUST 18, 2014
RECLAIMED: OCTOBER 27, 2023
RECORDED: CONWAY STUDIOS IN LOS ANGELES, CA

CHARTS & AWARDS

- PEAKED AT #1 ON THE BILLBOARD HOT 100 CHART
- (TAYLOR'S VERSION) PEAKED AT #28 ON THE BILLBOARD HOT 100 CHART
- CERTIFIED 10X PLATINUM BY THE RIAA
- WON "TOP STREAMING SONG" AT THE BILLBOARD MUSIC AWARDS IN 2015
- NOMINATED FOR 3 GRAMMYS IN 2015
- WON "SONG OF THE YEAR" AT THE IHEARTRADIO MUSIC AWARDS IN 2015
- WON "FAVORITE SONG" AT THE PEOPLE'S CHOICE AWARDS IN 2015
- TO DATE, THE ORIGINAL VERSION HAS BEEN STREAMED 1,267,555,924 TIMES
- (TAYLOR'S VERSION) HAS BEEN STREAMED 50,202,463 TIMES

IN TAYLOR'S WORDS

"I'VE HAD EVERY PART OF MY LIFE DISSECTED – MY CHOICES, MY ACTIONS, MY WORDS, MY BODY, MY STYLE, MY MUSIC. WHEN YOU LIVE YOUR LIFE UNDER THAT KIND OF SCRUTINY, YOU CAN EITHER LET IT BREAK YOU, OR YOU CAN GET REALLY GOOD AT DODGING PUNCHES. AND WHEN ONE LANDS, YOU KNOW HOW TO DEAL WITH IT. AND I GUESS THE WAY THAT I DEAL WITH IT IS TO SHAKE IT OFF."

DID YOU KNOW?

THE MUSIC VIDEO FOR SHAKE IT OFF HAS OVER 3 BILLION VIEWS. DIRECTED BY MARK ROMANEK, KNOWN FOR HIS WORK ON JOHNNY CASH'S "HURT" AND MICHAEL AND JANET JACKSON'S "SCREAM." THE MUSIC VIDEO WAS FILMED OVER THREE DAYS IN LOS ANGELES IN JUNE 2014.

MAX MARTIN HELPED CO-PRODUCE THE SONG WITH TAYLOR, AS HE DID FOR THE MAJORITY OF "1989". WHEN THE TRACK REACHED #1, THE SONG MARKED MAX MARTIN'S 18TH #1 AS A SONGWRITER, PLACING HIM IN THIRD PLACE AMONG WRITERS WITH THE MOST CHART-TOPPERS ON THE HOT 100.

TAYLOR NOTES: "FOUR YEARS AGO I PUT OUT A SONG CALLED 'MEAN' FROM THE PERSPECTIVE OF 'WHY ARE YOU PICKING ON ME? WHY CAN I NEVER DO ANYTHING RIGHT IN YOUR EYES?' IT WAS COMING FROM A SEMI-DEFEATED PLACE. FAST-FORWARD A FEW YEARS AND 'SHAKE IT OFF' IS LIKE, 'YOU KNOW WHAT? IF YOU'RE UPSET AND IRRITATED THAT I'M JUST BEING MYSELF, I'M GOING TO BE MYSELF MORE, AND I'M HAVING MORE FUN THAN YOU SO IT DOESN'T MATTER.'"

I WISH YOU WOULD

SEVENTH TRACK ON HER FIFTH ALBUM
RELEASED: OCTOBER 27, 2014
RECLAIMED: OCTOBER 27, 2023
RECORDED: LAMBY'S HOUSE IN NEW YORK, NY

CHARTS & AWARDS

- THE ORIGINAL VERSION DID NOT MAKE THE BILLBOARD HOT 100 CHART
- (TAYLOR'S VERSION) PEAKED AT #31 ON THE BILLBOARD HOT 100 CHART
- TO DATE, THE ORIGINAL VERSION HAS BEEN STREAMED 146,818,419 TIMES
- (TAYLOR'S VERSION) HAS BEEN STREAMED 43,458,537 TIMES

DID YOU KNOW?

TAYLOR NOTES HER BIGGEST INSPIRATION FOR THIS SONG COMES FROM CLASSIC JOHN HUGHES MOVIES LIKE "SIXTEEN CANDLES". SHE EXPLAINS THAT SHE OFTEN WATCHED THESE CLASSIC FILMS AND THINK: "OK, PAUSE, FREEZE FRAME: WHAT'S HE THINKING IN THIS MOMENT? WHAT'S SHE THINKING IN THIS MOMENT?'"

SIMILAR TO "STYLE", THIS SONG IS SPECULATED TO BE ABOUT HER FORMER BOYFRIEND, HARRY STYLES. TAYLOR HAS SAID IT WAS ONE OF THE FIRST TIMES SHE HAD BEEN ABLE TO BE FRIENDS WITH AN EX AFTER THEIR RELATIONSHIP ENDED. THIS SONG DESCRIBES HOW EVEN AFTER THEY HAD ENDED, BOTH HARBORED FEELINGS THEY DIDN'T HAVE THE NERVE TO ACT ON.

IN TAYLOR'S WORDS

"I THINK, FOR THIS SONG, WE WANTED TO CREATE A SORT OF JOHN HUGHES MOVIE VISUAL WITH PINING AND, YOU KNOW, ONE PERSON'S OVER HERE AND MISSES THE OTHER PERSON BUT IS TOO PRIDEFUL AND WON'T SAY IT. MEANWHILE THIS OTHER PERSON IS HERE AND MISSING THE SAME PERSON: THEY'RE MISSING EACH OTHER BUT NOT SAYING IT. AND I HAD THIS HAPPEN IN MY LIFE AND SO I WANTED TO KIND OF NARRATE IT IN A VERY CINEMATIC WAY WHERE IT'S LIKE YOU'RE SEEING TWO SCENES PLAY OUT AND THEN IN THE BRIDGE YOU'RE SEEING THE FINAL SCENE, WHERE IT RESOLVES ITSELF. SO IT SAYS, 'IT'S A CROOKED LOVE IN A STRAIGHT LINE DOWN, MAKES YOU WANNA RUN AND HIDE BUT IT MAKES YOU TURN RIGHT BACK AROUND.' IT KIND OF IS LIKE THAT DRAMATIC LOVE THAT'S NEVER REALLY QUITE WHERE IT NEEDS TO BE AND THAT TENSION THAT THAT CREATES."

BAD BLOOD

FOURTH SINGLE ON HER FIFTH ALBUM
RELEASED AS A SINGLE: MAY 17, 2015
RECLAIMED: OCTOBER 27, 2023
RECORDED: CONWAY STUDIOS IN LOS ANGELES, CA

CHARTS & AWARDS

- PEAKED AT #1 ON THE BILLBOARD HOT 100 CHART
- (TAYLOR'S VERSION) PEAKED AT #7 ON THE BILLBOARD HOT 100 CHART
- WON "BEST MUSIC VIDEO" AT THR 58TH ANNUAL GRAMMY AWARDS
- NOMINATED FOR 8 AWARDS AT THE MTV VIDEO MUSIC AWARDS
- WON "VIDEO OF THE YEAR" AND "BEST COLLABORATION" AT THE MTV VIDEO MUSIC AWARDS IN 2015
- TO DATE, THE ORIGINAL VERSION HAS BEEN STREAMED 548,074,629 TIMES
- (TAYLOR'S VERSION) HAS BEEN STREAMED 41,562,588 TIMES

DID YOU KNOW?

IT IS SPECULATED THAT THE TRACK IS DESCRIBING HER FEUD WITH KATY PERRY, SPECIFICALLY AFTER PERRY ATTEMPTED TO SABOTAGE HER CONCERT TOUR BY HIRING HER CURRENT DANCERS. THE TWO HAVE SINCE MADE UP AND ARE ON GOOD TERMS.

FOR THE WEEK CONCLUDING ON JULY 12, 2015, "BAD BLOOD" SET A NEW RECORD FOR THE HIGHEST NUMBER OF SINGLE-WEEK PLAYS IN THE 22-YEAR HISTORY OF THE POP SONGS CHART, SURPASSING THE PREVIOUS RECORD HELD BY WIZ KHALIFA AND CHARLIE PUTH'S "SEE YOU AGAIN."

TAYLOR ASSEMBLED MANY OF HER CLOSE CELEBRITY FRIENDS TO SHOOT THE "BAD BLOOD" MUSIC VIDEO. IN TOTAL, THERE ARE 17 CELEBRITY APPEARANCES. THE VIDEO SHATTERED VEVO'S 24-HOUR VIEWING RECORD AT THE TIME BY AMASSING 20.1 MILLION VIEWS WITHIN ITS INITIAL DAY OF RELEASE.

IN TAYLOR'S WORDS

"FOR YEARS, I WAS NEVER SURE IF WE WERE FRIENDS OR NOT. SHE WOULD COME UP TO ME AT AWARDS SHOWS AND SAY SOMETHING AND WALK AWAY, AND I WOULD THINK, 'ARE WE FRIENDS, OR DID SHE JUST GIVE ME THE HARSHEST INSULT OF MY LIFE?' THEN LAST YEAR, THE OTHER STAR CROSSED A LINE. SHE DID SOMETHING SO HORRIBLE. I WAS LIKE, 'OH, WE'RE JUST STRAIGHT-UP ENEMIES.' AND IT WASN'T EVEN ABOUT A GUY! IT HAD TO DO WITH BUSINESS. SHE BASICALLY TRIED TO SABOTAGE AN ENTIRE ARENA TOUR. SHE TRIED TO HIRE A BUNCH OF PEOPLE OUT FROM UNDER ME. AND I'M SURPRISINGLY NON-CONFRONTATIONAL – YOU WOULD NOT BELIEVE HOW MUCH I HATE CONFLICT. SO NOW I HAVE TO AVOID HER. IT'S AWKWARD, AND I DON'T LIKE IT."

WILDEST DREAMS

FIFTH SINGLE ON HER FIFTH ALBUM
RELEASED AS A SINGLE: AUGUST 31, 2015
RECLAIMED: OCTOBER 27, 2023
RECORDED: CONWAY STUDIOS IN LOS ANGELES, CA

CHARTS & AWARDS

- PEAKED AT #5 ON THE BILLBOARD HOT 100 CHART
- (TAYLOR'S VERSION) PEAKED AT #19 ON THE BILLBOARD HOT 100 CHART
- CERTIFIED 4X PLATINUM BY THE RIAA
- WON AS AN "AWARD WINNING SONG" AT THE BMI POP AWARDS IN 2016
- TO DATE, THE ORIGINAL VERSION HAS BEEN STREAMED 882,328,965 TIMES
- (TAYLOR'S VERSION) HAS BEEN STREAMED 582,181,398 TIMES

IN TAYLOR'S WORDS

"I THINK THE WAY I USED TO APPROACH RELATIONSHIPS WAS VERY IDEALISTIC. I USED TO GO INTO THEM THINKING, 'MAYBE THIS IS THE ONE – WE'LL GET MARRIED AND HAVE A FAMILY, THIS COULD BE FOREVER'. WHEREAS NOW I GO IN THINKING, 'HOW LONG DO WE HAVE ON THE CLOCK – BEFORE SOMETHING COMES ALONG AND PUTS A WRENCH IN IT, OR YOUR PUBLICIST CALLS AND SAYS THIS ISN'T A GOOD IDEA?'"

DID YOU KNOW?

THE MUSIC VIDEO FOR THE TRACK PREMIERED AT THE MTV VIDEO MUSIC AWARDS ON AUGUST 30, 2015. THE STORY IN THE VIDEO SURROUNDS TWO ACTORS AND THEIR LOVE AFFAIR WHILE FILMING A MOVIE IN THE AFRICAN SAVANNAH. SWIFT TAKES ON THE ROLE OF A FICTIONAL ACTRESS NAMED MARJORIE FINN, A NOD TO HER GRANDMOTHER MARJORIE FINLAY. HER COSTAR PORTRAYS A FICTIONAL ACTOR NAMED ROBERT KINGSLEY, A BLEND OF SWIFT'S GRANDFATHER'S NAME ROBERT AND HER FATHER'S MIDDLE NAME KINGSLEY. ALL PROCEEDS FROM THE VIDEO WERE DONATED TO WILDLIFE CONSERVATION THROUGH THE AFRICAN PARKS FOUNDATION ON AMERICA.

THE BEAT IN THE BACKGROUND OF THE SONG IS A SAMPLE OF TAYLOR SWIFT'S ACTUAL HEARTBEAT.

WHEN IT REACHED THE #10 SPOT ON THE BILLBOARD HOT 100 CHART, IT BECAME THE FIFTH TOP TEN SONG OF "1989".

HOW YOU GET THE GIRL

TENTH TRACK ON HER FIFTH ALBUM
RELEASED: OCTOBER 27, 2014
RECLAIMED: OCTOBER 27, 2023
RECORDED: CONWAY STUDIOS IN LOS ANGELES, CA

CHARTS & AWARDS

- THE ORIGINAL VERSION DID NOT MAKE THE BILLBOARD HOT 100 CHART
- (TAYLOR'S VERSION) PEAKED AT #40 ON THE BILLBOARD HOT 100 CHART
- CERTIFIED GOLD BY THE RIAA
- TO DATE, THE ORIGINAL VERSION HAS BEEN STREAMED 162,047,492 TIMES
- (TAYLOR'S VERSION) HAS BEEN STREAMED 38,478,626 TIMES

DID YOU KNOW?

TAYLOR PERFORMED "HOW YOU GET THE GIRL" AS AN ACOUSTIC SURPRISE SONG ON APRIL 30, 2023, DURING "THE ERAS TOUR" IN ATLANTA, GA.

THE SONG IS FEATURED IN A DIET COKE ADVERTISEMENT THAT WAS RELEASED LEADING UP TO "1989" AND FEATURE'S TAYLOR'S CAT OLIVIA BENSON.

TAYLOR REVEALED IN SEPTEMBER 2022, THAT IN WRITING EACH OF HER SONGS, THEY FALL INTO 3 DISTINCT CATEGORIES: "FOUNTAIN PEN", "QUILL PEN" OR "GLITTER GEL PEN". TAYLOR NOTES: "I CAME UP WITH THESE CATEGORIES BASED ON WHAT WRITING TOOL I IMAGINE HAVING IN MY HAND WHEN I SCRIBBLED IT DOWN, FIGURATIVELY." THIS SONG IS THOUGHT TO BE CATEGORIZED AS A "GLITTER GEL PEN" SONG WHICH INCLUDE LYRICS THAT ARE "FRIVOLOUS, CAREFREE, AND BOUNCY".

IN TAYLOR'S WORDS

"THE SONG 'HOW YOU GET THE GIRL' IS A SONG THAT I WROTE ABOUT HOW YOU GET THE GIRL BACK IF YOU RUINED THE RELATIONSHIP SOMEHOW AND SHE WON'T TALK TO YOU ANYMORE. LIKE, IF YOU BROKE UP WITH HER AND LEFT HER ON HER OWN FOR SIX MONTHS AND THEN YOU REALIZE YOU MISS HER. ALL THE STEPS YOU HAVE TO DO TO EDGE YOUR WAY BACK INTO HER LIFE. BECAUSE SHE'S PROBABLY PRETTY MAD AT YOU. SO IT'S KIND OF A TUTORIAL. IF YOU FOLLOW THE DIRECTIONS IN THE SONG, CHANCES ARE THINGS WILL WORK OUT. OR YOU MAY GET A RESTRAINING ORDER."

THIS LOVE

ELEVENTH TRACK ON HER FIFTH ALBUM
RELEASED: OCTOBER 27, 2014
RECLAIMED: OCTOBER 27, 2023
RECORDED: PAIN IN THE ART STUDIOS IN NASHVILLE, TN

CHARTS & AWARDS

- THE ORIGINAL VERSION DID NOT MAKE THE BILLBOARD HOT 100 CHART
- (TAYLOR'S VERSION) PEAKED AT #42 ON THE BILLBOARD HOT 100 CHART
- CERTIFIED PLATINUM BY THE RIAA
- TO DATE, THE ORIGINAL VERSION HAS BEEN STREAMED 104,126,090 TIMES
- (TAYLOR'S VERSION) HAS BEEN STREAMED 197,479,709 TIMES

DID YOU KNOW?

OF ALL OF THE SONGS ON "1989", THIS IS THE ONLY SONG WRITTEN COMPLETELY BY TAYLOR ALONE.

TAYLOR HAS PREVIOUSLY HIDDEN MESSAGES IN THE LYRIC BOOKLETS OF EACH SONG ON HER ALBUMS UNTIL 2014. THIS SPECIFIC SONG'S HIDDEN MESSAGE IS: "TIMING IS A FUNNY THING".

THE INITIAL EXCERPT OF "THIS LOVE (TAYLOR'S VERSION)" MADE ITS DEBUT IN THE TRAILER FOR THE 2022 TV SERIES THE SUMMER I TURNED PRETTY, WHICH PREMIERED ON MAY 5, 2022.

IN TAYLOR'S WORDS

"THE LAST TIME I WROTE A POEM THAT ENDED UP BEING A SONG, I WAS WRITING IN MY JOURNAL AND I WAS WRITING ABOUT SOMETHING THAT HAD HAPPENED IN MY LIFE - IT WAS ABOUT A YEAR AGO - AND I JUST WROTE THIS REALLY REALLY SHORT POEM. IT SAID, 'THIS LOVE IS GOOD /THIS LOVE IS BAD / THIS LOVE IS ALIVE BACK FROM THE DEAD / THESE HANDS HAD TO LET IT GO FREE / AND THIS LOVE CAME BACK TO ME.' AND I JUST WROTE IT DOWN, CLOSED THE BOOK AND PUT IT BACK ON MY NIGHT STAND [...] ALL OF A SUDDEN IN MY HEAD I JUST STARTED HEARING THIS MELODY HAPPEN, AND THEN I REALIZED THAT IT WAS GOING TO BE A SONG."

I KNOW PLACES

TWELFTH TRACK ON HER FIFTH ALBUM
RELEASED: OCTOBER 27, 2014
RECLAIMED: OCTOBER 27, 2023
RECORDED: PAIN IN THE ART STUDIOS IN NASHVILLE, TN

CHARTS & AWARDS

- THE ORIGINAL VERSION DID NOT MAKE THE BILLBOARD HOT 100 CHART
- (TAYLOR'S VERSION) PEAKED AT #36 ON THE BILLBOARD HOT 100 CHART
- CERTIFIED GOLD BY THE RIAA
- TO DATE, THE ORIGINAL VERSION HAS BEEN STREAMED 129,451,652 TIMES
- (TAYLOR'S VERSION) HAS BEEN STREAMED 39,603,658 TIMES

DID YOU KNOW?

TAYLOR SANG THE SONG ACOUSTICALLY AS A SURPRISE SONG IN TOKYO DURING HER "REPUTATION STADIUM TOUR" ON NOVEMBER, 20, 2018.

TAYLOR COLLABORATED WITH ONEREPUBLIC FRONTMAN RYAN TEDDER TO WRITE THE SONG, WITH TEDDER KNOWN FOR HIS INVOLVEMENT IN CRAFTING POP HITS SUCH AS "APOLOGIZE," "BLEEDING LOVE," "HALO," AND "COUNTING STARS."

TAYLOR'S COLLABORATION WITH POP PRODUCERS LIKE RYAN TEDDER AND MAX MARTIN THROUGHOUT THE ALBUM BUILT "1989" AS TAYLOR'S CLEAR TRANSITION TO POP. TAYLOR QUOTES: "I HAD TO CONVINCE MY NASHVILLE RECORD LABEL PRESIDENT IT WAS RIGHT FOR ME. I PRESENTED THE ALBUM TO HIM AND HE SAID, 'IT'S GREAT, IT'S THE BEST THING YOU'VE EVER DONE BUT CAN YOU PUT TWO COUNTRY SONGS ON IT?'"

IN TAYLOR'S WORDS

"I KIND OF WAS IN A PLACE WHERE I WAS LIKE, 'NO ONE IS GONNA SIGN UP FOR THIS. THERE ARE JUST TOO MANY CAMERAS POINTED AT ME. THERE ARE TOO MANY RIDICULOUS ELABORATIONS ON MY LIFE. IT'S JUST NOT EVER GONNA WORK.' BUT I DECIDED TO WRITE A LOVE SONG, JUST KIND OF LIKE, 'WHAT WOULD I SAY IF I MET SOMEONE REALLY AWESOME AND THEY WERE LIKE, HEY, I'M WORRIED ABOUT ALL THIS ATTENTION YOU GET?' SO I WROTE THIS SONG CALLED 'I KNOW PLACES' ABOUT, 'HEY, I KNOW PLACES WE CAN HIDE. WE COULD OUTRUN THEM.' I'M SO HAPPY THAT IT SOUNDS LIKE THE URGENCY THAT IT SINGS."

CLEAN

THIRTEENTH TRACK ON HER FIFTH ALBUM
RELEASED: OCTOBER 27, 2014
RECLAIMED: OCTOBER 27, 2023
RECORDED: THE HIDEAWAY IN ENGLAND

CHARTS & AWARDS

- THE ORIGINAL VERSION DID NOT MAKE THE BILLBOARD HOT 100 CHART
- (TAYLOR'S VERSION) PEAKED AT #30 ON THE BILLBOARD HOT 100 CHART
- CERTIFIED GOLD BY THE RIAA
- TO DATE, THE ORIGINAL VERSION HAS BEEN STREAMED 187,544,696 TIMES
- (TAYLOR'S VERSION) HAS BEEN STREAMED 46,938,424 TIMES

DID YOU KNOW?

THIS TRACK WAS TAYLOR'S FIRST AND ONLY COLLABORATION WITH BRITISH MUSICIAN IMOGEN HEAP. HEAP PLAYS PERCUSSION, DRUMS, MBIRA, VIBRAPHONE, AND KEYBOARD IN ADDITION TO PROVIDING BACKGROUND VOCALS FOR THE SONG.

TAYLOR SAYS OF THE COLLABORATION: "WE DID A ONE TAKE VOCAL AND IT WAS JUST SO INSPIRING TO SEE A WOMAN DO ALL THE TECHNICAL THINGS IN THE STUDIO THAT YOU USUALLY SEE MEN DO."

TAYLOR HAS PREVIOUSLY HIDDEN MESSAGES IN THE LYRIC BOOKLETS OF EACH SONG ON HER ALBUMS UNTIL 2014. THIS SPECIFIC SONG'S HIDDEN MESSAGE IS: "SHE LOST HIM BUT SHE FOUND HERSELF AND SOMEHOW THAT WAS EVERYTHING".

IN TAYLOR'S WORDS

"'CLEAN' I WROTE AS I WAS WALKING OUT OF LIBERTY IN LONDON. SOMEONE I USED TO DATE - IT HIT ME THAT I'D BEEN IN THE SAME CITY AS HIM FOR TWO WEEKS AND I HADN'T THOUGHT ABOUT IT...YOU GET USED TO NOT CALLING SOMEONE AT NIGHT TO TELL THEM HOW YOUR DAY WAS. YOU REPLACE THESE OLD HABITS WITH NEW HABITS. LIKE TEXTING YOUR FRIENDS IN A GROUP CHAT ALL DAY, AND PLANNING FUN DINNER PARTIES, AND GOING OUT ON ADVENTURES WITH YOUR GIRLFRIENDS. AND THEN ALL OF A SUDDEN ONE DAY YOU'RE IN LONDON AND YOU REALIZE YOU'VE BEEN IN THE SAME PLACE AS YOUR EX FOR TWO WEEKS AND YOU'RE FINE. AND YOU HOPE HE'S FINE. THE FIRST THOUGHT THAT CAME TO MY MIND WAS - I'M FINALLY CLEAN."

WONDERLAND

FOURTEENTH TRACK OF HER FIFTH ALBUM
RELEASED: OCTOBER 27, 2014
RECLAIMED: OCTOBER 27, 2023
RECORDED: CONWAY STUDIOS IN LOS ANGELES, CA

CHARTS & AWARDS

- PEAKED AT #51 THE BILLBOARD HOT 100 CHART
- (TAYLOR'S VERSION) PEAKED AT #39 ON THE BILLBOARD HOT 100 CHART
- CERTIFIED GOLD BY THE RIAA
- TO DATE, THE ORIGINAL VERSION HAS BEEN STREAMED 142,478,545 TIMES
- (TAYLOR'S VERSION) HAS BEEN STREAMED 38,674,298 TIMES

DID YOU KNOW?

THE SONG WEAVES A NARRATIVE OF AN IDEALIZED RELATIONSHIP WHERE TAYLOR AND HER LOVE INTEREST FIND SOLACE IN THEIR DREAM WORLD TOGETHER, DESPITE THE WARNINGS THAT THE RELATIONSHIP WAS UNSUSTAINABLE.

FANS HAVE SPECULATED THAT THE SONG MAY BE ABOUT HARRY STYLES, BASED ON THE "GREEN EYES" LINE IN THE PRE-CHORUS.

ON SEPTEMBER 29, 2018, IN HOUSTON, TEXAS, TTAYLOR PLAYED "WONDERLAND" AS THE SURPRISE PERFORMANCE DURING THE "REPUTATION STADIUM TOUR".

TAYLOR REVEALED IN SEPTEMBER 2022, THAT IN WRITING EACH OF HER SONGS, THEY FALL INTO 3 DISTINCT CATEGORIES: "FOUNTAIN PEN", "QUILL PEN" OR "GLITTER GEL PEN". TAYLOR NOTES: "I CAME UP WITH THESE CATEGORIES BASED ON WHAT WRITING TOOL I IMAGINE HAVING IN MY HAND WHEN I SCRIBBLED IT DOWN, FIGURATIVELY." THIS SONG IS THOUGHT TO BE CATEGORIZED AS A "FOUNTAIN PEN" SONG WHICH INCLUDE MODERN LYRICS FULL OF FAMILIAR REFERENCES AND VIVID IMAGERY.

IN TAYLOR'S WORDS

"I REALLY WANNA PLAY THIS ONE TONIGHT. I HAVEN'T PLAYED IT IN A VERY LONG TIME. I KINDA BASED IT OFF OF A TWISTED ALICE IN WONDERLAND. I'M INSANE. TRULY."

YOU ARE IN LOVE

FIFTEENTH TRACK OF HER FIFTH ALBUM
RELEASED: OCTOBER 27, 2014
RECLAIMED: OCTOBER 27, 2023

CHARTS & AWARDS

- PEAKED AT #83 THE BILLBOARD HOT 100 CHART
- (TAYLOR'S VERSION) PEAKED AT #43 ON THE BILLBOARD HOT 100 CHART
- TO DATE, THE ORIGINAL VERSION HAS BEEN STREAMED 136,357,409 TIMES
- (TAYLOR'S VERSION) HAS BEEN STREAMED 37,837,882 TIMES

DID YOU KNOW?

"YOU ARE IN LOVE" WAS FEATURED ON THE 1989 WORLD TOUR MOVIE AS THE FEATURED SURPRISE SONG ON HER SETLIST.

TAYLOR WROTE THE SONG BASED ON ANECDOTES FROM LENA DUNHAM AND JACK ANTANOFF ABOUT THEIR RELATIONSHIP. TAYLOR NOTES: "I'VE NEVER HAD THAT, SO I WROTE THAT SONG ABOUT THINGS THAT LENA [DUNHAM] HAS TOLD ME ABOUT HER AND JACK [ANTONOFF]. THAT'S JUST BASICALLY STUFF SHE'S TOLD ME. AND I THINK THAT THAT KIND OF RELATIONSHIP - GOD, IT SOUNDS LIKE IT WOULD JUST BE SO BEAUTIFUL - WOULD ALSO BE HARD. IT WOULD ALSO BE MUNDANE AT TIMES."

LENA DUNHAM DUBBED THIS HER "SOMEDAY WEDDING SONG." NEITHER LENA NOR JACK KNEW THE SONG WAS ABOUT THEM UNTIL AFTER THE ALBUM CAME OUT.

IN TAYLOR'S WORDS

"I WROTE IT WITH MY FRIEND JACK ANTONOFF WHO'S DATING MY FRIEND LENA. JACK SENT ME THIS SONG. IT WAS JUST AN INSTRUMENTAL TRACK HE WAS WORKING ON AND IMMEDIATELY I KNEW THE SONG IT NEEDED TO BE. AND I WROTE IT AS A KIND OF COMMENTARY ON WHAT THEIR RELATIONSHIP HAS BEEN LIKE. SO IT'S ACTUALLY ME LOOKING AND GOING, 'THIS HAPPENED AND THAT HAPPENED, THEN THAT HAPPENED AND THAT'S HOW YOU KNEW YOU ARE IN LOVE.'"

NEW ROMANTICS

SEVENTH SINGLE OF HER FIFTH ALBUM
RELEASED AS A SINGLE: FEBRUARY 23, 2016
RECLAIMED: OCTOBER 27, 2023
RECORDED: CONWAY STUDIOS IN LOS ANGELES, CA

CHARTS & AWARDS

- PEAKED AT #46 THE BILLBOARD HOT 100 CHART
- (TAYLOR'S VERSION) PEAKED AT #29 ON THE BILLBOARD HOT 100 CHART
- CERTIFIED GOLD BY THE RIAA
- TO DATE, THE ORIGINAL VERSION HAS BEEN STREAMED 261,211,360 TIMES
- (TAYLOR'S VERSION) HAS BEEN STREAMED 53,316,434 TIMES

DID YOU KNOW?

THE SONG'S TITLE ALLUDES TO THE LATE 1970S AND 1980S NEW ROMANTIC CULTURAL MOVEMENT, CHARACTERIZED BY FLAMBOYANT CLOTHING AND MAKEUP. THE SOUND OF THE SONG MIRRORS THE NEW WAVE MUSIC ASSOCIATED WITH THE NEW ROMANTIC ERA.

THE MUSIC VIDEO FOR THE TRACK BLENDS CONCERT AND BEHIND-THE-SCENES CLIPS FROM "THE 1989 WORLD TOUR" IN 2015, ACCOMPANIED BY TAYLOR'S VOICE-OVERS SHARING HER REFLECTIONS ON HER FANS.

IN TAYLOR'S WORDS

"PEOPLE WILL SAY, 'LET ME SET YOU UP WITH SOMEONE', AND I'M JUST SITTING THERE SAYING, 'THAT'S NOT WHAT I'M DOING. I'M NOT LONELY. I'M NOT LOOKING.' THEY JUST DON'T GET IT. I'VE LEARNED THAT JUST BECAUSE SOMEONE IS CUTE AND WANTS TO DATE YOU, THAT'S NOT A REASON TO SACRIFICE YOUR INDEPENDENCE AND ALLOW EVERYONE TO SAY WHATEVER THEY WANT ABOUT YOU. I'M NOT DOING THAT ANYMORE. IT'D TAKE SOMEONE REALLY SPECIAL FOR ME TO UNDERGO THE CIRCUMSTANCES I HAVE TO GO THROUGH TO EXPERIENCE A DATE. I DON'T KNOW HOW I WOULD EVER HAVE ANOTHER PERSON IN MY WORLD TRYING TO HAVE A RELATIONSHIP WITH ME, OR A FAMILY."

DESPITE ITS EXCLUSION FROM THE STANDARD EDITION OF 1989, ROLLING STONE NAMED "NEW ROMANTICS" ONE OF THE BEST SONGS OF THE 2010S, DENOUNCING SWIFT'S DECISION TO RELEGATE IT TO A BONUS TRACK AS "ONE OF POP'S GREATEST CRIMES."

1989

'SLUT!'

FIRST VAULT TRACK OF "1989 (TAYLOR'S VERSION)"
RELEASED: OCTOBER 27, 2023
RECORDED: ELECTRIC LADY STUDIOS IN NEW YORK, NY

CHARTS & AWARDS

- PEAKED AT #3 ON THE BILLBOARD HOT 100 CHART
- SPENT 3 WEEKS TOTAL ON THE CHART
- TO DATE, IT HAS BEEN STREAMED 111,644,493 TIMES

DID YOU KNOW?

TAYLOR NOTES THAT SHE FELT THE SONG HAD A STRONG CALIFORNIA VIBE THAT DIDN'T MESH WITH NEW YORK ESSENCE OF "1989", ULTIMATELY DECIDING TO REMOVE IT FROM THE ALBUM. IT ALSO SHARED SIMILAR THEMES TO "BLANK SPACE" WHICH WAS A MAJOR SINGLE FOR THE ALBUM.

SWIFT DEBUTED HER LIVE PERFORMANCE OF "SLUT!" FOR THE FIRST TIME IN BUENOS AIRES ON NOVEMBER 12, 2023, AS PART OF "THE ERAS TOUR".

THE SONG IS A CHEEKY REPLY TO THE MEDIA NAMING HER A "SERIAL DATER" AND SUBJECTING HER RELATIONSHIPS TO POP CULTURE JOKES AND SLUT-SHAMING.

IN TAYLOR'S WORDS

"THE SONG 'SLUT!' IS A SONG WE WROTE FOR 1989, AND IN IT I SORT OF CHEEKILY PLAY ON THE DISCUSSIONS AT THAT TIME IN MY LIFE AROUND MY DATING LIFE. AND THAT'S NOT THE ONLY TIME ON 1989 THAT I'VE DONE THAT. I DID THAT ON 'BLANK SPACE'. AND I THINK WHEN I CAME DOWN TO HAVING TO PICK SONGS FOR THE ALBUM I THINK I THOUGHT, 'OKAY, I'M GONNA CHOOSE 'BLANK SPACE'. AND UNFORTUNATELY, I HAD TO MAKE SOME TOUGH DECISIONS IN TERMS OF WHAT TO PUT ON THE TRACKLIST. BUT I LOVE THIS SONG BECAUSE I THINK IT'S REALLY DREAMY."

SAY DON'T GO

SECOND VAULT TRACK OF "1989 (TAYLOR'S VERSION)"
RELEASED: OCTOBER 27, 2023
RECORDED: ELECTRIC LADY STUDIOS IN NEW YORK, NY

CHARTS & AWARDS

- PEAKED AT #5 ON THE BILLBOARD HOT 100 CHART
- SPENT 5 WEEKS TOTAL ON THE CHART
- TO DATE, IT HAS BEEN STREAMED 92,941,052 TIMES

DID YOU KNOW?

TAYLOR COLLABORATED WITH MASTER SONGWRITER - DIANNE WARREN FOR "SAY DON'T GO". DIANE IS RESPONSIBLE FOR HITS LIKE "BECAUSE YOU LOVED ME" BY CÉLINE DION AND "I DON'T WANNA MISS A THING" BY AEROSMITH, AMONG MANY OTHERS. SHE MARKS THE FIRST SONGWRITER TO HAVE 7 DIFFERENT SONGS BY DIFFERENT ARTISTS CHARTING ON THE BILLBOARD HOT 100 AT THE SAME TIME.

SWIFT DEBUTED HER LIVE PERFORMANCE OF "SAY DON'T GO" FOR THE FIRST TIME IN SAO PAULO ON NOVEMBER 26, 2023, AS PART OF "THE ERAS TOUR".

ALTHOUGH RECORDED AS A DEMO IN WARREN'S STUDIO IN 2014, JACK ANTONOFF PRODUCED THE RE-RECORDING OF THE TRACK IN 2023. HE PLAYS MELLOTRON, ACOUSTIC GUITAR, ELECTRIC GUITAR AS WELL AS BACKGROUND VOCALS ON THE TRACK.

NOW THAT WE DON'T TALK

THIRD VAULT TRACK OF "1989 (TAYLOR'S VERSION)"
RELEASED: OCTOBER 27, 2023

CHARTS & AWARDS

- PEAKED AT #2 ON THE BILLBOARD HOT 100 CHART
- CERTIFIED GOLD BY THE RIAA
- SPENT 5 WEEKS TOTAL ON THE CHART
- TO DATE, IT HAS BEEN STREAMED 126,485,764 TIMES

DID YOU KNOW?

THE FIRST VERSE OF THE SONG LIKELY ALLUDES TO HARRY STYLES' RETURN FLIGHT FROM THE BRITISH VIRGIN ISLANDS AFTER THEIR BREAKUP. IN EARLY 2013, THEIR NEW YEAR'S HOLIDAY AS A COUPLE WAS CUT SHORT BY AN ALLEGED ARGUMENT, LEADING TAYLOR TO FLY BACK TO THE US ALONE JUST THREE DAYS AFTER ARRIVING.

"NOW THAT WE DON'T TALK" IS THE SHORTEST SONG OF ANY TRACK IN TAYLOR'S DISCOGRAPHY, JUST ABOVE "GLITCH" HER SECOND SHORTEST.

IN TAYLOR'S WORDS

"'NOW THAT WE DON'T TALK' IS ONE OF MY FAVORITE SONGS THAT WAS LEFT BEHIND. IT WAS SO HARD TO LEAVE IT BEHIND BUT I THINK WE WROTE IT A LITTLE BIT TOWARDS THE END OF THE PROCESS AND WE COULDN'T GET THE PRODUCTION RIGHT AT THE TIME. BUT WE HAD TONS OF TIME TO PERFECT THE PRODUCTION THIS TIME AND FIGURE OUT WHAT WE WANTED THE SONG TO SOUND LIKE! I THINK IT'S THE SHORTEST SONG I'VE EVER HAD, BUT I THINK IT PACKS A PUNCH. I THINK IT REALLY GOES IN. FOR THE SHORT AMOUNT OF TIME WE HAVE I THINK IT MAKES ITS POINT."

SUBURBAN LEGENDS

FOURTH VAULT TRACK OF "1989 (TAYLOR'S VERSION)"
RELEASED: OCTOBER 27, 2023

CHARTS & AWARDS

- PEAKED AT #10 ON THE BILLBOARD HOT 100 CHART
- SPENT 3 WEEKS TOTAL ON THE CHART
- TO DATE, IT HAS BEEN STREAMED 62,354,309 TIMES

DID YOU KNOW?

"SUBURBAN LEGENDS" PORTRAYS A HOPEFUL YET DOOMED ROMANCE FILLED WITH OBSTACLES, OFFERING A HINT OF FANTASY AS TAYLOR'S LYRICS EMBODY DESIRE, ELONGATING SYLLABLES IN PURSUIT OF THE UNATTAINABLE AND REVISITING FUTILE SCENARIOS.

ON NOVEMBER 17, 2023, DURING "THE ERAS TOUR" IN RIO DE JANEIRO, TAYLOR PERFORMED THE SECOND SURPRISE SONG, "SUBURBAN LEGENDS," ACOUSTICALLY ON THE PIANO.

IS IT OVER NOW?

FIFTH VAULT TRACK OF "1989 (TAYLOR'S VERSION)"
RELEASED: OCTOBER 27, 2023

CHARTS & AWARDS

- PEAKED AT #1 ON THE BILLBOARD HOT 100 CHART
- CERTIFIED GOLD BY THE RIAA
- SPENT 5 WEEKS TOTAL ON THE CHART
- TO DATE, IT HAS BEEN STREAMED 170,896,649 TIMES

DID YOU KNOW?

DURING HER CONCERT ON NOVEMBER 11, 2023, IN BUENOS AIRES, ARGENTINA, "IS IT OVER NOW?" WAS THE FIRST SURPRISE SONG. TAYLOR DECIDED TO BLEND IT WITH THE BRIDGE OF "OUT OF THE WOODS." INTERESTINGLY, IT IS SPECULATED THAT BOTH SONGS REVOLVE AROUND THE SAME RELATIONSHIP.

WHEN THE TRACK REACHED #1, IT DETHRONED HER OWN TRACK "CRUEL SUMMER". EXACTLY NINE YEARS PRIOR IN 2014, TAYLOR MADE HISTORY AS THE FIRST FEMALE ARTIST TO REPLACE HERSELF AT NO. 1 ON THE CHART ON MULTIPLE OCCASIONS, FIRST ACHIEVING THIS FEAT WHEN "BLANK SPACE" REPLACED "SHAKE IT OFF."

IN TAYLOR'S WORDS

"'IS IT OVER NOW?' WAS A SONG I WANTED TO END THE ALBUM BECAUSE I THINK IT'S A FUNNY PLAY ON WORDS OF LIKE, 'IS THE ALBUM OVER NOW?' AND I ALWAYS SAW THIS SONG AS SORT OF A SISTER TO 'OUT OF THE WOODS' AND 'I WISH YOU WOULD'. I KIND OF SAW THOSE SONGS AS SIMILAR. SO UNFORTUNATELY WHEN WE WERE MAKING THESE DECISIONS ON WHAT TO PUT ON 1989 AND WHAT TO LEAVE BEHIND I HAD TO MAKE SOME TOUGH CHOICES. AND NOW THAT DOESN'T MATTER ANYMORE BECAUSE YOU GUYS ARE GONNA HEAR ALL THE SONGS. SO, I AM SO HAPPY ABOUT THIS ONE BEING OUT! I REALLY LOVE THE, 'LET'S FAST FORWARD TO 300 TAKEOUT COFFEES LATER' SECTION, I FEEL LIKE HEADBANGING TO IT EVERY TIME IT COMES ON."

reputation

RELEASED: NOVEMBER 10, 2017
TO BE RECLAIMED

...Ready for it?

SECOND SINGLE ON HER SIXTH ALBUM
RELEASED AS A SINGLE: OCTOBER 24, 2017
RECORDED: MXM STUDIOS IN LOS ANGELES, CA & STOCKHOLM, SWEDEN

DID YOU KNOW?

ON NOVEMBER 11, 2017, TAYLOR PERFORMED THE TRACK FOR THE FIRST TIME ON SATURDAY NIGHT LIVE EPISODE #1730. THE TRACK WAS FIRST TEASED ON A COLLEGE FOOTBALL GAME FEATURING FLORIDA STATE UNIVERSITY VS. THE UNIVERSITY OF ALABAMA.

THE SONG IS WRITTEN IN THE E MINOR KEY AT A TEMPO OF 80 BEATS PER MINUTE.

THE SONG IS ONE OF FEW THAT START WITH AN ELIPSES (...) - OTHERS INCLUDING BRITNEY SPEARS' "...BABY ONE MORE TIME" AND METALLICA'S "...AND JUSTICE FOR ALL".

LYRICS IN THE SONG REFER TO ELIZABETH TAYLOR AND HER FAMOUS RELATIONSHIP WITH RICHARD BURTON, OFTEN FOUND IN GOSSIP COLUMNS AND KNOWN FOR THEIR PASSION AND DYSFUNCTION,

CHARTS & AWARDS

- PEAKED AT #4 ON THE BILLBOARD HOT 100 CHART
- SPENT 20 WEEKS ON THE CHARTS
- CERTIFIED RIAA DOUBLE PLATINUM
- WON AS AN "AWARD WINNING SONG" AT THE 2019 BMI AWARDS
- TO DATE, THE TRACK HAS BEEN STREAMED 603,957,981 TIMES

in taylor's words

"IT INTRODUCES A METAPHOR YOU MAY HEAR MORE OF THROUGHOUT THE REST OF THE ALBUM, WHICH IS THIS CRIME AND PUNISHMENT METAPHOR, WHERE IT TALKS ABOUT ROBBERS, AND THIEVES, AND HEISTS, AND ALL THAT. AND I FOUND THAT TO BE A REALLY INTERESTING METAPHOR, BUT TWISTED IT IN DIFFERENT WAYS THROUGHOUT THE ALBUM. THE WAY THAT IT'S PRESENTED IN '...READY FOR IT?' IS BASICALLY, FINDING YOUR PARTNER IN CRIME, AND IT'S LIKE 'OH MY GOD, WE'RE THE SAME, WE'RE THE SAME, OH MY GOD! LET'S ROB BANKS TOGETHER, THIS IS GREAT!'"

End Game

FEATURING ED SHEERAN, FUTURE
THIRD SINGLE ON HER SIXTH ALBUM
RELEASED AS A SINGLE: OCTOBER 24, 2017
RECORDED: MXM STUDIOS IN LOS ANGELES, CA & STOCKHOLM, SWEDEN

DID YOU KNOW?

FROM ED ON WRITING HIS FEATURE: "I ACTUALLY WROTE [MY VERSE] IN, I REMEMBER WHERE IT WAS, I WAS IN A HOTEL ROOM IN NEW YORK, IN BED AT ABOUT EIGHT O'CLOCK IN THE MORNING. I WOKE UP 'CAUSE FOR SOME REASON I, LIKE, DREAMED IT IN MY HEAD WHAT I WAS GONNA DO. [...] I WOKE UP AND THEN, LIKE, TYPED IT ALL OUT AND THEN RECORDED IT LIKE A DAY LATER AND SENT IT TO [TAYLOR]."

"END GAME" SERVED AS THE SECOND SURPRISE SONG IN BUENOS AIRES DURING "THE ERAS TOUR" ON NOVEMBER 11,2023.

THE MUSIC VIDEO FOR THE TRACK WAS FILMED BY JOSEPH KAHN WHO HAD PREVIOUSLY DIRECTED SIX OF TAYLOR'S MUSIC VIDEOS PRIOR TO THIS. THE VIDEO WAS FILMED IN LONDON, MIAMI, AND TOKYO. IN THE LONDON SCENE, TAYLOR PLAYS THE GAME SNAKE ON HER PHONE, HINTING AT THE "SNAKE" REPUTATION THE MEDIA HAD FALSELY GIVEN HER.

CHARTS & AWARDS

- PEAKED AT #18 ON THE BILLBOARD HOT 100 CHART
- SPENT 14 WEEKS ON THE CHARTS
- CERTIFIED RIAA PLATINUM
- WON AS AN "AWARD WINNING SONG" AT THE 2019 BMI AWARDS
- TO DATE, THE TRACK HAS BEEN STREAMED 439,427,764 TIMES

TAYLOR HAS LONG FELT A CONNECTION TO THE NUMBER 13. SHE USES THE PHRASE 'REPUTATION' 13 TIMES ON THE TRACK.

FUTURE AND ED SHEERAN'S COLLABORATION ON THIS TRACK WAS TEASED PRIOR TO ITS RELEASE, AS THEIR NAMES WERE WRITTEN IN THE GRAFFITI WALLS OF THE "...READY FOR IT" MUSIC VIDEO.

I Did Something Bad

THIRD TRACK ON HER SIXTH ALBUM
RELEASED: NOVEMBER 10, 2017
RECORDED: MXM STUDIOS IN LOS ANGELES, CA & STOCKHOLM, SWEDEN

DID YOU KNOW?

TAYLOR NOTES THE INSPIRATION FOR THIS SONG COMES FROM THE "GAME OF THRONES" SERIES. SPECIFICALLY, SHE REFERENCES THE PLOT LINE WHERE THE TWO HOUSE STARK SISTERS CONSPIRE TO ELIMINATE AN ENEMY WHO BETRAYED THEM.

SEVERAL LYRICS FROM THE BRIDGE OF THE SONG APPEARED IN THE "...READY FOR IT" MUSIC VIDEO PRIOR TO ITS RELEASE.

THIS TRACK IS THE FIRST SONG TAYLOR PUBLISHED WITH AN EXPLICIT LYRIC.

THE IDEA FOR THE SOUNDS ON THE CHORUS REFRAIN CAME TO TAYLOR IN A DREAM; PRODUCERS LOWERED AND SYNTHESIZED HER VOICE TO CREATE THE SOUND.

CHARTS & AWARDS

- THE TRACK DID NOT CHART ON THE BILLBOARD HOT 100
- CERTIFIED RIAA GOLD
- TO DATE, THE TRACK HAS BEEN STREAMED 378,980,904 TIMES

in taylor's words

"I KIND OF GREW UP THINKING, 'IF I'M NICE, AND IF I TRY TO DO THE RIGHT THING, YOU KNOW, MAYBE I CAN JUST, LIKE, ACE THIS WHOLE THING [LIFE].' AND IT TURNS OUT I CAN'T. IT'S SOMETHING I'VE HAD TO RECONCILE WITHIN MYSELF IN THE LAST COUPLE OF YEARS — THAT SORT OF 'GOOD' COMPLEX. BECAUSE FROM THE TIME I WAS A KID I'D TRY TO BE KIND, BE A GOOD PERSON. TRY REALLY HARD. BUT YOU GET WALKED ALL OVER SOMETIMES. AND HOW DO YOU RESPOND TO BEING WALKED ALL OVER? YOU CAN'T JUST SIT THERE AND EAT YOUR SALAD AND LET IT HAPPEN. 'I DID SOMETHING BAD' WAS ABOUT DOING SOMETHING THAT WAS SO AGAINST WHAT I WOULD USUALLY DO."

Don't Blame Me

FOURTH TRACK ON HER SIXTH ALBUM
RELEASED: NOVEMBER 10, 2017
RECORDED: MXM STUDIOS IN LOS ANGELES, CA & STOCKHOLM, SWEDEN

DID YOU KNOW?

THE TRACK CONTAINS A POP CULTURE REFERENCE TO THE CHARACTER DAISY FROM "THE GREAT GATSBY". CHARACTER ANALYSES OF DAISY BUCHANAN DESCRIBE HER AS HAVING A BEAUTIFUL VOICE THAT MAKES HER IRRESISTIBLE AND DANGEROUS TO MEN.

DUE TO THE POPULARITY OF THE TRACK IN 2022 ON THE APP TIKTOK, THE SONG RE-ENTERED THE GLOBAL 200 CHARTS 5 YEARS AFTER ITS RELEASE.

TAYLOR'S ESTIMATED TO HAVE A 3.6 OCTAVE VOCAL RANGE. HE VOCAL RANGE FOR THE TRACK IS D3-35, SHOWCASING TAYLOR'S LOWER REGISTER. E6 IS THE LOWEST END OF TAYLOR'S RANGE.

THE IDEA FOR THE SOUNDS ON THE CHORUS REFRAIN CAME TO TAYLOR IN A DREAM; PRODUCERS LOWERED AND SYNTHESIZED HER VOICE TO CREATE THE SOUND.

CHARTS & AWARDS

- THE TRACK DID NOT CHART ON THE BILLBOARD HOT 100
- CERTIFIED RIAA GOLD
- TO DATE, THE TRACK HAS BEEN STREAMED 895,382,968 TIMES

in taylor's words

"THREE THINGS CAN REALLY CHANGE SOMEONE – LOVE, DRUGS AND RELIGION."

Delicate

SIXTH SINGLE ON HER SIXTH ALBUM
RELEASED AS A SINGLE: MARCH 12, 2018
RECORDED: MXM STUDIOS IN LOS ANGELES, CA & STOCKHOLM, SWEDEN

DID YOU KNOW?

WHEN PERFORMING THE TRACK ON THE "REPUTATION STADIUM TOUR", TAYLOR FLOATED IN A GOLDEN BASKET AS SHE SANG TO THE CROWD.

"DELICATE" WAS THE LONGEST CHARTING SONG BY A SOLO FEMALE OF THE 2010 DECADE.

DURING THE TIME 100 GALA AT THE LINCOLN CENTER FOR THE PERFORMING ARTS ON APRIL 23, 2019, SWIFT WAS HONORED AS ONE OF THE "100 MOST INFLUENTIAL PEOPLE" OF THE YEAR AND DELIVERED AN ACOUSTIC RENDITION OF THE SONG.

CHARTS & AWARDS

- PEAKED AT #12 ON THE BILLBOARD HOT 100 CHART
- SPENT 35 WEEKS TOTAL ON THE CHART
- CERTIFIED RIAA PLATINUM X6
- WON "BEST MUSIC VIDEO" AT THE IHEARTRADIO MUSIC AWARDS IN 2019
- NOMINATED FOR "CHOICE POP SONG" AT THE TEEN CHOICE AWARDS IN 2018
- TO DATE, THE TRACK HAS BEEN STREAMED 860,185,691 TIMES

in taylor's words

"THIS IS A SONG WHERE THE IDEA OF REPUTATION IS DEFINITELY SOMETHING THAT I PLAY ON FOR THE ENTIRE ALBUM BUT WHEN THE ALBUM STARTED OFF IT'S MUCH MORE BOMBASTIC. 'I DON'T CARE WHAT YOU SAY ABOUT ME! I DON'T CARE SAY ABOUT MY REPUTATION. BLAH.' BUT, LIKE, THEN IT HITS THIS POINT ON TRACK 5 WHERE IT'S LIKE WHAT HAPPENS WHEN YOU MEET SOMEONE WHO YOU REALLY WANT IN YOUR LIFE AND THEN YOU START WORRYING ABOUT WHAT THEY'VE HEARD BEFORE THEY MET YOU? YOU START TO WONDER LIKE, 'COULD SOMETHING FAKE, LIKE YOUR REPUTATION, AFFECT SOMETHING REAL LIKE SOMEONE GETTING TO KNOW YOU?' YOU START TO WONDER HOW IT ALL MATTERS. THIS IS THE FIRST POINT OF VULNERABILITY IN THE RECORD WHERE YOU'RE LIKE, 'OH, MAYBE THIS DOES ACTUALLY MATTER A LITTLE BIT,' AND QUESTIONING THE REALITY AND THE PERCEPTION OF A REPUTATION AND HOW MUCH WEIGHT IT ACTUALLY HAS. SO THIS IS CALLED 'DELICATE.'"

Look What You Made Me Do

FIRST SINGLE ON HER SIXTH ALBUM
RELEASED AS A SINGLE: AUGUST 25, 2017
RECORDED: ROUGH CUSTOMER STUDIOS IN BROOKLYN, NY

DID YOU KNOW?

AS THE LEAD SINGLE AND THE FIRST RELEASE AFTER A YEAR OUT OF THE PUBLIC EYE, THIS SONG SERVES AS TAYLOR'S CHOICE TO TAKE BACK HER OWN NARRATIVE.

THE OFFICIAL CREDITS FOR THE SONG CONFIRM THAT THE CHORUS INTENTIONALLY INCORPORATES AN INTERPOLATION OF THE HOOK FROM RIGHT SAID FRED'S 1991 HIT "I'M TOO SEXY."

THE MUSIC VIDEO SET RECORDS ON VEVO AND YOUTUBE, ACCUMULATING A HISTORIC 43.2 MILLION VIEWS WITHIN ITS FIRST DAY.

CHARTS & AWARDS

- PEAKED AT #1 ON THE BILLBOARD HOT 100 CHART
- SPENT 20 WEEKS TOTAL ON THE CHART
- CERTIFIED RIAA PLATINUM X8
- NOMINATED FOR "BEST MUSIC VIDEO" AND "BEST LYRICS" AT THE IHEARTRADIO MUSIC AWARDS IN 2019
- NOMINATED FOR "BEST ART DIRECTION, BEST EDITING, AND BEST VISUAL EFFECTS" AT THE MTV VIDEO MUSIC AWARDS IN 2019
- TO DATE, THE TRACK HAS BEEN STREAMED 1,014,166,156 TIMES

in taylor's words

"IT ACTUALLY STARTED WITH JUST A POEM THAT I WROTE ABOUT MY FEELINGS, AND IT'S BASICALLY ABOUT REALIZING THAT YOU COULDN'T TRUST CERTAIN PEOPLE, BUT REALIZING YOU APPRECIATE THE PEOPLE YOU CAN TRUST. REALIZING THAT YOU CAN'T JUST LET EVERYONE IN, BUT THE ONES YOU CAN LET IN, YOU NEED TO CHERISH. AND IT HAD ALL THE VERSES IN IT, JUST BASICALLY AS IS. WHEN THE BEAT HIT, WE WERE LIKE 'OH, LOOK WHAT YOU MADE ME DO, LOOK WHAT YOU MADE ME DO,' AND WE WERE JUST LIKE, 'OH MY GOD, WE'VE GOTTA EDIT OUT THE REST OF THE WORDS, AND JUST DO THAT.' THE MOST IMPORTANT PART OF THE SONG IS, 'I DON'T TRUST NOBODY, AND NOBODY TRUSTS ME, I'LL BE THE ACTRESS STARRING IN YOUR BAD DREAMS. OH, I'M SORRY, THE OLD TAYLOR CAN'T COME TO THE PHONE RIGHT NOW. WHY? OH, 'CAUSE SHE'S DEAD.'"

So It Goes...

SEVENTH TRACK ON HER SIXTH ALBUM
RELEASED: NOVEMBER 10, 2017
RECORDED: MXM STUDIOS IN LOS ANGELES, CA & STOCKHOLM, SWEDEN

DID YOU KNOW?

ALONGSIDE MAIN PRODUCERS MAX MARTIN AND SHELLBACK, TAYLOR JOINED FORCES WITH OSCAR GÖRRES FOR THE TRACK. GÖRRES HAS ALSO CONTRIBUTED TO PROJECTS LIKE CHER LLOYD'S "I WISH," TORI KELLY'S "UNBREAKABLE SMILE," AND DNCE'S "BE MEAN."

THE SONG BECAME SUCH A FAN FAVORITE FROM THE ALBUM THAT TAYLOR ADDED THE SONG TO THE REGULAR SETLIST FOR "THE REPUTATION STADIUM TOUR" AFTER SEEING REQUESTS ON SOCIAL MEDIA.

THE PHRASE "SO IT GOES" IS DRAWN FROM KURT VONNEGUT'S 1969 NOVEL, SLAUGHTERHOUSE-FIVE, WHERE IT IS REPEATEDLY EMPLOYED BY THE AUTHOR AS A NARRATIVE TRANSITION TO ANOTHER SUBJECT WHENEVER A DEATH OCCURS. THIS IS A CALLBACK TO "THE OLD TAYLOR" BEING DEAD.

IN ADDITION TO "END GAME" LYRICS, THERE WERE ALSO LYRICS FROM THIS TRACK HIDDEN IN THE "...READY FOR IT" MUSIC VIDEO.

CHARTS & AWARDS

- THE TRACK DID NOT CHART ON THE BILLBOARD HOT 100
- CERTIFIED RIAA GOLD
- TO DATE, THE TRACK HAS BEEN STREAMED 153,585,270 TIMES

Gorgeous

FIFTH SINGLE ON HER SIXTH ALBUM
RELEASED AS A SINGLE: JANUARY 12, 2018
RECORDED: MXM STUDIOS IN LOS ANGELES, CA & STOCKHOLM, SWEDEN

DID YOU KNOW?

DAUGHTER OF BLAKE LIVELY AND RYAN REYNOLDS, JAMES REYNOLDS IS THE BABY VOICE AT THE START OF THE TRACK. AT A SECRET SESSION, TAYLOR REVEALED SHE PLAYED "GORGEOUS" ON GUITAR FOR BLAKE AND RYAN AT THE BEACH, AND AFTER THEIR CHILD JAMES KEPT REPEATING "GORGEOUS," TAYLOR RECORDED A VOICE MEMO CAPTURING THE MOMENT. THIS MADE JAMES REYNOLDS TAYLOR'S YOUNGEST COLLABORATOR AND THE ONLY FEMALE COLLABORATOR ON THE ALBUM.

"GORGEOUS" WAS THE FIRST SONG FROM "REPUTATION" THAT TAYLOR PLAYED DURING "THE ERAS TOUR" ON APRIL 29, 2023 IN ATLANTA, GA.

CLAIMING THE TOP SPOT ON THE DIGITAL SONGS CHART, IT MARKED SWIFT'S 14TH NUMBER-ONE ENTRY, SOLIDIFYING HER RECORD FOR THE MOST NUMBER-ONE DEBUTS ON THE CHART.

CHARTS & AWARDS

- PEAKED AT #13 ON THE BILLBOARD HOT 100 CHART
- SPENT 4 WEEKS TOTAL ON THE CHART
- CERTIFIED RIAA PLATINUM
- TO DATE, THE TRACK HAS BEEN STREAMED 525,051,944 TIMES

in taylor's words

"THIS IS A SONG ABOUT THE UNIVERSAL FACT THAT YOU WILL ACT STUPID AROUND SOMEONE THAT YOU THINK IS HOT."

Getaway Car

NINTH TRACK ON HER SIXTH ALBUM
RELEASED: NOVEMBER 10, 2017
RECORDED: ROUGH CUSTOMER STUDIOS IN BROOKLYN, NY

DID YOU KNOW?

JACK ANTONOFF COLLABORATED WITH TAYLOR ON THE TRACK. HE NOTES: "IT'S THE ONLY TIME IN MY LIFE THAT A LIGHTNING-IN-A-BOTTLE MOMENT, A PURE MOMENT OF CRAZY WRITING, WAS CAUGHT ON FILM. IT'S RARE THAT YOU JUST, LIKE, BLURT OUT A WHOLE SONG. BUT THERE'S PIECES, LIKE THAT BRIDGE, WHERE WE'RE JUST GOING BACK AND FORTH AND YELLING THINGS. IT'S SORT OF LIKE, 'WHOA! OH, MY GOD, WHAT HAPPENED? IT CAN HAPPEN LIKE THAT?' THAT'S WHEN IT FEELS LIKE A MOVIE."

THE SONG IS BELIEVED TO BE ABOUT TOM HIDDLESTON AND HOW TAYLOR SWIFT USED THEIR BRIEF RELATIONSHIP TO BREAK UP WITH HER THEN-BOYFRIEND, CALVIN HARRIS.

JACK JOINED TAYLOR LIVE ON STAGE TO PERFORM THE TRACK AS A SURPRISE SONG DURING "THE ERAS TOUR" IN EAST RUTHERFORD, NJ ON MAY 26, 2023.

CHARTS & AWARDS

- IT DID NOT PEAK ON BILLBOARD HOT 100 CHART, BUT IT DID ACHIEVE SUCCESS IN AUSTRALIA MAKING #26 ON THE AUSTRALIAN DIGITAL TRACKS CHART AS WELL AS BEING CERTIFIED PLATINUM BY THE AUSTRALIAN RIAA
- CERTIFIED RIAA GOLD
- TO DATE, THE TRACK HAS BEEN STREAMED 525,051,944 TIMES

King of my Heart

TENTH TRACK ON HER SIXTH ALBUM
RELEASED: NOVEMBER 10, 2017
RECORDED: MXM STUDIOS IN LOS ANGELES, CA & STOCKHOLM, SWEDEN

DID YOU KNOW?

TAYLOR ON CREATING THE TRACK: "I'VE ALWAYS WANTED TO STRUCTURE A SONG WHERE EACH INDIVIDUAL SECTION OF THE SONG SOUNDED LIKE A MOVE FORWARD IN THE RELATIONSHIP, BUT STILL BE LISTENABLE. SO, I WANTED THE VERSE TO SEEM LIKE ITS OWN PHASE OF A RELATIONSHIP, THE PRE-CHORUS TO SOUND LIKE ITS OWN PHASE OF A RELATIONSHIP, AND THE CHORUS TO SOUND LIKE ITS OWN PHASE OF A RELATIONSHIP. AND I WANTED THEM TO HAVE THEIR OWN IDENTITY, BUT SEEM LIKE THEY WERE GETTING DEEPER AND MORE FAST-PACED AS THE SONG WENT ON. SO FINALLY, I WAS ABLE TO ACHIEVE THAT IN A SONG.»

TAYLOR HAS CONFIRMED THE SONGS THAT REFERENCE A TRUE LOVE ARE ABOUT HER NOW EX-BOYFRIEND JOE ALWIN. THE PRE-CHORUS THROWS SHADE AT TWO OF HER PRIOR EX-BOYRIENDS, CALVIN HARRIS AND TOM HIDDLESTON, WHO COINCIDENTALLY DRIVE A RANGE ROVER AND JAGUAR, RESPECTIVELY.

TAYLOR SWIFT INCLUDED "KING OF MY HEART" IN HER PERFORMANCES DURING THE REPUTATION STADIUM TOUR FROM MAY 8, 2018, IN GLENDALE, ARIZONA, TO NOVEMBER 21, 2018, IN TOKYO, JAPAN.

CHARTS & AWARDS

- IT DID NOT PEAK ON BILLBOARD HOT 100 CHART
- TO DATE, THE TRACK HAS BEEN STREAMED 227,436,646 TIMES

in taylor's words

"I THINK IT'S REALLY INTERESTING WHEN PEOPLE TALK ABOUT THEIR LOVE STORIES. THERE SEEMS TO BE THESE DEFINITIVE PHASES, AND IT DOESN'T MATTER HOW LONG THAT PHASE LASTS, THERE SEEMS TO BE A MOMENT WHEN YOU KNEW IT TRANSITIONED INTO THE NEXT PHASE. PEOPLE WILL BE LIKE, 'OH MY GOD, WE WERE FRIENDS FOR SIX YEARS, AND THERE WAS THIS MOMENT, AND WE KNEW, AND THEN IT CHANGED. THEN THERE WAS A MOMENT AND IT GOT DEEPER, AND THEN THERE WAS A MOMENT AND WE KNEW. EVERYBODY HAS A DIFFERENT STORY WITH HOW THEY CONNECT WITH SOMEONE ELSE. AND WHAT I FIND INTERESTING ARE THE MOMENTS WHERE IT SWITCHES, BECAUSE YOU ALWAYS HOPE THAT THAT SWITCH IS GOING TO MOVE YOU FORWARD AND NOT BACKWARD. BECAUSE, IT CAN HAPPEN BOTH WAYS. IT CAN HAPPEN EITHER WAY."

Dancing With Our Hands Tied

ELEVENTH TRACK ON HER SIXTH ALBUM
RELEASED: NOVEMBER 10, 2017
RECORDED: MXM STUDIOS IN LOS ANGELES, CA & STOCKHOLM, SWEDEN

DID YOU KNOW?

TAYLOR NOTES THAT THE SONG WAS INSPIRED BY AN INCIDENT THAT OCCURRED AFTER RETURNING TO LOS ANGELES AFTER HAVING A YEAR OF PRIVACY WITH JOE ALWIN IN THE UNITED KINGDOM. BACK IN CALIFORNIA, SHE WENT TO THE GYM FOR THE FIRST TIME ONLY TO BE ACCOSTED BY PAPARAZZI WHO SHOUTED RUDE COMMENTS ABOUT HER WEIGHT. FEELING OVERWHELMED, SHE GOT THE IDEA FOR THE TRACK AS SHE WONDERED HOW SHE WOULD HAVE A NORMAL RELATIONSHIP IN THIS ENVIRONMENT.

SWEDISH WRITER-PRODUCER OSCAR HOLTER, KNOWN FOR CO-WRITING "BON APPÉTIT" FOR KATY PERRY, COLLABORATED WITH MAX MARTIN AND SHELLBACK IN BOTH WRITING AND PRODUCING THE SONG.

AUSTIN SWIFT, TAYLOR SWIFT'S BROTHER, CONSIDERS THIS TRACK FROM "REPUTATION" TO BE HIS FAVORITE.

CHARTS & AWARDS

- IT DID NOT PEAK ON BILLBOARD HOT 100 CHART
- CERTIFIED RIAA GOLD
- TO DATE, THE TRACK HAS BEEN STREAMED 213,846,502 TIMES

Dress

TWELFTH TRACK ON HER SIXTH ALBUM
RELEASED: NOVEMBER 10, 2017
RECORDED: MXM STUDIOS IN LOS ANGELES, CA & STOCKHOLM, SWEDEN

DID YOU KNOW?

AS MENTIONED DURING HER PRIVATE "REPUTATION SECRET SESSIONS", THE SONG CHRONICLES THE START OF TAYLOR'S RELATIONSHIP WITH JOE ALWIN.

DURING THE "REPUTATION WORLD TOUR", TAYLOR HAD A DEDICATED SPOT FOR THE SONG ON THE REGULAR SET LIST. DURING THE PERFORMANCE, TAYLOR SWIFT PAID TRIBUTE TO LOÏE FULLER, A PIONEER IN ARTS AND DANCE. A WHITE-ROBED DANCER PERFORMED THE SERPENTINE DANCE, CREATED BY FULLER AND FEATURED IN EARLY EDISON FILMS. FOLLOWING "DRESS," SCREENS DISPLAYED A DEDICATION TO FULLER, RECOGNIZING HER CONTRIBUTIONS TO THE ARTS AND HER ADVOCACY FOR ARTISTS' OWNERSHIP OF THEIR WORK.

PRIOR TO WRITING THIS TRACK, TAYLOR MENTIONED A "DRESS" IN 13 OF HER OTHER SONGS.

CHARTS & AWARDS

- IT DID NOT PEAK ON BILLBOARD HOT 100 CHART
- CERTIFIED RIAA PLATINUM
- TO DATE, THE TRACK HAS BEEN STREAMED 264,843,004 TIMES

in taylor's words

"THIS SONG WAS ONE OF THOSE THINGS WHERE ALMOST EVERY LINE IS SOMETHING THAT I CAME UP WITH LIKE A YEAR BEFORE, AND THEN WHEN I WAS WRITING THE SONG, I JUST CHERRY PICKED, AND I WAS LIKE, 'LIKE THAT, LIKE THAT, LIKE THAT, LIKE THAT.' AND I WAS REALLY PROUD OF THE HOOK OF THIS BECAUSE IT SOUNDS LIKE A PICKUP LINE, AND YET IT IS A LOVE SONG ABOUT DEEP AND TENDER FEELINGS."

This is Why We Can't Have Nice Things

THIRTEENTH TRACK ON HER SIXTH ALBUM
RELEASED: NOVEMBER 10, 2017
RECORDED: ROUGH CUSTOMER STUDIOS IN BROOKLYN, NY

DID YOU KNOW?

TAYLOR DREW INSPIRATION FROM "HARD KNOCK LIFE" IN "ANNIE" FOR HER SONG'S PRODUCTION. SHE APPRECIATED THE VIBRANT SOUND OF CHILDREN'S VOICES IN MUSICALS, PROMPTING HER TO INCORPORATE IT INTO HER OWN WORK.

SIMILAR TO "DELICATE", THE SONG DRAWS ON IMAGERY FROM "THE GREAT GATSBY" THROUGHOUT THE LYRICS.

THE SONG ALSO MAKES SPECIFIC REFERENCE TO ELEMENTS OF HER ONGOING FUED WITH KANYA WEST. TAYLOR AND KANYE'S RIFT BEGAN IN 2009 AFTER HE INTERRUPTED HER AT THE MTV VMAS. THOUGH THEY RECONCILED IN 2015 WHEN SHE PRESENTED HIM WITH A "THE VANGUARD AWARD", THEIR FEUD FLARED UP AGAIN IN THE FOLLOWING YEAR WITH KANYE'S RELEASE OF "FAMOUS."

OF NOTE, "THIS IS WHY WE CAN'T HAVE NICE THINGS" WAS ORIGINALLY SLATED AS THE CLOSING TRACK FOR THE REPUTATION ALBUM. THIS CHOICE MIGHT EXPLAIN ITS ROLE AS THE FINAL SONG IN TAYLOR'S "REPUTATION STADIUM TOUR" (2018), MARKING THE FIRST TIME A NON-SINGLE CONCLUDED ONE OF HER TOURS.

CHARTS & AWARDS

- IT DID NOT PEAK ON BILLBOARD HOT 100 CHART
- TO DATE, THE TRACK HAS BEEN STREAMED 190,434,889 TIMES

in taylor's words

"IT'S A SONG ABOUT WHEN PEOPLE TAKE NICE THINGS FOR GRANTED. LIKE FRIENDSHIP, OR TRUSTING PEOPLE, OR BEING OPEN OR WHATEVER. LETTING PEOPLE IN ON YOUR LIFE, TRUSTING PEOPLE, RESPECT. THOSE ARE ALL REALLY NICE THINGS."

Call It What You Want

FOURTEENTH TRACK ON HER SIXTH ALBUM
RELEASED: NOVEMBER 10, 2017
RECORDED: ROUGH CUSTOMER STUDIOS IN BROOKLYN, NY

DID YOU KNOW?

ON SATURDAY NIGHT LIVE'S 43RD SEASON, TAYLOR SWIFT PERFORMED AN ACOUSTIC VERSION OF THE SONG ALONGSIDE "...READY FOR IT?".

TAYLOR COLLABORATED WITH JACK ANTONOFF FOR THIS TRACK ALONG WITH FOUR OTHERS ON "REPUTATION". JACK NOTES ABOUT THE PRODUCTION. OF THE SONG: " IT WAS MADE WITH AN MPC, LIVE KICK, DX7 STRINGS AND SAMPLES OF TAYLOR'S VOICE AS THE INTRO AND THROUGHOUT. MAKING HER VOICE INTO AN INSTRUMENT."

TAYLOR REVEALED IN SEPTEMBER 2022, THAT IN WRITING EACH OF HER SONGS, THEY FALL INTO 3 DISTINCT CATEGORIES: "FOUNTAIN PEN", "QUILL PEN" OR "GLITTER GEL PEN". TAYLOR NOTES: "I CAME UP WITH THESE CATEGORIES BASED ON WHAT WRITING TOOL I IMAGINE HAVING IN MY HAND WHEN I SCRIBBLED IT DOWN, FIGURATIVELY." THIS SONG IS THOUGHT TO BE CATEGORIZED AS A "FOUNTAIN PEN" SONG WHICH INCLUDE MODERN LYRICS FULL OF FAMILIAR REFERENCES AND VIVID IMAGERY.

CHARTS & AWARDS

- PEAKED AT #27 ON THE BILLBOARD HOT 100 CHART
- SPENT 2 TOTAL WEEKS ON THE CHART
- CERTIFIED RIAA PLATINUM
- TO DATE, THE TRACK HAS BEEN STREAMED 344,872,648 TIMES

in taylor's words

"THE WAY I FEEL THE ALBUM IS, AS FAR AS A STORYLINE, IS I FEEL LIKE IT STARTS WITH JUST GETTING OUT ANY KIND OF REBELLION, OR ANGER, OR ANGST, OR WHATEVER. AND THEN, LIKE, FALLING IN LOVE, AND REALIZING THAT YOU KIND OF SETTLE INTO WHAT YOUR PRIORITIES ARE, AND YOUR LIFE CHANGES, BUT YOU WELCOME IT BECAUSE IT'S SOMETHING THAT MATTERS TO YOU. AND THIS LAST PART OF THE ALBUM FEELS LIKE SETTLING INTO WHERE I AM NOW. SO IT STARTED WITH WHERE I WAS WHEN I STARTED MAKING THE ALBUM, AND ENDS WITH KIND OF MY EMOTIONAL STATE NOW. AND THIS SONG, I THINK, REALLY REFLECTS THAT PROBABLY THE BEST ON THE ALBUM."

New Years Day

FOURTH SINGLE ON HER SIXTH ALBUM
RELEASED AS A SINGLE: NOVEMBER 27, 2017
RECORDED: ROUGH CUSTOMER STUDIOS IN BROOKLYN, NY

DID YOU KNOW?

BEFORE THE ALBUM DROPPED, TAYLOR PREMIERED A LIVE RECORDING OF THE SONG ON THE NOVEMBER 9, 2017 EPISODE OF THE ABC SERIES "SCANDAL".

TAYLOR COLLABORATED WITH JACK ANTONOFF FOR THIS TRACK ALONG WITH FOUR OTHERS ON "REPUTATION". JACK NOTES THAT THIS WAS THE FASTEST TRACK TO RECORD AND ONLY RECORDED IT ONCE. HE ALSO CITED JONI MITCHELL AS INSPIRATION FOR CAPTURING EMOTIONAL HONESTY DURING THE RECORDING SESSION.

WHEN THE SONG CHARTED ON THE BILLBOARD HOT COUNTRY SONGS CHART AND THE COUNTRY DIGITAL SONG SALES CHART, IT WAS HER 40TH AND 33RD ENTRY TO EACH CHART RESPECTIVELY.

OLIVIA RODRIGO USED AN INTERPOLATION OF "NEW YEARS DAY" ON THE SONG "1 STEP FORWARD, 3 STEPS BACK" ON HER FIRST ALBUM, "SOUR".

CHARTS & AWARDS

- DEBUTED AT #40 ON THE BILLBOARD HOT COUNTRY SONGS CHART
- TO DATE, THE TRACK HAS BEEN STREAMED 163,130,801 TIMES

in taylor's words

"TWO NEW YEAR'S EVE'S AGO, I FOUND MYSELF IN THE MIDST OF A VERY INCREDIBLE 3 A.M. MOMENT WHERE YOU FEEL LIKE YOU'RE INVINCIBLE AND YOU END UP LIKE JUMPING IN A POOL IN THE WINTER. AND YOU FEEL SUPER UNTOUCHABLE IN THAT MOMENT. AND THEN THE NEXT MORNING YOU FEEL VERY FRAGILE. AND YOU'RE LIKE, 'THIS IS LOVE! THIS IS WHAT LOVE REALLY IS.' WE ALL WANNA FIND SOMEONE TO KISS AT MIDNIGHT, THAT'S COOL OR WHATEVER, BUT WHO'S GONNA WANT TO HANG OUT WITH YOU THE NEXT DAY WHEN YOU'RE LIKE 'ADVIL OR NOTHING.' SO THIS IS A SONG ABOUT REAL LOVE AND FINDING SOMEONE TO HANG OUT WITH ON NEW YEAR'S DAY."

Lover

RELEASED: AUGUST 23, 2019

"Whimsical, Romantic, Intimate, Poignant"

I Forgot That You Existed

FIRST TRACK OF HER SEVENTH ALBUM
RELEASED: AUGUST 23, 2019
RECORDED: ELECTRIC FEEL STUDIOS IN WEST HOLLYWOOD, CA

DID YOU KNOW?

FOUR YEARS AFTER ITS RELEASE, TAYLOR PERFORMED THE SONG FOR THE FIRST TIME ON AUGUST 24TH, 2023 IN MEXICO CITY.

VIBRANT, AIRY, AND EFFERVESCENT, THE SONG FEATURES HER REFLECTING ON PAST CONFLICTS AND CONTROVERSIES, ULTIMATELY REALIZING THEIR INSIGNIFICANCE IN HER LIFE NOW. TAYLOR NOTES THAT THE "REPUTATION STADIUM TOUR" TRANSFORMED HER PERSPECTIVE AND MADE HER EXTREMELY RESILIENT.

SWIFT COLLABORATED WITH THE RENOWNED PRODUCERS LOUIS BELL AND FRANK DUKES, KNOWN FOR THEIR INVOLVEMENT IN MAJOR HITS LIKE CAMILA CABELLO'S "HAVANA" AND JONAS BROTHERS' "SUCKER," IN CRAFTING THE SONG.

CHARTS & AWARDS

- PEAKED AT #28 ON THE BILLBOARD HOT 100 CHART
- CERTIFIED RIAA PLATINUM
- TO DATE, THE TRACK HAS BEEN STREAMED 306,526,838 TIMES

IN TAYLOR'S WORDS

"REPUTATION' WAS PRETTY MUCH LIKE A COPING MECHANISM. IT WAS LIKE GOING THROUGH ALL THE STAGES OF GRIEF OVER THE LOSS OF ONE'S REPUTATION; KIND OF LIKE THROWING A FUNERAL FOR SOMETHING THAT MAYBE WASN'T EVEN GOOD FOR YOU TO HAVE IN THE FIRST PLACE. IN DOING THAT, AND IN PICKING THE FIRST SONG AND WRITING THE FIRST SONG ON THIS ALBUM, I WANTED TO COMPLETE THE CYCLE OF GRIEVING, ALMOST, AND THE CYCLE OF WHEN YOU GO THROUGH SOME DRAMA OR SOME FRUSTRATING STUFF IN YOUR LIFE WHERE A RELATIONSHIP ENDS, OR YOU'RE GOING THROUGH THIS TURMOIL IN YOUR LIFE, THERE'S ALL THESE PHASES YOU GO THROUGH. AND THEN, WHEN YOU'RE REALLY DONE WITH IT, YOU HIT INDIFFERENCE. THE ACTUAL DEFINITION OF GETTING OVER SOMETHING IS A SHRUG. I WROTE THE SONG AND I WANTED IT TO BE JUST AS SIMPLE AS THE EMOTION OF INDIFFERENCE IS."

Cruel Summer

FOURTH SINGLE OF HER SEVENTH ALBUM
RELEASED AS A SINGLE: JUNE 20, 2023
RECORDED: ELECTRIC LADY STUDIOS IN NEW YORK, NY

DID YOU KNOW?

THE TRACK WAS AN IMMEDIATE FAN FAVORITE AND RECEIVED UNIVERSAL ACCLAIM IN ADDITION TO BEING TAYLOR'S FAVORITE TRACK ON LOVER. DUE TO ITS POPULARITY, IT WAS RELEASED AS A SINGLE 4 YEARS AFTER THE RELEASE OF LOVER WITH HUGE COMMERCIAL SUCCESS.

AFTER THE RELEASE OF THE SONG AS A SINGLE, IT BECAME TAYLOR'S TENTH #1 ON THE BILLBOARD HOT 100 CHART.

TAYLOR DROPPED HINTS ABOUT THE SONG'S TITLE BEFORE UNVEILING THE TRACKLIST. IN THE "YOU NEED TO CALM DOWN" MUSIC VIDEO, ELLEN DEGENERES WAS SPOTTED GETTING A TATTOO OF THE SONG'S TITLE AT 2:03. ANOTHER EASTER EGG SHOWED UP IN THE "LOVER" MUSIC VIDEO WHERE TWO OF THE BOARD GAMES PLAYED ARE LYRICS FROM THIS TRACK.

IN ADDITION TO TAYLOR'S LONG TIME COLLABORATOR JACK ANTONOFF, TAYLOR COLLABORATED WITH THE MUSICIAN ST.VINCENT ON WRITING THE TRACK; HE ALSO PLAYS THE LEAD GUITAR MELODY.

CHARTS & AWARDS

- THE ORIGINAL RELEASE OF THE TRACK PEAKED AT #29 IN 2019
- THE SINGLE PEAKED AT #1 ON THE BILLBOARD HOT 100 CHART IN 2023
- CERTIFIED RIAA 6X PLATINUM
- TO DATE, THE TRACK HAS BEEN STREAMED 1,466,908,081 TIMES

IN TAYLOR'S WORDS

"THIS SONG IS ONE THAT I WROTE "BOUT THE FEELING OF A SUMMER ROMANCE, AND HOW OFTEN TIMES A SUMMER ROMANCE CAN BE LAYERED WITH ALL THESE FEELINGS OF PINING AWAY AND SOMETIMES EVEN SECRECY. IT DEALS WITH THE IDEA OF BEING IN A RELATIONSHIP WHERE THERE'S SOME ELEMENT OF DESPERATION AND PAIN IN IT, WHERE YOU'RE YEARNING FOR SOMETHING THAT YOU DON'T QUITE HAVE YET. IT'S JUST RIGHT THERE, AND YOU JUST CAN'T REACH IT. SO, THIS HAS SOME OF MY FAVORITE LYRICS IN IT, AND IT WAS SO FUN TO WRITE THIS."

Lover

THIRD SINGLE OF HER SEVENTH ALBUM
RELEASED AS A SINGLE: AUGUST 16, 2019
RECORDED: ELECTRIC LADY STUDIOS IN NEW YORK, NY

DID YOU KNOW?

TAYLOR CO-DIRECTED THE MUSIC VIDEO FOR "LOVER" WITH DREW KIRSCH. THE MUSIC VIDEO STARS TAYLOR'S FORMER BACK-UP DANCER CHRISTOPHER OWNS AS HER LOVE INTEREST.

ON SEPTEMBER 9, 2019, SHE FEATURED "LOVER" IN THE LINEUP FOR HER EXCLUSIVE "CITY OF LOVER" CONCERT IN PARIS.

TAYLOR SAYS OF A PARTICULAR LINE IN THE SONG'S BRIDGE: "IN LIFE, YOU ACCUMULATE SCARS, YOU ACCUMULATE HURT, YOU ACCUMULATE MOMENTS OF LEARNING AND DISAPPOINTMENT AND STRUGGLE AND ALL THAT. AND IF SOMEONE'S GONNA TAKE YOUR HAND, THEY BETTER TAKE YOUR HAND, SCARS AND ALL."

CHARTS & AWARDS

- THE SINGLE PEAKED AT #10 ON THE BILLBOARD HOT 100 CHART
- SPENT 22 WEEKS ON THE CHART
- WON THE "TEN SONGS I'D WISH I'D WRITTEN" AWARD AT THE NASHVILLE SONGWRITER AWARDS
- NOMINATED FOR "SONG OF THE YEAR AT THE 63RD GRAMMY AWARDS
- NOMINATED FOR "BEST ART DIRECTION" AT THE MTV MUSIC VIDEO AWARDS IN 2020
- CERTIFIED RIAA 4X PLATINUM
- TO DATE, THE TRACK HAS BEEN STREAMED 1,119,714,602 TIMES

IN TAYLOR'S WORDS

"THIS SONG IS REALLY SPECIAL TO ME BECAUSE I WROTE IT ALONE WHEN I COULDN'T SLEEP ONE NIGHT IN MY NASHVILLE APARTMENT. I JUST WANDERED OVER TO THE PIANO, I HAD THIS MELODY THAT WAS KEEPING ME AWAKE, I COULDN'T REALLY GET PAST IT, AND IT ENDED UP BEING THE CHORUS MELODY FOR 'LOVER.' I WANTED TO PAINT A PICTURE OF TWO PEOPLE WHO ARE LEARNING TO LIVE TOGETHER FOR THE FIRST TIME. REALIZING YOU CAN MAKE YOUR OWN TRADITIONS, YOU CAN STAY UP AS LATE AS YOU WANT, YOU CAN KEEP THE CHRISTMAS LIGHTS UP AS LATE AS YOU WANT, YOU CAN LET YOUR FRIENDS STAY OVER IF THE NIGHT GOES TOO LONG, BECAUSE THIS IS YOUR LIFE AND YOUR FAMILY THAT YOU'RE CHOOSING. "

The Man

FOURTH SINGLE OF HER SEVENTH ALBUM
RELEASED AS A SINGLE: JANUARY 28, 2020
RECORDED: ELECTRIC LADY STUDIOS IN NEW YORK, NY

DID YOU KNOW?

SWIFT COLLABORATED WITH JOEL LITTLE, CO-WRITING AND CO-PRODUCING THE SYNTH-POP DANCE TRACK. THE NEW ZEALAND PRODUCER ALSO PLAYED A ROLE IN THREE OTHER LOVER TRACKS, INCLUDING THE HIT SINGLES "YOU NEED TO CALM DOWN" AND "ME!".

DIRECTED BY SWIFT IN HER OFFICIAL SOLO DIRECTORIAL DEBUT, THE MUSIC VIDEO FEATURES A BRIEF APPEARANCE BY HER FATHER, SCOTT, AS A TENNIS UMPIRE. TAYLOR WAS TRANSFORMED INTO DIFFERENT MALE CHARACTERS WITH HER NOTING THE TRANSFORMATIONS TOOK OVER 6 HOURS. SOCIAL MEDIA INFLUENCERS LOREN GRAY AND DOMINIC TOLIVER, ALONG WITH ACTRESS JAYDEN BARTELS, MAKE CAMEO APPEARANCES.

TAYLOR SAYS OF THE SONGS MESSAGE: "WE [WOMEN] HAVE TO CURATE AND CATER EVERYTHING, BUT WE HAVE TO MAKE IT LOOK LIKE AN ACCIDENT. BECAUSE IF WE MAKE A MISTAKE, THAT'S OUR FAULT, BUT IF WE STRATEGIZE SO THAT WE WON'T MAKE A MISTAKE, WE'RE CALCULATING. THERE IS A BIT OF A DAMNED-IF-WE-DO, DAMNED-IF-WE-DON'T THING HAPPENING IN MUSIC."

CHARTS & AWARDS

- PEAKED AT #23 ON THE BILLBOARD HOT 100 CHART
- SPENT 8 WEEKS ON THE CHART
- CERTIFIED RIAA PLATINUM
- TO DATE, THE TRACK HAS BEEN STREAMED 633,367,712 TIMES

IN TAYLOR'S WORDS

"THIS IS A SONG THAT I HAVE WANTED TO WRITE FOR A VERY LONG TIME BUT NEVER KNEW EXACTLY HOW TO. I OFTEN THINK ABOUT WHAT MY CAREER AND THE HEADLINES ABOUT IT WOULD HAVE BEEN LIKE, IF I HAD BEEN A MAN INSTEAD OF A WOMAN. NOT, 'WHAT WOULD I DO DIFFERENTLY?', BUT IF I HAD THE SAME ACCOMPLISHMENTS, THE SAME MISTAKES, THE SAME DATING HISTORY, THE SAME STATEMENTS… WHAT WOULD HAVE BEEN DIFFERENT? SO 'THE MAN' IS ABOUT WHAT WOULD HAVE BEEN, IF I HAD BEEN A DUDE AND MY APPROXIMATIONS OF IT."

The Archer

FIFTH TRACK OF HER SEVENTH ALBUM
RELEASED: AUGUST 23, 2019
RECORDED: ELECTRIC LADY STUDIOS IN NEW YORK, NY

DID YOU KNOW?

IN THIS INTROSPECTIVE BALLAD, TAYLOR EMPLOYS ROMANTIC ARCHERY IMAGERY, SHARING A NUANCED CONFESSION ABOUT RELATIONSHIP INSECURITIES. ALLUDING TO THE ANCIENT GOD CUPID, SHE EXPLORES THE DUAL IMPACT OF HIS ARROWS, INCITING INTENSE DESIRE OR PROMPTING A DESIRE TO FLEE. SWIFT'S LYRICS HINT AT HER FIRSTHAND EXPERIENCE WITH BOTH EMOTIONAL EXTREMES.

THE TITLE "THE ARCHER" ALSO NODS TO SWIFT'S ZODIAC SUN-SIGN, SAGITTARIUS.

TAYLOR INTERPOLATES LYRICS FROM "HUMPTY DUMPTY" IN THE TRACK

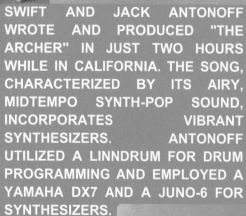

SWIFT AND JACK ANTONOFF WROTE AND PRODUCED "THE ARCHER" IN JUST TWO HOURS WHILE IN CALIFORNIA. THE SONG, CHARACTERIZED BY ITS AIRY, MIDTEMPO SYNTH-POP SOUND, INCORPORATES VIBRANT SYNTHESIZERS. ANTONOFF UTILIZED A LINNDRUM FOR DRUM PROGRAMMING AND EMPLOYED A YAMAHA DX7 AND A JUNO-6 FOR SYNTHESIZERS.

CHARTS & AWARDS

- PEAKED AT #38 ON THE BILLBOARD HOT 100 CHART
- SPENT 3 WEEKS ON THE CHART
- CERTIFIED RIAA PLATINUM
- TO DATE, THE TRACK HAS BEEN STREAMED 322,171,102 TIMES

IN TAYLOR'S WORDS

"MAYBE IN OUR LIVES IF WE'VE BEEN LET DOWN, OR THINGS HAVEN'T TURNED OUT THE WAY THAT WE WANTED TO IN RELATIONSHIPS. OFTEN TIMES WE CAN KIND OF HAVE THIS PHANTOM FEAR OF TRAGEDY, WHERE YOU'RE LIKE, IF YOU EVER FIND SOMETHING REALLY GREAT, OR A SITUATION THAT IS SOLID, OR A SITUATION WHERE YOUR TRUST ISN'T BEING BROKEN… SOMETIMES YOU HAVE TO DEAL WITH YOUR DEMONS FROM ALL THOSE TIMES THAT IT DIDN'T WORK. YOU HAVE TO STOP YOURSELF FROM THINKING THE WORST IS ALWAYS GOING TO HAPPEN. AND THIS IS A SONG THAT TOUCHES ON ANXIETY, AND HOW TO BREAK PATTERNS AND CYCLES THAT AREN'T HEALTHY, BECAUSE WE LEARN A LOT IN LIFE. SOME OF THE LESSONS ARE GOOD, AND SOME OF THE HABITS ARE GOOD, AND SOME OF THE HABITS ARE BAD. SO IT'S A SONG ABOUT HAVING TO UNLEARN SOME BAD LESSONS THAT YOU LEARNED IN THE PAST."

I Think He Knows

SIXTH TRACK OF HER SEVENTH ALBUM
RELEASED: AUGUST 23, 2019
RECORDED: ELECTRIC LADY STUDIOS IN NEW YORK, NY

DID YOU KNOW?

FOUR YEARS AFTER ITS RELEASE, TAYLOR PERFORMED "I THINK HE KNOWS" FOR THE FIRST TIME DURING HER SIXTH HEADLINING CONCERT TOUR, "THE ERAS TOUR".

TAYLOR INITIALLY HINTED AT "I THINK HE KNOWS" IN THE MUSIC VIDEO FOR "YOU NEED TO CALM DOWN," SHOWCASING A SCENE WITH THE ENTRANCE OF A NEIGHBORHOOD FEATURING A STREET SIGN FOR "16TH AVENUE."

THE SONG IS SPECULATED TO BE ABOUT HER NOW EX-BOYFRIEND JOE ALWYN IN REFERENCE TO HIS "BOY-ISH LOOK" AND "INDIGO EYES".

THE SONG MARKED ANOTHER COLLABORATION WITH JACK ANTONOFF IN BOTH THE WRITING AND PRODUCTION OF THE TRACK. THE CHORD PROGRESSION IS G-E MINOR-C-D WHICH IS A POPULAR PROGRESSION IN TAYLOR'S REPERTOIRE INCLUDING TRACKS LIKE "TEARDROPS ON MY GUITAR" AND "SPEAK NOW".

CHARTS & AWARDS

- PEAKED AT #51 ON THE BILLBOARD HOT 100 CHART
- SPENT 1 WEEK ON THE CHART
- CERTIFIED RIAA PLATINUM
- TO DATE, THE TRACK HAS BEEN STREAMED 238,611,108 TIMES

IN TAYLOR'S WORDS

"BASICALLY, I WAS PLAYING AROUND WITH THE IDEA OF QUIET CONFIDENCE. THERE'S SOMETHING SO SICK ABOUT QUIET CONFIDENCE; SOMEBODY WHO, THEY'RE NOT ARROGANT, THEY'RE NOT COCKY, LIKE, THAT'S OBNOXIOUS. BUT, THERE ARE CERTAIN PEOPLE WHO JUST WALK IN AND THEY DON'T NEED TO BE ARROGANT BECAUSE THERE'S SOMETHING BEAMING FROM WITHIN THEM THAT THEY PROBABLY AREN'T EVEN IN CONTROL OF. AND WHEN YOU MEET A PERSON LIKE THIS, YOU'RE LIKE, 'WHY DO I WANT TO WALK OVER THERE AND TALK TO THAT PERSON?' I CAN'T EXPLAIN IT, BUT I THINK IT'S THIS QUALITY."

Miss Americana & The Heartbreak Prince

SIXTH TRACK OF HER SEVENTH ALBUM
RELEASED: AUGUST 23, 2019
RECORDED: GOLDEN AGE STUDIOS IN LOS ANGELES, CA

DID YOU KNOW?

THE TITLE OF TAYLOR'S 2020 NETFLIX DOCUMENTARY, "MISS AMERICANA," DIRECTED BY LANA WILSON, WAS INSPIRED BY THE SONG "MISS AMERICANA & THE HEARTBREAK PRINCE." THE DOCUMENTARY PROVIDES AN IN-DEPTH LOOK INTO TAYLOR'S LIFE AND CAREER OVER SEVERAL YEARS.

CAPTURING SWIFT'S POLITICAL DISENCHANTMENT, "MISS AMERICANA & THE HEARTBREAK PRINCE" STANDS AS A PROTEST SONG. IT CLEVERLY EMPLOYS HIGH SCHOOL IMAGERY TO CRITIQUE THE PRESENT AMERICAN POLITICAL LANDSCAPE, DRAWING A METAPHORICAL COMPARISON BETWEEN POLITICS AND A HIGH SCHOOL SETTING.

TAYLOR REVEALED IN SEPTEMBER 2022, THAT IN WRITING EACH OF HER SONGS, THEY FALL INTO 3 DISTINCT CATEGORIES: "FOUNTAIN PEN", "QUILL PEN" OR "GLITTER GEL PEN". TAYLOR NOTES: "I CAME UP WITH THESE CATEGORIES BASED ON WHAT WRITING TOOL I IMAGINE HAVING IN MY HAND WHEN I SCRIBBLED IT DOWN, FIGURATIVELY." THIS SONG IS THOUGHT TO BE CATEGORIZED AS A "FOUNTAIN PEN" SONG WHICH INCLUDE MODERN LYRICS FULL OF FAMILIAR REFERENCES AND VIVID IMAGERY.

CHARTS & AWARDS

- PEAKED AT #49 ON THE BILLBOARD HOT 100 CHART
- SPENT 1 WEEK ON THE CHART
- CERTIFIED RIAA PLATINUM
- TO DATE, THE TRACK HAS BEEN STREAMED 296,248,008 TIMES

IN TAYLOR'S WORDS

"THERE ARE SO MANY INFLUENCES THAT GO INTO THAT PARTICULAR SONG. I WROTE IT A COUPLE OF MONTHS AFTER MIDTERM ELECTIONS, AND I WANTED TO TAKE THE IDEA OF POLITICS AND PICK A METAPHORICAL PLACE FOR THAT TO EXIST. AND SO I WAS THINKING ABOUT A TRADITIONAL AMERICAN HIGH SCHOOL, WHERE THERE'S ALL THESE KINDS OF SOCIAL EVENTS THAT COULD MAKE SOMEONE FEEL COMPLETELY ALIENATED. AND I THINK A LOT OF PEOPLE IN OUR POLITICAL LANDSCAPE ARE JUST FEELING LIKE WE NEED TO HUDDLE UP UNDER THE BLEACHERS AND FIGURE OUT A PLAN TO MAKE THINGS BETTER."

Paper Rings

EIGHTH TRACK OF HER SEVENTH ALBUM
RELEASED: AUGUST 23, 2019
RECORDED: GOLDEN AGE STUDIOS IN LOS ANGELES, CA

DID YOU KNOW?

MORE FROM TAYLOR ON THE TRACK: "I WROTE "PAPER RINGS" WITH THIS IDEA OF THROWBACK SOUNDS. WE DIDN'T WANT TO USE ANY SOUNDS THAT WERE VERY MODERN ON THIS SONG. THE SONG TALKS ABOUT TRUE LOVE AND IF YOU REALLY FIND TRUE LOVE, YOU PROBABLY DON'T REALLY CARE WHAT THE SYMBOLISM OF THAT LOVE IS. MATERIAL THINGS WOULDN'T MATTER TO YOU ANYMORE IF YOU FOUND SOMEONE THAT YOU JUST WANTED TO LIVE YOUR LIFE WITH."

THE SONG IS WRITTEN IN THE MUSICAL KEY OF A MAJOR AND WITH A TEMPO OF 104 BEATS PER MINUTE.

TAYLOR REVEALED IN SEPTEMBER 2022, THAT IN WRITING EACH OF HER SONGS, THEY FALL INTO 3 DISTINCT CATEGORIES: "FOUNTAIN PEN", "QUILL PEN" OR "GLITTER GEL PEN". TAYLOR NOTES: "I CAME UP WITH THESE CATEGORIES BASED ON WHAT WRITING TOOL I IMAGINE HAVING IN MY HAND WHEN I SCRIBBLED IT DOWN, FIGURATIVELY." THIS SONG IS THOUGHT TO BE CATEGORIZED AS A "GLITTER GEL PEN" SONG WHICH INCLUDE LYRICS THAT ARE "FRIVOLOUS, CAREFREE, AND BOUNCY".

CHARTS & AWARDS

- PEAKED AT #49 ON THE BILLBOARD HOT 100 CHART
- SPENT 1 WEEK ON THE CHART
- CERTIFIED RIAA PLATINUM
- TO DATE, THE TRACK HAS BEEN STREAMED 296,248,008 TIMES

IN TAYLOR'S WORDS

"PART OF THE TEMPLATE FOR WHAT I WANTED TO DO WITH SOME OF THE SONGS [ON LOVER] WAS IMAGINING THAT I WAS IN A WEDDING BAND AT A RECEPTION, PLAYING THE LOVE SONGS THAT THE BRIDE AND GROOM WANTED TO HEAR IN 1978 OR SOMETHING. 'PAPER RINGS' IS BASICALLY JUST REMINISCING ON FUN MEMORIES. YOUR WHOLE LIFE YOU TALK WITH YOUR FRIENDS ABOUT, 'OH MY GOD, DO YOU WANNA GET MARRIED? WHAT WOULD YOU WANT YOUR RING TO LOOK LIKE?' I DON'T KNOW, I FEEL LIKE IF YOU REALLY LOVE SOMEONE YOU WOULD BE LIKE, 'I DON'T CARE'. THE BRIDGE WAS INSPIRED BY SOME FUN PUNK GIRL GROUPS, IN THE WAY THEY USED TO SING AND SHOUT IN A REALLY UNAPOLOGETIC WAY. I MADE THIS ONE WITH JACK [ANTONOFF] AND YOU CAN HEAR HIM COUNTING IN THE CHORUS – LIKE THAT'S HOW MUCH WE WANTED TO SOUND LIKE A WEDDING BAND. IT'S A REALLY FUN ONE, I REALLY LIKE THIS ONE."

Cornelia Street

NINTH TRACK OF HER SEVENTH ALBUM
RELEASED: AUGUST 23, 2019
RECORDED: GOLDEN AGE STUDIOS IN LOS ANGELES, CA

DID YOU KNOW?

IN JUNE 2016, TAYLOR SWIFT SETTLED INTO 23 CORNELIA STREET IN NEW YORK'S WEST VILLAGE, RENTING THE TOWNHOUSE DURING RENOVATIONS ON HER TRIBECA APARTMENT. SHORTLY AFTER MOVING IN, SHE MET AND STARTED DATING BRITISH ACTOR JOE ALWYN. THIS SONG VIVIDLY CAPTURES SWIFT'S REFLECTIONS ON THE INITIAL STAGES OF THEIR RELATIONSHIP DURING HER TIME ON CORNELIA STREET.

SWIFT PENNED THE BALLAD INDEPENDENTLY AND COLLABORATED WITH FREQUENT PARTNER JACK ANTONOFF IN ITS CO-PRODUCTION. ANTONOFF, CREDITED AS A CO-WRITER ON EIGHT OF THE 18 TRACKS ON LOVER, HAS BEEN A CONSISTENT COLLABORATOR WITH THE SONGSTRESS.

TAYLOR PLAYED "CORNELIA STREET" LIVE FOR THE FIRST TIME DURING "THE ERAS TOUR" IN MEXICO CITY CONCERT ON AUGUST 26, 2023.

SWIFT ALSO SAYS OF THE TRACK: "IT'S ABOUT THE THINGS THAT TOOK PLACE AND THE MEMORIES THAT TOOK PLACE ON THAT STREET... ALL THE NOSTALGIA. SOMETIMES WE BOND OUR MEMORIES TO THE PLACES THAT THEY HAPPEN."

CHARTS & AWARDS

- PEAKED AT #57 ON THE BILLBOARD HOT 100 CHART
- SPENT 1 WEEK ON THE CHART
- CERTIFIED RIAA PLATINUM
- TO DATE, THE TRACK HAS BEEN STREAMED 281,000,933 TIMES

IN TAYLOR'S WORDS

"IT'S ABOUT THE THINGS THAT TOOK PLACE, THE MEMORIES THAT WERE MADE ON THAT STREET. I RENTED AN APARTMENT THERE AND JUST WANTED TO WRITE A SONG ABOUT ALL THE NOSTALGIA OF, YOU KNOW, SOMETIMES IN OUR LIVES WE KIND OF BOND OUR MEMORIES TO THOSE PLACES WHERE THOSE MEMORIES HAPPENED. IT'S JUST SOMETHING WE DO IF WE ROMANTISIZE LIFE, WHICH I TEND TO DO. AND SO, I WROTE THIS SONG ABOUT GOING BACK OVER THE MEMORIES OF THINGS THAT HAPPENED IN THIS PARTICULAR PLACE, AND IT ENDED UP BEING ONE OF MY FAVORITE SONGS. I WROTE THIS ONE ALONE."

London Boy

ELEVENTH TRACK OF HER SEVENTH ALBUM
RELEASED: AUGUST 23, 2019
RECORDED: ELECTRIC LADY STUDIOS IN NEW YORK, NY

DID YOU KNOW?

LONDON BOY WAS CRAFTED AND CO-PRODUCED BY TAYLOR SWIFT ALONGSIDE JACK ANTONOFF AND AMERICAN PRODUCER SOUNWAVE. SINGER/SONGWRITER CAUTIOUS CLAY RECEIVES ADDITIONAL WRITING CREDIT DUE TO THE INTERPOLATION OF HIS SONG "COLD WAR."

THE START OF THE SONG INCLUDES A SPOKEN-WORD SEGMENT BY ENGLISH ACTOR IDRIS ELBA FROM HIS APPEARANCE ON "THE LATE LATE SHOW" WITH JAMES CORDEN IN 2017.

ON SEPTEMBER 2, 2019, TAYLOR SWIFT PRESENTED THE FIRST LIVE PERFORMANCE OF "LONDON BOY" DURING BBC RADIO 1'S LIVE LOUNGE.

CHARTS & AWARDS

- PEAKED AT #62 ON THE BILLBOARD HOT 100 CHART
- SPENT 1 WEEK ON THE CHART
- CERTIFIED RIAA GOLD
- TO DATE, THE TRACK HAS BEEN STREAMED 250,160,953 TIMES

IN TAYLOR'S WORDS

"WITH THIS SONG, I WROTE ABOUT WHAT IT WAS LIKE TO SAY, 'BYE GUYS, I'M GONNA BE HERE [IN LONDON] FOR A LONG TIME.' THERE'S A VOICE THAT YOU'LL HEAR IN THE BEGINNING OF [THE SONG] AND IT'S IDRIS ELBA'S TALKING ABOUT LONDON. IN THE BRIDGE, THERE'S A NAME CHECK OF STELLA MCCARTNEY. I WENT OVER TO HER PLACE, PLAYED HER THE SONG AND SHE WAS LIKE, 'OH MY GOD, LET'S DO SOMETHING!' AND I WAS LIKE, 'OKAY!' AND THAT'S WHY WE HAVE A MERCH COLLABORATION."

Soon You'll Get Better

FEATURING THE CHICKS
TWELFTH TRACK OF HER SEVENTH ALBUM
RELEASED: AUGUST 23, 2019
RECORDED: ELECTRIC LADY STUDIOS IN NEW YORK, NY

DID YOU KNOW?

THE MUSIC VIDEO FOR THE ALBUM'S LEAD SINGLE, "ME!," INCLUDED A SUBTLE NOD WITH A PICTURE OF THE CHICKS, THE COUNTRY TRIO FEATURED ON THIS TRACK.

ON APRIL 18, 2020, TAYLOR SWIFT PERFORMED A HEARTFELT SOLO PIANO VERSION OF "SOON YOU'LL GET BETTER" FOR THE LADY GAGA-CURATED ONE WORLD: TOGETHER AT HOME EVENT. THE BENEFIT AIMED TO RAISE FUNDS FOR THE WORLD HEALTH ORGANIZATION'S "COVID-19 SOLIDARITY RESPONSE FUND"

"ROLLING STONE" DESCRIBES THIS TRACK AS THE "MOST VULNERABLE LYRICS SWIFT HAS WRITTEN IN HER ENTIRE CAREER".

THE SONG IS KNOWN TO BE DESCRIBING THE HEARTBREAKING CANCER DIAGNOSIS AND TREATMENT OF HER MOTHER, ANDREA SWIFT. ANDREA IS A TWO-TIME BREAST CANCER SURVIVOR.

CHARTS & AWARDS

- PEAKED AT #63 ON THE BILLBOARD HOT 100 CHART
- SPENT 1 WEEK ON THE CHART
- TO DATE, THE TRACK HAS BEEN STREAMED 128,509,845 TIMES

IN TAYLOR'S WORDS

"THERE'S A SONG CALLED 'SOON YOU'LL GET BETTER' THAT WAS REALLY, REALLY HARD TO WRITE, AND IT WAS A FAMILY DECISION TO EVEN PUT ON THE ALBUM, AND I THINK SONGS LIKE THAT THAT ARE REALLY HARD FOR YOU TO WRITE EMOTIONALLY, MAYBE THEY'RE HARD TO WRITE AND HARD TO SING BECAUSE THEY'RE REALLY TRUE. WE AS A FAMILY DECIDED TO PUT THIS ON THE ALBUM. IT'S SOMETHING I'M SO PROUD OF. I CAN'T SING IT. IT'S HARD TO EMOTIONALLY DEAL WITH THAT SONG."

False God

THIRTEENTH TRACK OF HER SEVENTH ALBUM
RELEASED: AUGUST 23, 2019
RECORDED: ELECTRIC LADY STUDIOS IN NEW YORK, NY

DID YOU KNOW?

IN THE SONG, TAYLOR CLEARLY IDENTIFIES THE "FALSE GOD" AS THE INTENSE LOVE BETWEEN HER AND HER PARTNER. SHE COMPARES THEIR COMMITMENT TO THAT OF A DEVOTEE TO THEIR DEITY, EXPRESSING A HINT OF CONCERN ABOUT THE INTENSE NATURE OF THEIR RELATIONSHIP.

UNLIKE "DON'T BLAME ME," WHERE SEXUALITY AND SPIRITUALITY ARE ALSO INTERTWINED, "FALSE GOD" SUGGESTS THAT TAYLOR RECOGNIZES THE POTENTIAL UNHEALTHY NATURE OF THIS RELATIONSHIP.

TAYLOR SWIFT PERFORMED "FALSE GOD" FOR THE FIRST TIME ON SATURDAY NIGHT LIVE'S OCTOBER 5, 2019, EPISODE, DELIVERING A LIVE RENDITION WITH A JAZZY, SLINKY VIBE ACCOMPANIED BY SAXOPHONIST LENNY PICKETT.

CHARTS & AWARDS

- PEAKED AT #77 ON THE BILLBOARD HOT 100 CHART
- SPENT 1 WEEK ON THE CHART
- CERTIFIED RIAA PLATINUM
- TO DATE, THE TRACK HAS BEEN STREAMED 196,312,860 TIMES

You Need to Calm Down

SECOND SINGLE ON HER SEVENTH ALBUM
RELEASED AS A SINGLE: JUNE 14, 2019
RECORDED: GOLDEN AGE STUDIOS IN LOS ANGELES, CA

DID YOU KNOW?

THE MUSIC VIDEO FOR THE SONG PREMIERED ON GOOD MORNING AMERICA AND WAS OFFICIALLY RELEASED ON JUNE 17, 2019. IT INCLUDES APPEARANCES BY NUMEROUS LGBTQ+ CELEBRITIES, SUCH AS HAYLEY KIYOKO, LAVERNE COX, THE CAST OF QUEER EYE, AND TODRICK HALL, WHO ALSO CO-EXECUTIVE PRODUCED THE VIDEO.

THE LAUNCH OF "YOU NEED TO CALM DOWN" CONTRIBUTED TO A NOTABLE INCREASE IN INDIVIDUAL CONTRIBUTIONS TO GLAAD, AN AMERICAN LGBT NON-GOVERNMENTAL ORGANIZATION, AS THE SONG'S LYRICS EXPLICITLY MENTION THE ORGANIZATION.

THE SONG'S TITLE WAS HINTED DURING THE INTRODUCTION OF THE MUSIC VIDEO FOR "ME!" WHEN BRENDON URIE EXCLAIMED THE TITLE IN FRENCH.

CHARTS & AWARDS

- PEAKED AT #2 ON THE BILLBOARD HOT 100 CHART
- SPENT 22 WEEKS ON THE CHART
- WON "FAVORITE MUSIC VIDEO" AT THE AMERICAN MUSIC AWARDS IN 2019
- NOMINATED FOR "BEST POP SOLO PERFORMANCE" AT THE 62ND GRAMMY AWARDS
- WON "VIDEO OF THE YEAR" AND "VIDEO FOR GOOD" AT THE MTV MUSIC VIDEO AWARDS IN 2019
- CERTIFIED RIAA 5X PLATINUM
- TO DATE, THE TRACK HAS BEEN STREAMED 833,530,837 TIMES

IN TAYLOR'S WORDS

"IT'S ABOUT HOW I'VE OBSERVED A LOT OF DIFFERENT PEOPLE IN OUR SOCIETY WHO JUST PUT SO MUCH ENERGY AND EFFORT INTO NEGATIVITY, AND IT JUST MADE ME FEEL LIKE, 'YOU NEED TO JUST CALM DOWN, LIKE YOU'RE STRESSING YOURSELF OUT. THIS SEEMS LIKE IT'S MORE ABOUT YOU THAN WHAT YOU'RE GOING OFF ABOUT. LIKE, JUST CALM DOWN."

Afterglow

FIFTEENTH TRACK ON HER SEVENTH ALBUM
RELEASED: AUGUST 23, 2019
RECORDED: ELECTRIC FEEL STUDIOS IN WEST HOLLYWOOD, CA

DID YOU KNOW?

TAYLOR PLAYED "AFTERGLOW" FOR THE FIRST TIME ON "THE ERAS TOUR" IN MEXICO CITY ON AUGUST 27, 2023 ABOUT 4 YEARS AFTER ITS RELEASE.

IN "AFTERGLOW," TAYLOR ACKNOWLEDGES HER OWN SHORTCOMINGS IN A ROMANTIC RELATIONSHIP AND TAKES RESPONSIBILITY FOR THE SIGNS OF ITS DETERIORATION. IN A SCRET SESSIONS CONCERT FOR FANS, SHE REVEALS SHE SENT THE LYRICS TO JOE ALWIN AFTER A FIGHT, CONFIRMING THE TRACK REFLECTS HER EXPERIENCES IN THAT RELATIONSHIP.

THE TITLE OF THIS SONG WAS HINTED AT IN TAYLOR SWIFT'S MUSIC VIDEO FOR HER SINGLE "LOVER," WHERE A HAND SPELLS OUT "AFTER" AND "GLOW" ON A SCRABBLE BOARD.

CHARTS & AWARDS

- PEAKED AT #75 ON THE BILLBOARD HOT 100 CHART
- SPENT 1 WEEK ON THE CHART
- CERTIFIED RIAA PLATINUM
- TO DATE, THE TRACK HAS BEEN STREAMED 325,440,765 TIMES

ME!

FEATURING BRENDON URIE
FIRST SINGLE ON HER SEVENTH ALBUM
RELEASED: APRIL 26, 2019
RECORDED: ELECTRIC LADY STUDIOS IN NEW YORK, NY

DID YOU KNOW?

ME! RECEIVED VERY MIXED REVIEWS FROM FANS AND CRITICS. ROLLING STONE CALLED IT "CAMPY", "BUBBLY" AND "A TOTALLY CANONICAL TAYLOR LEAD SINGLE".

CHARTS & AWARDS

- PEAKED AT #2 ON THE BILLBOARD HOT 100 CHART
- SPENT 20 WEEKS ON THE CHART
- CERTIFIED RIAA PLATINUM
- NOMINATED FOR "BEST MUSIC VIDEO" AT THE 2020 IHEARTRADIO MUSIC AWARDS
- WON "BEST VISUAL EFFECTS" AT THE 2019 MTV VIDEO MUSIC AWARDS
- TO DATE, THE TRACK HAS BEEN STREAMED 804,317,543 TIMES

THE MUSIC VIDEO FOR THE TRACK BROKE THE RECORD FOR "MOST VIEWS OF A NEW MUSIC VIDEO FROM A SOLO ARTIST IN 24 HOURS" ON YOUTUBE. TAYLOR FAMOUSLY MET AND ADOPTED HER CAT (BENJAMIN BUTTON) ON THE SET.

REPORTEDLY ON AUGUST 21, 2019, THE LYRIC "HEY, KIDS, SPELLING IS FUN!" WAS EXCLUDED FROM ALL DIGITAL AND STREAMING EDITIONS OF THE SONG, INCLUDING THE ALBUM VERSION.

IN TAYLOR'S WORDS

"THIS SONG IS SUCH A CELEBRATION AND IT'S SO PLAYFUL. WHEN I THOUGHT OF THIS MELODY, I WAS LIKE, 'IT'S SO CATCHY. WHAT DO WE WANT TO GET STUCK IN PEOPLE'S HEADS?' AND WHAT I WANTED WAS TO MAKE PEOPLE HAPPY ABOUT THEMSELVES BECAUSE I THINK EVERYONE IS SO NEUROTIC, AND INSECURE, AND ANXIOUS ABOUT THINGS. I THINK THERE SHOULD BE A WAY FOR US TO HAVE A SONG STUCK IN OUR HEADS THAT REINFORCES THE FACT THAT WE'RE DIFFERENT. AND OBVIOUSLY THERE ARE A LOT OF SONGS ABOUT, 'I'M SPECIAL,' BUT I HADN'T HEARD ONE RECENTLY THAT WAS ABOUT, 'I'M SPECIAL BECAUSE OF WHO I AM.'"

It's Nice to Have a Friend

SEVENTEENTH TRACK ON HER SEVENTH ALBUM
RELEASED: AUGUST 23, 2019
RECORDED: ELECTRIC FEEL STUDIOS IN WEST HOLLYWOOD, CA

DID YOU KNOW?

THE SONG FEATURES MINIMALIST PRODUCTION, INCORPORATING BACKGROUND SINGERS FROM A TORONTO YOUTH CHOIR WHO EMULATE THE AMBIANCE OF A CHURCH WEDDING. THE CHOIR IS FROM REGENT PARK SCHOOL OF MUSIC IN TORONTO, CA THAT HELPS CHILDREN DEVELOP THROUGH MUSIC. ROYALTIES FROM THE CHOIR'S SAMPLE HELPS SUPPORT THIS PROGRAM.

A REMIXED "IT'S NICE TO HAVE A FRIEND" IS FEATURED IN THE TRAILER FOR THE 2023 HORROR FILM "M3GAN", WITH TAYLOR'S VOICE DISTORTED FOR A CHILLING EFFECT.

CO-WRITTEN AND CO-PRODUCED BY SWIFT WITH LOUIS BELL AND FRANK DUKES, THE BALLAD HAS A DREAMY, DELICATE PRODUCTION WITH SUBTLE STEEL DRUM ELEMENTS, REMINISCENT OF DUKES AND BELL'S PREVIOUS CARIBBEAN-INFLUENCED HITS LIKE CAMILA CABELLO'S "HAVANA."

CHARTS & AWARDS

- PEAKED AT #92 ON THE BILLBOARD HOT 100 CHART
- SPENT 1 WEEK ON THE CHART
- TO DATE, THE TRACK HAS BEEN STREAMED 116,591,522 TIMES

IN TAYLOR'S WORDS

"THERE'S A SONG ON LOVER ABOUT FLASHBACK AND CHILDHOOD. IT COMPARES CHILDHOOD FRIENDSHIPS TO WHEN YOU FIND SOMEONE TO FALL IN LOVE WITH WHEN YOU'RE OLDER, CALLED 'IT'S NICE TO HAVE A FRIEND.' IT'S VERY NOSTALGIC."

Daylight

EIGHTEENTH TRACK ON HER SEVENTH ALBUM
RELEASED: AUGUST 23, 2019
RECORDED:METROPOLIS STUDIOS IN LONDON, UK

DID YOU KNOW?

THE SONG IS ONE OF 3 SOLO-WRITTEN SONGS ON "LOVER". TAYLOR NEARLY CHOSE IT AS THE TITLE TRACK. SHE NOTES: "«IT ALMOST WAS THE TITLE TRACK. I THOUGHT IT MIGHT BE A LITTLE BIT TOO SENTIMENTAL. I WAS KIND OF IN MY HEAD REFERRING TO THE ALBUM AS DAYLIGHT FOR A WHILE. BUT LOVER, TO ME, WAS A MORE INTERESTING TITLE, MORE OF AN ACCURATE THEME IN MY HEAD, AND MORE ELASTIC AS A CONCEPT."

IN A PIECE SHE PENNED FOR ELLE MAGAZINE IN MARCH 2019, TAYLOR HINTED AT THE SONG'S TITLE: "I'VE COME TO A REALIZATION THAT I NEED TO BE ABLE TO FORGIVE MYSELF FOR MAKING THE WRONG CHOICE, TRUSTING THE WRONG PERSON, OR FIGURATIVELY FALLING ON MY FACE IN FRONT OF EVERYONE. STEP INTO THE DAYLIGHT AND LET IT GO."

TAYLOR DEBUTED THE SONG AT THE "CITY OF LOVER" CONCERT AT THE OLYMPIA ON SEPTEMBER 9, 2019, IN PARIS, FRANCE.

CHARTS & AWARDS

- PEAKED AT #89 ON THE BILLBOARD HOT 100 CHART
- SPENT 1 WEEK ON THE CHART
- TO DATE, THE TRACK HAS BEEN STREAMED 297,699,206 TIMES

IN TAYLOR'S WORDS

"I CHOSE 'DAYLIGHT' AS THE LAST SONG ON THE ALBUM BECAUSE IT RECOGNIZES PAST DAMAGE AND PAIN BUT SHOWS THAT IT DOESN'T HAVE TO DEFINE YOU. FOR ME, THE REPUTATION ALBUM SEEMED LIKE NIGHTTIME. THE LOVER ALBUM FEELS COMPLETELY SUNLIT. I WROTE THIS ONE ALONE."

folklore

Released: July 24th, 2020

Atmospheric, Vintage, Poetic, Serene

the 1

First track on her eighth album
Released: July 24, 2020
Recorded: Kitty Committee Studios in Los, Angeles, CA

Did you know?

Charts & Awards

- *Peaked at #4 on the Billboard Hot 100 Chart*
- *Spent 6 weeks on the charts*
- *Certified RIAA 2x Platinum*
- *To date, the track has been streamed 490,217,543 times*

"The 1" made its debut on the global Spotify Top 200 songs chart at No. 2, amassing over 7.420 million streams. It achieved the second-largest opening day for a song by a female artist in 2020, following the lead single "cardigan" with 7.742 million streams.

Taylor co-produced the majority of the album "folklore" with Aaron Dessner who is the founding member of the band "The National". He revealed in an Interview that "the 1" was the second to last song written for the album, just before "hoax". Aaron's twin brother Bryce Dessner provided the orchestration for the track.

Speculation over the song's subject arose with a line in the chorus that refers to someone who "didn't show". Fans made the connection to lyrics in her previous track "The Moment I Knew" and proposed that the track could refer to her relationship with Jake Gyllenhaal.

In Taylor's Words

"Opening the album with that line applies to the situation that this song is written about where you're updating a former lover on what your life is like now and trying to be positive about it. But it was also about where I am creatively. I'm just saying 'Yes', I'm just putting out an album in the worst time you could put one out, I'm just making stuff with someone who I've always wanted to make stuff with, as long as I've been a fan of The National. I'm just going to say 'Yes' to stuff and it worked out."

cardigan

First single on her eighth album
Released as a single: July 27, 2020
Recorded: Kitty Committee Studios in Los, Angeles, CA

Charts & Awards

- Peaked at #1 on the Billboard Hot 100 Chart
- Spent 14 weeks on the charts
- Certified RIAA 4x Platinum
- Nominated for "Best Pop Solo Performance" and "Song of the Year" at the 64th Annual Grammy Awards
- Nominated for "Best Lyrics" at the iHeartRadio Music Awards in 2021
- Nominated for "Song of the Summer" at the MTV Video Music Awards in 2020
- To date, the track has been streamed 1,053,393,932 times

Did you know?

The song's lyrics explore a love remembered through the eyes of a female protagonist named Betty, one of the many fictional characters introduced in "folklore". Taylor notes the inspiration of the song started with "a cardigan that still bears the scent of loss 20 years later."

Securing the number-one position on the Billboard Hot 100, the song marked Taylor Swift's sixth career chart-topping single in the U.S.

Crafted and directed by Swift, the mesmerizing music video sees the singer immersed in an alternate realm as she plays her piano. The team behind the video included cinematographer Rodrigo Prieto, renowned for his collaborations with Martin Scorsese on films like "The Irishman" and "The Wolf of Wall Street."

In Taylor's Words

"The song is about a long lost romance, and why young love is often fixed so permanently within our memories. When looking back on it, why it leaves such an incredible mark and how special it made you feel; all the good things it made you feel, all the pain that it made you feel...The line about feeling like you were an old cardigan under someone's bed, but someone put you on and made you feel like you were their favorite."

the last great american dynasty

Third track on her eighth album
Released: July 24, 2020
Recorded: Kitty Committee Studios in Los, Angeles, CA

Charts & Awards

- Peaked at #13 on the Billboard Hot 100 Chart
- Spent 2 weeks on the charts
- Certified RIAA Platinum
- To date, the track has been streamed 310,026,997 times

Did you know?

In 2013, Taylor Swift bought the "Holiday House" mansion in Watch Hill, Rhode Island, for about $17 million and sings about its previous owner, the eccentric Rebekah Harkness.

Taylor says of Harkness: "It can be a real pearl-clutching moment for society when a woman owns her desires and wildness, and I love the idea that the woman in question would be too joyful in her freedom to even care that she's ruffling feathers, raising eyebrows or becoming the talk of the town."

Aaron Dessner crafted the instrumentals for "The Last Great American Dynasty," drawing inspiration from the electric guitars featured in Radiohead's album, "In Rainbows" (2007).

In Taylor's Words

"When [Aaron] sent me the track to 'the last great american dynasty' I had been wanting to write a song about Rebekah Harkness since 2013, probably. I'd never figured out the right way to do it because there was never a track that felt like it could hold an entire story of somebody's life and moving between generations. When I heard that [the track] I was like, 'Oh my God, I think this is my opening. I think this is my moment. I think I can write the Rebekah Harkness story!' It has that country music narrative device. In country music, it's like, 'This guy did this, then this woman did this, then they met...and their kid was me! I was that kid!' Which is the best because when you listen to country music it's like, 'Shivers everywhere, my whole body!'"

exile

Featuring Bon Iver
Second single on her eighth album
Released as a single: August 3, 2020
Recorded: Kitty Committee Studios in Los, Angeles, CA

Charts & Awards

- Peaked at #6 on the Billboard Hot 100 Chart
- Spent 5 weeks on the charts
- Certified RIAA Platinum
- To date, the track has been streamed 659,073,371 times

Did you know?

"Exile" was written by Taylor Swift, Joe Alwyn (credited as William Bowery), and Justin Vernon of Bon Iver, with production by Aaron Dessner and Alwyn.

Joe's involvement in the track started with him messing around on the piano. He says, "'It was completely off the cuff, an accident. She said, 'Can we try and sit down and get to the end together?' And so we did. It was as basic as some people made sourdough."

The lyrics follow a call-and-response format, with Taylor and Vernon singing over each other instead of engaging in dialogue, imparting an argumentative tone to the song, lacking a resolution. "When Taylor sent it to me as a voice memo, she sang both the male and female parts — as much as she could fit in without losing her breath. We talked about who she was imagining joining her, and she loves Justin [Vernon]'s voice in Bon Iver and Big Red Machine. She was like, 'Oh my God, I would die if he would do it. It would be so perfect.' I didn't want to put pressure on Justin as his friend, so I said, 'Well, it depends on if he's inspired by the song but I know he thinks you're rad.'"

In Taylor's Words

"'exile' is a song that was written about miscommunications in relationships, and in the case of this song I imagined that the miscommunications ended the relationship. They led to the demise of this love affair, and now these two people are seeing each other out for the first time, and they keep miscommunicating with each other. They can't quite get on the same page, they never were able to. And even in their end, even after they've broken up, they're still not hearing each other. So we imagined the beginning would be his side of the story, the second verse her side of the story, and the end would be the story of them talking over each other and not hearing each other. "

my tears ricochet

Fifth track on her eighth album
Released: July 24, 2020
Recorded: Kitty Committee Studios in Los, Angeles, CA

Did you know?

Charts & Awards

- Peaked at #16 on the Billboard Hot 100 Chart
- Spent 2 weeks on the charts
- Certified RIAA Platinum
- To date, the track has been streamed 392,432,995 times

In "my tears ricochet," the lyrics tell the story of a deceased woman's ghost confronting her once-beloved murderer at their own funeral.

"My Tears Ricochet" was the first song Swift wrote for "folklore", in isolation during the COVID-19 pandemic. Jack Antonoff collaborated with Taylor on the track and notes that "My Tears Ricochet' and 'August' are my favorite things we've done together."

Swift disclosed that she wrote the initial lyrics for "My Tears Ricochet" after watching Noah Baumbach's 2019 film "Marriage Story."

The song also metaphorically expresses Taylor's emotions of resentment and betrayal towards Scott Borchetta, the founder of her former record label Big Machine, who sold her back catalog masters to Scooter Braun.

In Taylor's Words

"It's definitely one of the saddest songs on the album. Picking a 'Track Five' is sort of a pressurized decision but I knew from day one this was probably going to be it. It's a song about karma, about greed, about how somebody could be your best friend and your companion and your most trusted person in your life and then they could go and become your worst enemy who knows how to hurt you because they were once your most trusted person. Writing this song, it kind of occurred to me that in all of the superhero stories the hero's greatest nemesis is the villain that used to be his best friend. When you think about that, you think about how there's this beautiful moment in the beginning of a friendship where these people have no idea that one day, they'll hate each other and try to take each other out. I mean, that's really sad and terrible."

mirrorball

Sixth track on her eighth album
Released: July 24, 2020
Recorded: Kitty Committee Studios in Los, Angeles, CA

Charts & Awards

- *Peaked at #26 on the Billboard Hot 100 Chart*
- *Spent 2 weeks on the charts*
- *Certified RIAA Platinum*
- *To date, the track has been streamed 350,346,032 times*

Did you know?

Taylor had planned "Lover Fest" as a live tour for her prior album. Due to the COVID-19 pandemic, the event was canclled. Following the cancellation, Taylor wrote this song capturing her feelings.

Mirrorball was the surprise song for the opening show of "The Eras Tour" in Glendale, AZ.

Laura Sisk is credited as a co-producer on the track and is a long time collaborator with Swift. She was initially introduced to her after working with her other frequent collaborator Jack Antonoff. Laura started working with Taylor on her "1989" album which won Laura her first grammy. They have collaborated on every one of Taylor's album or re-records since.

The song is written in the musical key of D major and with the main chord progression D-G-B minor-G. This is the identical main chord progression in her song "You are in Love" on her "1989" album.

In Taylor's Words

"On folklore there are a lot of songs that reference each other or have lyrical parallels and one of the ones that I like is the entire song 'this is me trying' then being referenced again in 'mirrorball,' … Sometimes when I'm writing to an instrumental track I'll push 'Play' and I'll immediately see a scene set and this was one of those cases. I just saw a lonely disco ball, twinkly lights, neon signs, people drinking beer by the bar, a couple of stragglers on the dance floor. Sort of a sad, moonlit, lonely experience in the middle of a town you've never been. I was just thinking that we have mirrorballs in the middle of a dance floor because they reflect light, they are broken a million times and that's what makes them so shiny. We have people like that in society, too. They hang there and every time they break it entertains us. And when you shine a light on them it's this glittering, fantastic thing. But then, a lot of the time when the spotlight isn't on them they're just still there, up on that pedestal but no one is watching them."

seven

Seventh track on her eighth album
Released: July 24, 2020
Recorded: Kitty Committee Studios in Los, Angeles, CA

Charts & Awards

- Peaked at #35 on the Billboard Hot 100 Chart
- Spent 2 weeks on the charts
- Certified RIAA Platinum
- To date, the track has been streamed 263,806,171 times

In Taylor's Words

"With 'seven' I was looking back. When I see a kid throwing a massive tantrum in a grocery store, part of me is like, 'Man, I feel you. When did I stop doing that when I was upset? When did I stop being so outraged that I would throw myself on the floor and throw the cereal at my mom?' So the idea is, 'Please, picture me in the trees before I learned civility. I used to scream anytime I wanted.' Obviously, we can't be throwing tantrums all the time and we learn that that's not the right thing to do. But there's something lost there, too."

Did you know?

"Seven" is used in a pivotal scene in the season 2 finale of the Netflix series "Heartstopper".

Fans have drawn parallels from this track to a track on taylor's seventh album - "It's Nice to Have a Friend". Both songs follow a storyline of two childhood friends growing together.

The narrative intertwines present and past viewpoints, featuring a 30-year-old narrator reflecting on her childhood in Pennsylvania. As she recalls the innocence of her friendship with an old companion, the narrator juxtaposes this with her younger, 7-year-old self, who was oblivious to her friend's experience of domestic violence but came to comprehend it in later years.

The song is a beautiful example of Taylor's higher vocal register over a minimalistic piano track. However, the highest note in the track ($E5$) is still several steps below the top note in her range ($D6$).

august

Eighth track on her eighth album

Released: July 24, 2020

Recorded: Kitty Committee Studios in Los, Angeles, CA

Charts & Awards

- Peaked at #23 on the Billboard Hot 100 Chart
- Spent 2 weeks on the charts
- Certified RIAA Gold
- To date, the track has been streamed 882,269,583 times

In Taylor's Words

"In my head, I've been calling the girl from 'august' either Augusta or Augustine. What happened in my head was: 'cardigan' is Betty's perspective from 20 or 30 years later, looking back on this love that was this tumultuous thing. I think Betty and James ended up together. So in my head, she ends up with him but he really put her through it. 'august' was obviously about the girl that James had this summer with. She seems like she's a bad girl, but really she's not. She's a really sensitive person who fell for him and she was trying to seem cool and like she didn't care because that's what girls have to do. And she was trying to let him think that she didn't care, but she did and she thought they had something very real. And then he goes back to Betty. So the idea that there is some bad, villain girl in any type of situation who 'takes your man' is a total myth because that's not usually the case at all. Everybody has feelings and wants to be seen and loved. And Augustine...that's all she wanted."

Did you know?

"august" is the second of three "folklore" tracks depicting a teenage love triangle with Betty, James, and an unnamed girl. Swift doesn't reveal why Inez and Augusta/Augustine's relationship ended, but in the third part, she explains that James was also dating his regular girlfriend, Betty as hinted in the chorus.

Rolling Stone named the performance of "August" along with "Cardigan" and "Willow" the 4th best Grammy Performance of All Time.

"Floklore" producer Aaron Dessner notes on this track: "This is maybe the closest thing to a pop song. It gets loud. It has this shimmering summer haze to it. It's kind of like coming out of 'seven' where you have this image of her in the swing and she's seven years old, and then in 'august' I think it feels like fast-forwarding to now. That's an interesting contrast. I think it's just a breezy, sort of intoxicating feeling."

this is me trying

Ninth track on her eighth album

Released: July 24, 2020

Recorded: Kitty Committee Studios in Los, Angeles, CA

Charts & Awards

- Peaked at #39 on the Billboard Hot 100 Chart
- Spent 1 week on the charts
- Certified RIAA Platinum
- To date, the track has been streamed 325,070,570 times

Did you know?

Swift crafted the lyrics "from the perspectives of three distinct characters". She notes they touch on the emotions she experienced in 2016 and 2017, saying "I just felt like I was worth absolutely nothing." Ex-boyfriend Joe Alwyn helped to co-produce the track.

Critics lauded "this is me trying" for Taylor's vocal performance and its poignant exploration of mental health, addiction, and emotional vulnerability. Rolling Stone said that the track is "the disturbingly witty tale of someone pouring her heart out, to keep herself from pouring more whiskey."

Taylor debuted the song live on March 18, 2023 as the first surprise song In Glendale, AZ during "The Eras Tour".

In Taylor's Words

"I've been thinking about people who are either suffering through mental illness, addiction or who have an everyday struggle. No one pats them on the back every day but every day they are actively fighting something. There are so many days that nobody gives them credit for that and so, how often must somebody who's in that sort of internal struggle wanna say to everyone in the room: 'You have no idea how close I am to going back to a dark place.' I had this idea that the first verse would be about someone who is in a life crisis and has just been trying and failing in their relationship, has been messing things up with people they love, has been letting everyone down and has driven to this overlook, this cliff, and is just in the car, going, 'I could do whatever I want in this moment and it could affect everything forever.' But this person backs up and drives home."

illicit affairs

Tenth track on her eighth album
Released: July 24, 2020
Recorded: Kitty Committee Studios in Los, Angeles, CA

Charts & Awards

- Peaked at #44 on the Billboard Hot 100 Chart
- Spent 1 week on the charts
- Certified RIAA Platinum
- To date, the track has been streamed 318,675,508 times

Did you know?

With a duration of three minutes and ten seconds, it stands as the briefest track on "folklore".

In 2006's "Should've Said No," Taylor Swift addressed infidelity, condemning a cheating boyfriend. Fast forward to Reputation's "Getaway Car," where Swift attempted to escape her own relationship by engaging with someone new. Now with this song, Taylor captures a nuanced view on the temptation to stray, acknowledging the accompanying heartbreak without passing judgment.

Taylor Swift teamed up with frequent collaborator Jack Antonoff to write and produce the song. Antonoff played percussion, bass, and guitar, while Evan Smith, Antonoff's bandmate in Bleachers, handled guitar, accordion, and saxophone.

In Taylor's Words

"This was the first album that I've ever let go of that need to be 100 percent autobiographical because I think I needed to do that. I felt like fans needed to hear a 'stripped from the headlines' account of my life and it actually ended up being a bit confining. Because there's so much more to writing songs than just what you're feeling and your singular storyline. And I think this was spurred on by the fact that I was watching movies every day, I was reading books every day, I was thinking about other people every day. I was kind of outside my own, personal stuff. I think that's been my favorite thing about this album: that it's allowed to exist on its own merit without it just being, 'Oh, people are listening to this because it tells them something that they could read in a tabloid'. It feels like a completely different experience."

invisible string

Eleventh track on her eighth album
Released: July 24, 2020
Recorded: Kitty Committee Studios in Los, Angeles, CA

Charts & Awards

- Peaked at #37 on the Billboard Hot 100 Chart
- Spent 2 weeks on the charts
- Certified RIAA Platinum
- To date, the track has been streamed 305,680,339 times

In Taylor's Words

"When I first heard the track that [Aaron] sent me I thought, 'I have to write something that matches it'. And pretty quickly I came upon the idea of fate. 'Cause sometimes I just go into a rabbit hole of thinking about how things happen and I love the romantic idea that every step you're taking, you're taking one step closer to what you're supposed to be, guided by this little invisible string. I wrote it right after I sent an ex a baby gift and I just remember thinking, 'This is a full signifier that life is great!'"

Did you know?

Taylor notes this love ode began with the imagery of "a lone thread that, whether for better or worse, connects you to your destiny." The concept of the "invisible string" alludes to an ancient Chinese folk myth involving a red thread of fate that binds two individuals together. According to the myth, the man and the woman are fated to cross paths, irrespective of time, place, or circumstances.

In the track, Taylor recalls how she used to dream about meeting someone in Centennial Park, a large park in Nashville, TN. The ice cream shop that her love, Joe Alwin, works at is actually named "Snogs' Frozen Yogurt" in London.

Taylor notes this invisible bond is colored golden and it is not the first time she has used this color to describe her love for someone. She also refers to a love that is golden in "The Best Day", "Dancing With Our Hands Tied", and "Daylight".

mad woman

Twelfth track on her eighth album
Released: July 24, 2020
Recorded: Kitty Committee Studios in Los, Angeles, CA

Charts & Awards

- Peaked at #47 on the Billboard Hot 100 Chart
- Spent 1 week on the charts
- Certified RIAA Gold
- To date, the track has been streamed 185,717,649 times

Did you know?

In the vein of her past songs like "Blank Space" and "Look What You Made Me Do," Taylor Swift relates the notion of a delusional woman to her own life in this track. Swift links her own anger to the tale of eccentric heiress Rebekah Harkness, the inspiration behind Folklore's "The Last Great American Dynasty." Harkness was criticized for her unconventional lifestyle, labeled as a "mad woman."

Co-producer Aaron Dessner notes the track is the "goth song" of the "folklore" album. He says: "It has a darkness that I think is cathartic, sort of witch-hunting and gaslighting and maybe bullying. Sometimes you become the person people try to pin you into a corner to be, which is not really fair."

Taylor touches on similar themes of double standards in "The Man" from "Lover" the album. In contrast, "mad woman" evokes a darkness and anger not seen previously.

In Taylor's Words

"[The song has] these ominous strings underneath it and I was like, 'Oh, this is female rage.' And then I was thinking the most rage provoking element of being a female is the gaslighting that happens. For centuries, we were just expected to absorb male behavior silently. And oftentimes, when we – in our enlightened and emboldened state – now respond to bad male behavior or somebody just doing something that's absolutely out of line and we respond, that response is treated like the offense itself. There's been situations recently with someone who's very guilty of this in my life and it's a person who makes me feel (or tries to make me feel) like I'm the offender by having any kind of defense to his offenses. It's like I have absolutely no right to respond or I'm crazy. I have no right to respond or I'm angry. I have no right to respond or I'm out of line. So [Aaron] provided the musical bed for me to make that point that I've been trying so hard to figure out how to make...How do I say why this feels so bad?"

epiphany

Thirteenth track on her eighth album
Released: July 24, 2020
Recorded: Kitty Committee Studios in Los, Angeles, CA

Charts & Awards

- Peaked at #57 on the Billboard Hot 100 Chart
- Spent 1 week on the charts
- Certified RIAA Gold
- To date, the track has been streamed 161,731,028 times

Did you know?

Taylor revealed in September 2022, that in writing each of her songs, they fall Into 3 distinct categories: "Fountain Pen", "Quill Pen" or "Glitter Gel Pen". Taylor notes: "I came up with these categories based on what writing tool I imagine having in my hand when I scribbled it down, figuratively." This song Is thought to be categorized as a "Quill Pen" song which include delicate and/or antiquated lyrics with structure inspired by Old English poetry.

In Taylor's Words

"I remember thinking, 'Maybe I wanna write a sports story.' Because I had just watched The Last Dance and I was thinking all in terms of sports, and winners, and underdogs. But actually, what I had been doing really frequently up until that point was I had been doing a lot of research on my grandfather who fought in World War II at Guadalcanal, which was an extremely bloody battle. And he never talked about it. Not with his sons, not with his wife. Nobody got to hear about what happened there. So my dad and his brothers did a lot of digging and found out that my granddad was exposed to some of the worst situations you could ever imagine as a human being. So I kind of tried to imagine what would happen in order to make you just never be able to speak about something. And when I was thinking about that I realized that there are people right now taking a twenty minute break in between shifts at a hospital who are having this kind of trauma happen to them right now, that they probably will never wanna speak about. And so I thought that this is an opportunity to maybe tell that story.»

In a salute to healthcare workers during the Covid-19 pandemic, the song's lyrics narrate the havoc unleashed by the global crisis. It draws a poignant comparison between doctors and nurses as frontline soldiers, mirroring their emotional turmoil with that experienced by the artist's grandfather, Dean, during the Battle of Guadalcanal.

Taylor wrote the lyrics to the track first, with Aaron Dessner creating the music to follow. He was aiming for "glacial, Icelandic sounds with distended chords and this almost classical feeling".

betty

Third single on her eighth album
Released as a single: August 17, 2020
Recorded: Kitty Committee Studios in Los, Angeles, CA

Charts & Awards

- Peaked at #42 on the Billboard Hot 100 Chart
- Spent 2 weeks on the charts
- Won as an "Award Winning Song" at the BMI awards London in 2021
- To date, the track has been streamed 300,558,766 times

Did you know?

Joe Alwin, under the pseudonym "William Bowery" wrote the chorus for the song. He says: "I'd probably had a drink and was just stumbling around the house. We couldn't decide on a film to watch that night, and she was like, 'Do you want to try and finish writing that song you were singing earlier?' And so we got a guitar and did that."

The lone track on Folklore co-produced by both Jack Antonoff and Aaron Dessner together, "Betty" draws inspiration for its sound from Bob Dylan's albums The Freewheelin' Bob Dylan (1963) and John Wesley Harding (1967), according to Swift.

In Taylor's Words

"I just heard Joe singing the entire fully formed chorus of 'betty' from another room. And I was just like, 'Hello.' It was a step that we would never have taken, because why would we have ever written a song together? So this was the first time we had a conversation where I came in and I was like, 'Hey, this could be really weird, and we could hate this, so because we're in quarantine and there's nothing else going on, could we just try to see what it's like if we write this song together?' So he was singing the chorus of it, and I thought it sounded really good from a man's voice, from a masculine perspective. And I really liked that it seemed to be an apology. I've written so many songs from a female's perspective of wanting a male apology that we decided to make it from a teenage boy's perspective apologizing after he loses the love of his life because he's been foolish."

In the love triangle trilogy of songs, this is the only song that names all three characters, possibly inspired by the children of Swift's friends Blake Lively and Ryan Reynolds—James, Inez, and the unnamed Betty, whose name wasn't publicly revealed at the time.

peace

Fifteenth track on her eighth album
Released: July 24, 2020
Recorded: Kitty Committee Studios in Los, Angeles, CA

Charts & Awards

- Peaked at #58 on the Billboard Hot 100 Chart
- Spent 1 week on the charts
- To date, the track has been streamed 180,950,986 times

Did you know?

"Peace" was a song written to track. Taylor felt "immediate sense of serenity" when she heard it, which lead her to write within that lyrical theme.

Producer Aaron Dessner has expressed multiple times that "peace" is his favorite song on "folklore". He says of the track: "I have in my life suffered from depression and I'm a hard person to be in a relationship with or be married to because I go up and down. And I can't help this, it's like a chemical thing that happens sometimes. And music is a way of dealing with that for me. And somehow this song captures the fragility of what's that like, of being in a relationship with someone who may or may not have peace."

Justin Vernon of the band Bon Iver is credited on the song for providing the "pulse" or rhythmic beat heard in the backing of the track.

In Taylor's Words

"I think this is a song that is extremely personal to me. There are times when I feel like with everything that's in my control, I can make myself seem like someone who doesn't have an abnormal life and I try that every day. It's like, 'How do I make my friends, and family, and my loved ones not see this big elephant that's in the room for our normal life?' Because I don't want the elephant in the room. If you're gonna be in my life I feel like there's a certain amount that comes with it that I can't stop from happening. I can't stop from you getting a call in the morning that says, 'The tabloids are writing this today.' I can't help it if there's a guy with a camera two miles away with a telescope lense taking pictures of you. I can't stop those things from happening. And so this song was basically like, 'Is it enough? Is the stuff that I can control enough to block out the things that I can't?' So it makes me really emotional to hear this song."

hoax

Sixteenth track on her eighth album
Released: July 24, 2020
Recorded: Kitty Committee Studios in Los, Angeles, CA

Charts & Awards

- Peaked at #71 on the Billboard Hot 100 Chart
- Spent 1 week on the charts
- Certified RIAA Gold
- To date, the track has been streamed 161,430,568 times

Did you know?

Violinist, Rob Moose, from Bon Iver arranged and recorded the strings for "Hoax," in addition to his contributions to "Exile" and "The Last Great American Dynasty". Dessner enlisted Moose due to his connection with Bon Iver's lead singer, Justin Vernon.

"Hoax" was the final track written for "folklore". Taylor struggled with where to go with the song, but notes, "I was really happy when [Aaron] pushed me forward like, 'Do the thing that makes you uncomfortable.' Because I think that's what makes it a song to me that really stands out."

Taylor uses lyrics in the first verse of this track to call back to her prior works "Holy Ground" from "RED" and "Look What You Made Me Do" from "reputation".

In Taylor's Words

"The word 'hoax' is another one that I love. I love that is has an 'x' and the way it looks and sounds. I think with this song being the last one on the album it kind of embodied all the things that this album was thematically: confessions, incorporating nature, emotional volatility and ambiguity at the same time, love that isn't just easy. And it's the most symbolic and poetic thing, listing all these things that this person is to you. That line, 'You know it still hurts underneath my scars from when they pulled me apart' – anyone in my life knows what I'm singing about there but everybody has that situation in their life where you let someone in and they get to know you and they know exactly what buttons to push to hurt you the most. That thing where the scars healed over but there's still phantom pain. ... To me that sounds like what love really is. Who would you be sad with? And who would you deal with when they were sad? And like, gray skies every day for months, would you still stay?"

the lakes

Bonus track on her eighth album
Released: August 18, 2020
Recorded: Kitty Committee Studios in Los, Angeles, CA

Charts & Awards

- Did not chart on the Billboard Hot 100 Chart
- Certified RIAA Gold
- To date, the track has been streamed 128,011,303 times

In Taylor's Words

"We'd gone to the Lake District in England a couple years ago. In the 19th century you had a lot of poets like William Wordsworth and John Keats who'd spend a lot of time there. And there was a poet district, these artists that moved there. They were heckled for it and made fun of for being these eccentrics and kind of odd artists who decided that they just wanted to live there. I remember thinking, 'I could see this.' You live in a cottage and you got wisteria growing up the outside of it...of course they escaped like that. And they had their own community of other artists who'd done the same thing. I've always, in my career since I was probably about twenty, written about this cottage backup plan that I have. I have been writing about that forever."

Did you know?

Taylor revealed in September 2022, that in writing each of her songs, they fall Into 3 distinct categories: "Fountain Pen", "Quill Pen" or "Glitter Gel Pen". Taylor notes: "I came up with these categories based on what writing tool I imagine having in my hand when I scribbled it down, figuratively." This song Is thought to be categorized as a "Quill Pen" song which include delicate and/or antiquated lyrics with structure inspired by Old English poetry.

Taylor performed the song for the first time on "The Eras Tour" in Chicago, IL on June 2, 2023.

Initially envisioning this as a grand orchestral piece, co-writer and co-producer Jack Antonoff found that Swift preferred a much smaller rendition. He shared "I had gotten lost in the string arrangements and all this stuff."

evermore

Released: December 11th, 2020

Ethereal, Introspective, Mystical, Melancholic

willow

First single on her ninth album
Released: December 11, 2020
Recorded: Long Pond Studios in Hudson Valley, NY

Charts & Awards

- *Peaked at #1 on the Billboard Hot 100 Chart*
- *Spent 20 weeks on the charts*
- *Certified RIAA 2x Platinum*
- *Nominated for "Best Art Direction" at the MTV Video Music Awards in 2021*
- *Nashville Songwriter's Awards named the song under the award of "Ten Songs I Wish I'd Written" in 2021*
- *To date, the track has been streamed 724,464,387 times*

Did you know?

"Willow" catapulted to No. 1 on the Billboard Hot 100, marking Taylor Swift as the first artist to debut both an album and a single at number one simultaneously on two occasions, following her previous achievement with "folklore" and "cardigan" in 2020.

Aaron Dessner co-produced this track along with 13 others on "evermore". It is the only song in Swift's discography to include a glockenspiel.

Directed by Taylor Swift, the music video serves as a continuation of the narrative introduced in the lead single from Folklore's, "Cardigan." It commences with Swift at her piano immediately following the events of "Cardigan," transitioning into another enchanting and fantastical realm.

In Taylor's Words

"I liked opening the album with ['willow'] because I loved the feeling that I got, immediately upon hearing the instrumental that Aaron created for it. It felt strangely witchy, like somebody making a love potion, dreaming up the person that they want and desire, and trying to figure out how to get that person in their life. And all the misdirection, and bait and switch, and complexity that goes into seeing someone, feeling a connection, wanting them, and trying to make them a part of your life. It's tactical at times, it's confusing at times, it's up to fate, it's magical. It felt a bit magical and mysterious, which is what I want people to feel going into an album that was a collection of these stories that were going to take them in all kinds of directions. I just wanted to start them off with a setting of the vibe."

champagne problems

Second track on her ninth album

Released: December 11, 2020

Recorded: Long Pond Studios in Hudson Valley, NY

Charts & Awards

- Peaked at #21 on the Billboard Hot 100 Chart
- Spent 2 weeks on the charts
- Certified RIAA 2x Platinum
- To date, the track has been streamed 517,136,439 times

Did you know?

Crafting this piano ballad, Taylor Swift collaborated with "William Bowery," the pen name for her actor boyfriend, Joe Alwyn. He is also acknowledged as a songwriter for two additional songs on Evermore: "coney island" and the "evermore"

"Champagne Problems" is one of the tracks that showcases Swift's lower register of her vocal range. The vocals on this track span from E_3 to G_4, although still not her lowest (A_2).

In Taylor's Words

"Joe and I really love sad songs. He started that one and came up with the melodic structure of it. I say it was a surprise that we started writing together, but in a way it wasn't cause we had always bonded over music and had the same musical tastes. He's always the person who's showing me songs by artists and then they become my favorite songs. 'champagne problems' was one of my favorite bridges to write. I really love a bridge where you tell the full story in the bridge. You really shift gears in that bridge. I'm so excited to one day be in front of a crowd, when they all sing, 'She would've made such a lovely bride, what a shame she's fucked in the head'. Cause I know it's so sad, but it's those songs like 'All Too Well'. Performing that song is one of the most joyful experiences I ever go through when I perform live, so when there's a song like 'champagne problems' where you know it's so sad...I love a sad song, you know?"

Taylor says, "two longtime college sweethearts had very different plans for the same night, one to end it and one who brought a ring." The Dom Perignon line mentioned has a clear double meaning for the situation; the man purchased pricey champagne to celebrate his engagement with loved ones, but he also "bought into" a falsehood, believing his girlfriend's love to be true.

gold rush

Third track on her ninth album
Released: December 11, 2020
Recorded: Long Pond Studios in Hudson Valley, NY

Did you know?

Charts & Awards

- Peaked at #40 on the Billboard Hot 100 Chart
- Spent 1 week on the charts
- Certified RIAA Gold
- To date, the track has been streamed 251,015,577 times

This song leans closest to pop on Evermore, fittingly produced by Jack Antonoff instead of Aaron Dessner, who worked on the rest of the album.

In either Folklore or Evermore, this is the only track where Taylor Swift explicitly mentions the word "folklore."

When this song came out, many fans wondered if Swift was referring to the Philadelphia Eagles football team or the '70s rock band the Eagles in her lyrics. She confirmed live during "The Eras Tour" noting "I love the band the Eagles. But guys, like come on. I'm from Philly. Of course, it's the team."

In Taylor's Words

"'gold rush' takes place inside a single daydream where you get lost in thought for a minute and then snap out of it."

Taylor revealed in September 2022, that in writing each of her songs, they fall Into 3 distinct categories: "Fountain Pen", "Quill Pen" or "Glitter Gel Pen". Taylor notes: "I came up with these categories based on what writing tool I imagine having in my hand when I scribbled it down, figuratively." This song Is thought to be categorized as a "Fountain Pen" song which include modern lyrics full of familiar references and vivid imagery.

'tis the damn season

Fourth track on her ninth album
Released: December 11, 2020
Recorded: Long Pond Studios in Hudson Valley, NY

Did you know?

"'tis the damn season' is the counterpart to "dorothea", another "evermore" track that takes the perspective of a former lover's point of view.

Charts & Awards

- Peaked at #39 on the Billboard Hot 100 Chart
- Spent 2 weeks on the charts
- Certified RIAA Gold
- To date, the track has been streamed 228,021,929 times

Aaron Dessner wrote the music for "'tis the damn season" years before evermore, considering it among his favorite works and explaining that it holds the distinction of being his favorite track on the album.

In Taylor's Words

Swift wrote the lyrics for "'tis the damn season" the night after rehearsing for Folklore: The Long Pond Studio Sessions. Producer Aaron Dessner recalled they spent the night playing, drinking, and chatting. The next morning, Swift surprised him by singing a song she had written in the middle of the night.

"[It's about] Dorothea, the girl who left her small town to chase down Hollywood dreams - and what happens when she comes back for the holidays and rediscovers an old flame."

Prior to evermore's surprise release, Taylor offered a sneak peek of "'tis the damn season" on December 9, 2020, through an Instagram story featuring a picture of herself in an Entertainment Weekly feature.

tolerate it

Fifth track on her ninth album
Released: December 11, 2020
Recorded: Long Pond Studios in Hudson Valley, NY

Charts & Awards

- Peaked at #45 on the Billboard Hot 100 Chart
- Spent 1 week on the charts
- Certified RIAA Gold
- To date, the track has been streamed 245,170,008 times

Did you know?

The Inspiration for this song came after Taylor read the novel "Rebecca" by Dapne du Maurier.

"Tolerate It" was written to track. Aaron Dessner says of the song: "When I wrote the piano track to 'tolerate it,' right before I sent it to her, I thought, 'This song is intense.' It's in 10/8, which is an odd time signature. And I did think for a second, 'Maybe I shouldn't send it to her, she won't be into it.' But I sent it to her, and it conjured a scene in her mind, and she wrote this crushingly beautiful song to it and sent it back. I think I cried when I first heard it. It just felt like the most natural thing, you know?"

This song is written in the musical key of A major and with a tempo of 75 BPM. It's Taylor's 5th slowest song she's written, with "It's Nice to Have A Friend" at the top of the list (70 BPM).

In Taylor's Words

"When you watch a film or you read a book and there's a character that you identify with, most of the time you identify with them because they're targeting something in you that feels that you've been there. That's why we relate to characters. When I was reading Rebecca by Daphne du Maurier I was thinking, 'Her husband just tolerates her. She's doing all these things, trying so hard to impress him and he's just tolerating her the whole time.' There was a part of me that could relate to that because at some point in my life I felt that way. So I ended up writing this song 'tolerate it' that's all about trying to love someone who's ambivalent."

no body, no crime

Featuring HAIM

Second single on her ninth album

Released as a single: January 11, 2021

Recorded: Long Pond Studios in Hudson Valley, NY

Charts & Awards

- Peaked at #34 on the Billboard Hot 100 Chart
- Spent 2 weeks on the charts
- Certified RIAA Gold
- To date, the track has been streamed 240,000,531 times

In Taylor's Words

"Working with the HAIM sisters on 'no body, no crime' was pretty hilarious because it came about after I wrote a pretty dark murder mystery song and had named the character Este, because she's the friend I have who would be stoked to be in a song like that. I had finished the song and was nailing down some lyric details and texted her, 'You're not going to understand this text for a few days but... which chain restaurant do you like best?' and I named a few. She chose Olive Garden and a few days later I sent her the song and asked if they would sing on it. It was an immediate 'YES.'"

Did you know?

Swift mentioned that the song was influenced by her "obsession with true crime podcasts/documentaries" and has expressed that if her music career took a different turn, she would consider an alternative path as a police detective.

"No body, no crime" made its live debut at Swift's Seattle, WA show on July 22, 2023, where HAIM, her opening act, joined her for the performance.

Swift and the Haim sisters have been friends for many years and Taylor notes she "can't figure out why we hadn't collaborated sooner". Despite their collaboration, this is the only song on "evermore" that Taylor wrote completely on her own.

happiness

Seventh track on her ninth album
Released: December 11, 2020
Recorded: Long Pond Studios in Hudson Valley, NY

Charts & Awards

- *Peaked at #52 on the Billboard Hot 100 Chart*
- *Spent 1 week on the charts*
- *Certified RIAA Gold*
- *To date, the track has been streamed 161,626,455 times*

Did you know?

"Happiness" includes numerous lyrical allusions to F. Scott Fitzgerald's classic novel, "The Great Gatsby". In the second verse, Swift makes a reference to a quote about Daisy's desire for her daughter to be "a fool—that's the best thing a girl can be in this world, a beautiful little fool." Taylor has referenced "The Great Gatsby" directly in two other songs in her repertoire.

In Taylor's Words

"[It is] the realization that maybe the only path to healing is to wish happiness on the one who took it away from you."

While wrapping up the recording of evermore, Taylor concurrently worked on "Fearless (Taylor's Version)", recording both "happiness" and "You Belong With Me (Taylor's Version)" on the same day.

Since 2019, Aaron Dessner, the producer and co-writer, had been developing the composition, originally intending it to be a Big Red Machine song.

dorothea

Eighth track on her ninth album
Released: December 11, 2020
Recorded: Long Pond Studios in Hudson Valley, NY

Charts & Awards

- Peaked at #67 on the Billboard Hot 100 Chart
- Spent 1 week on the charts
- To date, the track has been streamed 148,825,755 times

Did you know?

The song mirrors Dorothea's Christmas reunion with her high school boyfriend from "'Tis the Damn Season," occurring several years later after the aspiring actress has found success.

JT Bates, who played drums and percussion, contributed to four Evermore tracks as recruited by producer Aaron Dessner, with Dessner praising Bates for his exceptional skills.

In a Q&A session, Taylor disclosed that Dorothea attended the same school as Betty, James, and Inez from "betty," despite their storylines not crossing paths.

Taylor debuted "dorothea" on July 8, 2023, at her second Kansas City show as part of "The Eras Tour".

coney island

Featuring The National
Third single on her ninth album
Released as a single: January 18, 2021
Recorded: Long Pond Studios in Hudson Valley, NY

Charts & Awards

- Peaked at #63 on the Billboard Hot 100 Chart
- Spent 1 week on the charts
- Certified RIAA Gold
- To date, the track has been streamed 156,034,692 times

Did you know?

Twin brothers Aaron and Bryce Dessner sent Taylor instrumentals from their band, The National, including what became "coney island." Taylor and Joe Alwyn wrote the lyrics, and after hearing the demo, the Dessner brothers envisioned Matt Berninger singing it with Bryan Devendorf on drums.

Released on December 11, 2020, just before her 31st birthday on December 13, Evermore holds significance for Taylor Swift, as 13 is her lucky number, and turning 31 symbolizes the number in reverse. Additionally, the song's location, Coney Island, is part of Brooklyn Community District 13.

Taylor debuted "coney Island" In Atlanta, GA on the same day that the National released their new album: "First Two Pages Of Frankenstein".

In Taylor's Words

"I think I might have been coming from a place of somebody who's been in a relationship for decades and wakes up one day and realizes that they've taken their partner completely for granted. So whether you want to look at it from the perspective of somebody who's in a new or a very longstanding relationship, it just really speaks to if two people are trying to communicate but they're two ships passing in the night. They're trying to love each other but the signals are somehow missing each other. I just found that interesting and we're really proud of this one. There were elements of it that immediately reminded me of Matt Berninger's vocal stylings and his writing and I targeted some of the lyrics of the second verse to sound like what he might do. I hoped that he might want to sing on it because we already had two members of The National on the song with Aaron and Bryce. So we got our wish and Matt sang on this song. He did such a great job, I'm a huge fan of the band and really honored that this was able to come together with The National."

ivy

Tenth track on her ninth album
Released: December 11, 2020
Recorded: Long Pond Studios in Hudson Valley, NY

Charts & Awards

- Peaked at #61 on the Billboard Hot 100 Chart
- Spent 1 week on the charts
- Certified RIAA Gold
- To date, the track has been streamed 186,889,261 times

Did you know?

Taylor revealed at the "Nashville Songwriter Awards" in September 2022, that in writing each of her songs, they fall Into 3 distinct categories: "Fountain Pen", "Quill Pen" or "Glitter Gel Pen". Taylor notes: "I came up with these categories based on what writing tool I imagine having in my hand when I scribbled it down, figuratively." This song is thought to be categorized as a "Quill Pen" song which include delicate and/or antiquated lyrics with structure inspired by Old English poetry.

Built upon the metaphor of ivy vines embracing stone to symbolize enduring love, the song draws inspiration from Miller Williams' 1997 poem "Compassion."

Fans have made the connection that the song may describe the life of Emily Dickinson and her alleged affair. In the Apple TV+ series "Dickinson," portraying the life of the renowned poet, this song plays during the closing credits of season 3.

cowboy like me

Featuring Marcus Mumford
Eleventh track on her ninth album
Released: December 11, 2020
Recorded: Scarlet Pimpernel Studios in the United Kingdom

Charts & Awards

- *Peaked at #71 on the Billboard Hot 100 Chart*
- *Spent 1 week on the charts*
- *To date, the track has been streamed 158,128,225 times*

Did you know?

Taylor Swift premiered "cowboy like me" on March 25, 2023, during her second Las Vegas show on "The Eras Tour", with a special guest appearance by Marcus Mumford.

Josh Kaufman, the winner of The Voice's sixth season, contributes lap steel guitar, harmonica, and mandolin to the track.

The song was recorded in Marcus Mumford's home studio in the countryside of Devon, England.

In Taylor's Words

"I'm such a Mumford & Sons fan. I just think he's brilliant, and has one of the most gorgeous voices in the world. So I'm like, 'Will he sing something, please?' But I didn't want to be weird about it, so I'm like, 'I wonder if fate will have him wander into the studio at the right time.' So sure enough, we're recording a song, and he wanders in at the perfect time and just kind of started humming a harmony. And I turned to him as if I hadn't been thinking of it the whole time, and I was like, 'Oh! You sound really good on that harmony! I wonder if you might sing on this song?' And he said, 'Yep, I would love to!' So essentially, because of Marcus Mumford we have a lot of the songs that probably we wouldn't have been able to put out evermore as quickly as we did. And we also have a gorgeous harmony on a song called 'cowboy like me.'"

long story short

Twelfth track on her ninth album
Released: December 11, 2020
Recorded: Long Pond Studios in Hudson Valley, NY

Charts & Awards

- Peaked at #68 on the Billboard Hot 100 Chart
- Spent 1 week on the charts
- To date, the track has been streamed 158,128,225 times

Did you know?

"Long Story Short" reflects Taylor Swift's personal redemption after the challenges of 2016, including the public humiliation following a fake edit of a leaked phone call with Kanye West in July of that year.

Except for the title track, this is only track in which "evermore" is mentioned on the album.

At 158 BPM, the song Is one of taylor's fastest tempo tunes. Her fastest song to date is "ME!" from the "Lover" album at 185 BPM.

marjorie

Thirteenth track on her ninth album
Released: December 11, 2020
Recorded: Long Pond Studios in Hudson Valley, NY

Charts & Awards

- Peaked at #68 on the Billboard Hot 100 Chart
- Spent 1 week on the charts
- To date, the track has been streamed 170,916,699 times

Did you know?

Both "epiphany," a song about her grandfather on folklore, and this track about her grandmother share the distinction of being the thirteenth track on their respective albums.

The outro includes a recording of Taylor Swift's grandmother, Marjorie Finlay, singing opera. Swift's mother found old LPs of Marjorie's performances, and the vinyl was sent to producer Aaron Dessner, who incorporated her voice into the song.

"Marjorie" served as the precursor to "Peace," the fifteenth track on Folklore; the drone in the bridge of "Marjorie" is sampled in "Peace."

In Taylor's Words

"The experience writing that song was really surreal because I was kind of a wreck at times writing that, I'd sort of break down sometimes. It was hard to actually sing it in the vocal booth sounding like I had sort of a break, because it was just really emotional. I think that one of the hardest forms of regret to sort of work through is the regret of being so young when you lost someone that you didn't have the perspective to learn and appreciate who they were fully. I'd open up my grandmother's closet and she had beautiful dresses from the sixties. I wish I asked her where she wore every single one of them, things like that. She was a singer and my mom will look at me so many times a year and say: "oh, you're just like her". You know, some mannerism that I don't recognize as being anymore as being anyone other than mine. (...) One of the things about this song that still kind of rips me apart when I listen to it, is that she's singing with me on this song."

closure

Fourteenth track on her ninth album
Released: December 11, 2020
Recorded: Long Pond Studios in Hudson Valley, NY

Did you know?

The sound of a machine breaking down is heard at the start of the track. It is speculated that this may metaphorically refer to Taylor's old record label "Big Machine Records".

"Closure" mainly uses a dissonant 5/4 time signature and incorporates Taylor's vocals filtered through the Messina, a vocal modifier often used by the band Bon Iver.

Charts & Awards

- Peaked at #82 on the Billboard Hot 100 Chart
- Spent 1 week on the charts
- To date, the track has been streamed 106,306,363 times

In Taylor's Words

"Evermore deals a lot in endings of all sorts, shapes, and sizes. All the kinds of ways we can end a relationship, a friendship, something toxic. And the pain that goes along with that, the phases of it."

In the accompanying notes for Evermore, Swift describes the tracks as "17 tales," exploring narratives beyond her own life. However, there's speculation that in this track she may be addressing her former label boss, Scott Borchetta, who sold her masters, or music manager Scooter Braun, who purchased them.

evermore

Featuring Bon Iver
Fourteenth track on her ninth album
Released: December 11, 2020
Recorded: Long Pond Studios in Hudson Valley, NY

Charts & Awards

- Peaked at #57 on the Billboard Hot 100 Chart
- Spent 1 week on the charts
- To date, the track has been streamed 182,797,722 times

Did you know?

"Evermore" made its debut in Swift's sixth headlining concert tour, "The Eras Tour", being the second surprise song performed during her show in Cincinnati on June 30, 2023.

Taylor revealed that she wrote the song and its lyrics just before the 2020 presidential election, describing the process "almost preparing for the worst to happen and trying to see some sort of glimmer at the end of the tunnel."

A duet with Bon Iver's Justin Vernon, this is the only Evermore track where he is featured, while he is credited as a backing vocalist in the other two songs, "Marjorie" and "Ivy."

In Taylor's Words

"When Joe wrote the piano, I based the vocal melody on the piano, and we sent it to Justin, who then added that bridge. And Joe had written the piano part so that the tempo speeds up, and it changes. The music completely changes to a different tempo in the bridge. And Justin really latched onto that, and just 100% embraced it and wrote this beautiful sort of... The clutter of all your anxieties in your head, and they're all speaking at once. And we got the bridge back, and then I wrote this narrative of, 'When I was shipwrecked, I thought of you.' That sort of thing, where there was this beacon of hope, and then in the end, you realize the pain wouldn't be forever."

right where you left me

First bonus track on her ninth album
Released: December 18, 2020
Recorded: Long Pond Studios in Hudson Valley, NY

Charts & Awards

- Did not chart on the Billboard Hot 100 Chart
- Certified RIAA Gold
- To date, the track has been streamed 261,929,966 times

Did you know?

With Aaron Dessner as a surprise guest, "right where you left me" had its first live acoustic performance on guitar during one of Taylor's shows on "The Eras Tour" in Santa Clara on July 28, 2023.

Dessner added two songs, "Right Where You Left Me" and "Happiness," to Evermore at the last minute. When he informed the engineer Jon Low about the need to mix two more songs before the deadline, Low expressed skepticism with a look that conveyed, "We're not going to make it."

In Taylor's Words

"'right where you left me' is a song about a girl who stayed forever in the exact spot where her heart was broken, completely frozen in time."

it's time to go

Second bonus track on her ninth album
Released: December 18, 2020
Recorded: Long Pond Studios in Hudson Valley, NY

Charts & Awards

- *Did not chart on the Billboard Hot 100 Chart*
- *To date, the track has been streamed 261,929,966 times*

Did you know?

In "It's Time to Go," Swift portrays situations where relationships have ended, including the dissolution of a friendship in the first verse. Fans speculate this may refer to Karlie Kloss, Swift's friend from 2014 to 2016, suggesting a fallout after Kloss associated with Swift's adversary, Scooter Braun.

the song is written in the musical key of C major and at a tempo of 152 BPM.

Taylor debuted the track live in Sao Paulo on November 26, 2023 during "The Eras Tour".

In Taylor's Words

"it's time to go' is about listening to your gut when it tells you to leave. How you always know before you know, you know?"

Midnights

Released: October 21, 2022

Honest, Free, Transformational, Diverse

Lavender Haze

Second Single on her Tenth Album
Released as a single: November 29, 2022
Recorded: Rough Customer Studios in Brooklyn, NY

Did you know?

The song was written with input from six different writers Including: Taylor, Jack Antonoff, Zoe Kravitz, Mark Anthony Spears, Jahaan Akli Sweet, and Sam Dew.

The music video is described by Swift as the "mood of Midnights, like a sultry sleepless 70's fever dream." Taylor wrote and directed the video herself and co-stared alongside Transgender activist and actor Laith Ashley De La Cruz.

With this song and six others reaching #2 on the charts, Taylor surpassed Madonna, breaking their tie and securing the record for the artist with the most number two hits on the chart. Additionally, Taylor became the first artist to concurrently hold positions in the Top 10 spots of the Hot 100.

Charts & Awards

- Peaked at #2 on the Billboard Hot 100 Charts
- Spent 29 weeks on the chart
- Certified RIAA Platinum
- To date, the track has been streamed 610,446,173 times

In Taylor's Words

"I happened upon the phrase 'lavender haze' when I was watching Mad Men. And I looked it up, because I thought it sounded cool, and it turns out that it's a common phrase used in the 50s where they would just describe being in love. Like, if you were in a lavender haze, that meant that you were in that all-encompassing love glow, and I thought that was really beautiful. And I guess theoretically when you're in the lavender haze, you'll do anything to stay there, and not let people bring you down off of that cloud. And I think a lot of people have to deal with this now, not just quote-unquote 'public figures,' because we live in the era of social media and if the world finds out that you're in love with somebody, they're going to weigh in on it. Like my relationship, for six years we've had to dodge weird rumors, tabloid stuff, and we just ignore it. So this song is about the act of ignoring that stuff to protect the real stuff."

Maroon

Second track on her Tenth Album
Released: October 21, 2022
Recorded: Rough Customer Studios in Brooklyn, NY

Did you know?

Swift Introduced her new album "Midnights" during 13 video episodes titled 'Midnights Mayhem with Me'. Maroon was revealed as the second track on episode five.

"Maroon" was released on October 21, 2022, almost exactly 10 years after "Red"'s debut on October 22, 2012. This synth-pop ballad mirrors the intense emotional exploration found in "Red".

Jack Antonoff and his Bleachers bandmate Evan Smith collectively played all seven instruments featured on the track.

"Maroon" is the most played surprise song of the acoustic set of "The Eras Tour", having been played 3 times in Los Angeles, East Rutherford, and Mexico City.

Charts & Awards

- Peaked at #3 on the Billboard Hot 100 Charts
- Spent 7 weeks on the chart
- Certified RIAA Platinum
- To date, the track has been streamed 395,241,256 times

In Taylor's Words

"Midnights is about all of these nights throughout my life, like things that kept me up, memories you keep going back to. So this one was a memory, just something I wrote about from a long time ago, but it took place in New York."

Anti-Hero

First Single on her Tenth Album
Released: October 21, 2022
Recorded: Rough Customer Studios in Brooklyn, NY

Did you know?

In the second verse, a famous line about a "baby" is actually a reference to a line from Tina Fey's character in the sitcom "30 Rock".

"Anti-Hero" secured Taylor Swift's ninth Hot 100 chart-topper by debuting at the #1 position.

In the music video for the track, Taylor attends her own funeral after being killed by her daughter-in-law. Stand-up Mike Birbiglia and comedian John Early play Swift's sons, alongside Mary Elizabeth Ellis from "It's Always Sunny in Philadelphia" as her daughter-in-law. Two of the ghosts in the video are played by her brother, Austin Swift, and the other by her lawyer.

Taylor Swift performed "Anti-Hero" live for the first time when she made a surprise appearance at The 1975's London O2 concert on January 12, 2023.

Charts & Awards

- Peaked at #1 on the Billboard Hot 100 Charts
- Spent 53 weeks on the chart
- Certified RIAA 6x Platinum
- Won "Top Selling Song" at the Billboard Music Awards In 2023
- Nominated for "International Song of the Year" at the Brit Awards in 2023
- Won "Song of the Year" at the iHeartRadio Music Awards in 2023
- Won 6 MTV VMAs in 2023 for the song
- To date, the track has been streamed 1,295,670,367 times

In Taylor's Words

"'Anti-Hero' is one of my favorite songs I've ever written. I really don't think I've delved this far into my insecurities in this detail before. You know, I struggle a lot with the idea that my life has become unmanagably sized and not to sound too dark, I struggle with the idea of not feeling like a person...This song really is a guided tour throughout all the things I tend to hate about myself. We all hate things about ourselves, and it's all those aspects of the things we dislike and like about ourselves that we have to come to terms with if we are going to be this person. Yeah, I like 'Anti-Hero' a lot because I think it's honest."

Snow On The Beach

Featuring Lana Del Rey
Fourth track on her Tenth Album
Released: October 21, 2022
Recorded: Rough Customer Studios in Brooklyn, NY

Did you know?

Lana Del Rey clarified after fans felt her vocals weren't brought enough to the forefront: "If I think somebody's song is perfect, I will act as a producer in it. I can mimic almost anyone. So I am all over the first version of 'Snow on the Beach,' but I layer and match her vocals perfectly, so you would never even know that I was completely all over that first song. She wanted me to sing the whole thing, but if it ain't broke, don't fix it!"

Swift and Del Rey, along with Jack Antonoff, collaborated on writing "Snow On The Beach." Antonoff, a longstanding collaborator with Swift, also served as a co-producer for Lana Del Rey's album "Chemtrails Over The Country Club."

If you listen closely, you can hear the subtle Christmas-y sleigh bells in the background of the track.

Dylan O'Brien, known for his role in The Maze Runner, plays drums on the song, having formed a close friendship with Swift and Antonoff since being cast by the pop star in her "All Too Well" short film.

Charts & Awards

- Peaked at #4 on the Billboard Hot 100 Charts
- Spent 8 weeks on the chart
- Certified RIAA Platinum
- To date, the track has been streamed 383,642,091 times

In Taylor's Words

"'Snow On The Beach,'' featuring Lana Del Rey, is track 4 on Midnights, and I can not get through that sentence without grinning because I am such a massive fan of Lana Del Rey, more on that later. The song is about falling in love with someone at the same time as they're falling in love with you, in this sort of in this cataclysmic, faded moment where you realize someone feels exactly the same way that you feel, at the same moment, and you're kind of looking around going, "Wait, is this real? Is this a dream? Is this for real? Is it really happening? Kinda like it would be if you were to see snow falling on a beach. And Lana Del Rey is, in my opinion, one of the best musical artists ever, the fact that I get to exist at the same time as her is an honor and a privilege, and the fact that she would be so generous as to collaborate with us on this song is something I'm gonna be grateful for life. Absolutely love her and I really hope you love this song as much as I do."

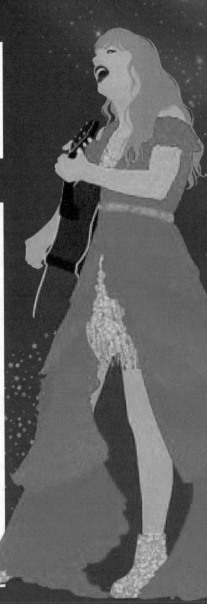

You're On Your Own Kid

Fifth track on her Tenth Album
Released: October 21, 2022
Recorded: Rough Customer Studios in Brooklyn, NY

Did you know?

Stevie Nicks notes this track is her favorite by Taylor, and immensely helped in processing the death of her former bandmate, Christine McVie: "Thank you to Taylor Swift for doing this thing for me, and that is writing a song called 'You're On Your Own, Kid'. That is the sadness of how I feel. As long as Chris was, even on the other side of the world, we didn't have to talk on the phone. We really weren't phone buddies. Then we would go back to Fleetwood Mac, and we would walk in and it would be like, 'Little sister, how are you?' It was like never a minute had passed, never an argument in our entire 47 years. So, when it was the two of us, the two of us were on our own, kids, we always were. And now, I'm having to learn to be on my own, kid, by myself. So, you help me to do that. Thank you."

As Taylor's sings in the lyrics of the bridge, fans at Taylor's "The Eras Tour" turned trading beaded bracelets into a fun activity, showcasing their colorful armfuls on social media.

Before the album was released, she incorporated the title into her New York University commencement speech on May 18, 2022. She said: "Scary news is: You're on your own now. Cool news is: You're on your own now." She was awarded an honorary Doctor of Fine Arts degree at the ceremony.

On April 14, 2023, Swift debuted a live performance of "You're On Your Own, Kid" at Raymond James Stadium in Tampa, Florida.

Charts & Awards

- Peaked at #8 on the Billboard Hot 100 Charts
- Spent 6 weeks on the chart
- Certified RIAA Platinum
- To date, the track has been streamed 469,870,097 times

Midnight Rain

Sixth track on her Tenth Album
Released: October 21, 2022
Recorded: Rough Customer Studios in Brooklyn, NY

Did you know?

Some fans suggest she's referencing her 2016 summer fling with British actor Tom Hiddleston, particularly the viral photos of them joyfully jumping into the ocean during Independence Day celebrations.

The song kicks off with a distorted voice, later joining Swift in a call-and-response during the chorus—surprisingly, it's her own pitched-down voice.

This is the album's sole track with the word "midnight" in the title and also incorporates the record's name in its final lines.

Vulture highlighted "Midnight Rain" as an example of Swift's R&B-infused album, praising its genre reset and potential for innovative directions. Critics also noted similarities in production, particularly vocal manipulation, to Jack Antonoff's work on Lorde's "Melodrama."

Charts & Awards

- Peaked at #5 on the Billboard Hot 100 Charts
- Spent 8 weeks on the chart
- Certified RIAA 2x Platinum
- To date, the track has been streamed 383,642,091 times

In Taylor's Words

"Sometimes sleep is as evasive as happiness. Isn't it mystifying how quickly we vacillate between self love and loathing at this hour? One moment, your life looks like a night sky of gleaming stars. The next, the fog has descended. [...] The boy's devastated face as he peeled out of your driveway. The family man he is now. What must they all think of you?"

Question...?

Seventh track on her Tenth Album
Released: October 21, 2022
Recorded: Rough Customer Studios in Brooklyn, NY

Charts & Awards

- Peaked at #7 on the Billboard Hot 100 Charts
- Spent 5 weeks on the chart
- Certified RIAA Platinum
- To date, the track has been streamed 264,235,225 times

Did you know?

"Question...?" begins with an interpolation from "Out of the Woods," both songs thought to reflect Taylor's relationship with Harry Styles in 2012-2013, though unconfirmed.

In the chorus, the crowd of applause heard was a combination of cheering recorded from Jack Antonoff, Dylan O'Brien, Austin Swift and Antonoff's sister, Rachel.

The last series of questions in the chorus refer back to two songs from "1989": "How You Get The Girl" and "All You Had To Do Was Stay. In "Question...?", Taylor echoes the expression "I remember" at the start, a motif also prominently present in the chorus and bridge of "Out of the Woods."

"Question...?" had its surprise debut on May 20, 2023, during Taylor's "The Eras Tour" in Foxborough, MA.

In Taylor's Words

"Maybe it's that one urgent question you meant to ask someone years ago but didn't. Someone that slipped through the cracks in your history, and they are too far gone now anyway. All the ghost ships that have sailed and sailed away, but at this hour, they've anchored in your harbor. They sit with flags waving, bright and beautiful. And it's almost like it's real."

Vigilante Shit

Eighth track on her Tenth Album
Released: October 21, 2022
Recorded: Rough Customer Studios in Brooklyn, NY

Did you know?

Throughout the track, Swift hints at "dressing for revenge", a term often linked to Princess Diana's stylish response to Prince Charles' affair.

"Vigilante Shit" is the first time Taylor has used profanity in a song title, although she has been using explicit language since her 2017 track "I Did Something Bad."

Charts & Awards

- Peaked at #10 on the Billboard Hot 100 Charts
- Spent 6 weeks on the chart
- Certified RIAA Gold
- To date, the track has been streamed 329,840,406 times

In Taylor's Words

The song has a tempo of 80 BPM, on the shorter end for the range of Taylor's songs; It is also the shortest song on the standard edition of "Midnights" at 2 minutes and 44 seconds.

The song is the only track on "Midnights" that Taylor wrote completely alone.

"Why are you still up at this hour? Because you're cosplaying vengeance fantasies, where the bad bad man is hauled away in handcuffs and you get to watch it happen. You laugh into the mirror with a red wine snarl. You look positively deranged."

Bejeweled

Ninth track on her Tenth Album
Released: October 21, 2022
Recorded: Rough Customer Studios in Brooklyn, NY

Did you know?

Taylor also says of the track: "'Bejeweled' is a song that I think it's really about finding confidence when you feel that it's been taken away, for whatever reason, You know, you're feeling insecure, you're feeling taken for granted... One of the things we love to do at night, 'cause we love to go dancing, we love to put on an outfit that makes us feel good, and we love to feel like we're still bejeweled."

In "Bejeweled," Swift revisits the upbeat pop vibe of her 2010s albums, departing from the folk sound of Folklore and Evermore and mirroring her return to pop music.

Charts & Awards

- Peaked at #6 on the Billboard Hot 100 Charts
- Spent 9 weeks on the chart
- Won "TikTok Bop of the Year" at the iHeartRadio Music Awards in 2023
- Nominated for "Favorite Song" at the Nickelodeon Kids' Choice Awards in 2023
- Certified RIAA Platinum
- To date, the track has been streamed 435,473,291 times

In Taylor's Words

"Some midnights, you're out and you're buzzing with electric current — an adventurer in pursuit of rapturous thrill. Music blaring from speakers and the reckless intimacy of dancing with strangers. Something in this shadowy room to make you feel shiny again. On these nights, you know that there are facets of you that only glow in the dark."

Swift wrote and directed a Cinderella-inspired video featuring a comic take on the fairy tale. Swift stars as "House Wench," with Laura Dern as the Stepmommy, the Haim sisters as stepsisters, Dita Von Teese as the fairy goddess, Pat McGrath as "Queen Pat," and Jack Antonoff as Prince Charming. The end of the video features the instrumental version of "Enchanted" and "Long Live", at the time serving as a foreshadowing to the release of "Speak Now (Taylor's Version)."

Labyrinth

Tenth track on her Tenth Album
Released: October 21, 2022
Recorded: Rough Customer Studios in Brooklyn, NY

Did you know?

November 9, 2023, marked the debut of Swift's live performance of "Labyrinth." She delivered a piano rendition during the Buenos Aires concert as part of "The Eras Tour".

SImilar to "You're On Your Own Kid", Taylor teased lyrics in the first verse of the song in her commencement speech at New York University.

Taylor wrote and produced the song with Jack Antonoff, who plays five instruments on the track. Antonoff co-wrote 11 out of the album's 13 tracks and co-produced all 13 of the standard version.

Swift Introduced her new album "Midnights" during 13 video episodes titled 'Midnights Mayhem with Me'. "Labyrinth" was revealed as the tenth track on episode eleven.

Charts & Awards

- Peaked at #14 on the Billboard Hot 100 Charts
- Spent 5 weeks on the chart
- Certified RIAA Gold
- To date, the track has been streamed 230,482,914 times

In Taylor's Words

"Why can't you sleep? Maybe you lie awake in the aftershock of falling headlong into a connection that feels like some surreal cataclysmic event. Like spontaneous combustion. [...] Maybe you were trying to mastermind matters of the heart again. You've gotten lost in the labyrinth of your head, where the fear wraps its claws around the fragile throat of true love. Will you be able to save it in time? Save it from who? Well, it obvious. From you."

Karma

Third Single on her Tenth Album
Released as a single: May 1, 2023
Recorded: Rough Customer Studios in Brooklyn, NY

Did you know?

"Karma" took shape when Jack Antonoff approached co-producer Mark Anthony Spears (Sounwave) for additional ideas to contribute to the album's synth-pop vibe. Spears says: "'Karma' was just a last-minute Hail Mary. I remembered I was working with my guy Keanu and had something that was too perfect not to send to her. As soon as I sent it, Jack was instantly like, 'This is the one. Playing it for Taylor now. We're going in on it.' The next day, I heard the final product with her vocals on it."

On May 26, 2023, a remix with Ice Spice was launched as part of the extended version of "Midnights" known as "Midnights (The Till Dawn Edition)". Taylor has collaborated with four other rappers in the past Including B.o.B, Future, Kendrick Lamar, and Nicki Minaj.

During Swift's 2023 Eras Tour, "Karma" served as the grand finale, concluding the show with fireworks, visuals, and confetti.

Charts & Awards

- Peaked at #2 on the Billboard Hot 100 Charts
- Spent 30 weeks on the chart
- Certified RIAA Platinum
- Nominated for "Song of the Summer" at the MTV Video Music Awards in 2023
- To date, the track has been streamed 610,256,234 times

In Taylor's Words

"So one of the themes about Midnights is how you're feeling in the middle of the night. And that can be intense self-hatred, you go through these very polarizing emotions when you're up late at night and you're brain just spirals, it can spiral downward or it can spiral way up and you can just be really feeling yourself. 'Karma' is written from a perspective of feeling like really happy, really proud of the way your life is, feeling like this must be a reward for doing stuff right. And it's a song that I really love because I think we all need some of those moments. You know, we can't just be beating ourselves up all the time. You have to have these moments where you're like, 'You know what, karma is my boyfriend and that's it.'"

Sweet Nothing

Twelfth track on her Tenth Album
Released October 21, 2022
Recorded: Rough Customer Studios in Brooklyn, NY

Did you know?

It is speculated that the track is about former actor partner, Joe Alwyn, as he was filming in Wicklow, Ireland for the TV series "Conversations With Friends." Joe is credited under his pseudonym as a writer on the track.

Interestingly, the song's lyrics also could correspond to a story Paul McCartney, a Beatles member and Taylor's friend, shared in a 2001 ABC interview about his wife Linda. Paul notes, "I would go out for a run, think of some words, get home from the run, write them down, and make a cup a tea for Linda. I'd make a little tray, and go up, and then I'd say, 'Hey, by the way, do you want to hear some poetry?' She'd always say, 'Yeah.' And having listened, she would say 'What a mind.' Though the lines may not have been supreme, she wasn't merely being kind."

The McCartney family also vacationed in Wicklow, Ireland, in the summer of 1971 as a retreat from The Beatles' breakup aftermath. Taylor mentions the Irish town in the first verse.

Charts & Awards

- Peaked at #15 on the Billboard Hot 100 Charts
- Spent 5 weeks on the chart
- Certified RIAA Gold
- To date, the track has been streamed 233,779,009 times

Mastermind

Thirteenth track on her Tenth Album
Released October 21, 2022
Recorded: Rough Customer Studios in Brooklyn, NY

Did you know?

Taylor also says of the track: "'Mastermind' is a song that I put last on the album because I'm really proud of it. I love that when we were making the song, we wanted the verse to sound like romance and sort of a Heroes type of soundtrack. And then we wanted the chorus to sound like a villain has just entered the room. The idea that you're flipping this narrative and you have been planning and plotting things and making them look like an accident. I think that's sort of an inside joke between me and my fans: that I tend to do that. And so, this song is the romantic version of that."

Swift Introduced her new album "Midnights" during 13 video episodes titled 'Midnights Mayhem with Me'. "Mastermind" was revealed on episode one.

In a 2023 interview, Swift disclosed that her inspiration for the song stemmed from watching the 2017 film "Phantom Thread."

In the first line of the song, Taylor makes a reference to a classic shakespeare motif of "star-crossed lovers"; many speculate this could be a call back to the first time she references a shakespearean convention in "Love Story".

Charts & Awards

- Peaked at #13 on the Billboard Hot 100 Charts
- Spent 5 weeks on the chart
- Certified RIAA Platinum
- To date, the track has been streamed 283,679,247 times

In Taylor's Words

"Remember that last scene? I thought, wouldn't it be fun to have a lyric about being calculated? It's something that's been thrown at me like a dagger, but now I take it as a compliment."

The Great War

First Bonus track on her Tenth Album
Released October 21, 2022
Recorded: Long Pond Studios in Hudson, NY

Did you know?

Taylor describes her lover placing a poppy in her hair in the 3rd verse. The red poppy, growing abundantly on the Western Front during World War I, has become a symbol of remembrance. Western countries often use poppies on or before Remembrance Day each year to honor the significance of the occasion.

Swift co-wrote and co-produced "The Great War" with Aaron Dessner, along with two other tracks on "Midnights" - "High Infidelity" and "Would've, Could've, Should've."

In Tampa, Florida, on April 14, 2023, Aaron Dessner joined Swift onstage for the live premiere of "The Great War."

Aaron Dessner says of his collaboration on "Midnights": "Eventually she obviously made most of Midnights with Jack and it became something different, but we made 'Would've, Could've, Should've, 'High Infidelity', 'The Great War' and 'Hits Different' together. And it was great to be a part of that record in that way. It was really special."

Charts & Awards

- Peaked at #26 on the Billboard Hot 100 Charts
- Spent 4 weeks on the chart
- Certified RIAA Gold
- To date, the track has been streamed 236,632,384 times

Bigger Than The Whole Sky

Second Bonus track on her Tenth Album
Released October 21, 2022
Recorded: Rough Customer Studios in Brooklyn, NY

Did you know?

On November 19, 2023, during "The Eras Tour" in Rio de Janeiro, Taylor paid tribute to fan Ana Clara Benevides, who had passed away two days earlier, by performing an acoustic rendition of "Bigger Than The Whole Sky" on the piano. Ana Clara had fainted at Taylor's show and tragically succumbed, possibly due to a cardiac arrest in the city's heatwave.

The song features ambiguous lyrics conveying sorrow and heartbreak for a person the narrator has never encountered, causing some critics and listeners to speculate that the song revolves around the theme of miscarriage.

The chord progression for the song Is F sharp-C sharp-G sharp minor-B major. This progression is very similar to huge hits like "You Belong With Me" and "Shake It Off", with just 1 chord in reverse order.

Swift co-wrote and co-produced the track with Jack Antonoff, who plays synthesizer, piano, slide guitar, electric guitar, acoustic guitar, and bass on the track.

Charts & Awards

- Peaked at #21 on the Billboard Hot 100 Charts
- Spent 4 weeks on the chart
- Certified RIAA Gold
- To date, the track has been streamed 153,441,151 times

Paris

Third Bonus track on her Tenth Album
Released October 21, 2022
Recorded: Rough Customer Studios in Brooklyn, NY

Charts & Awards

- Peaked at #32 on the Billboard Hot 100 Charts
- Spent 3 weeks on the chart
- Certified RIAA Gold
- To date, the track has been streamed 156,347,750 times

Did you know?

On September 9, 2019, she held a "City of Lover" concert at the Olympia theater in Paris, shortly after releasing her romantic album "Lover," with Joe Alwyn by her side in the French capital.

"Paris" is the third song by Taylor Swift with a city in its title, joining the likes of "Welcome to New York" from "1989" and "London Boy" from the "Lover" album.

Mikey Hart, handling synthesizer, organ, and theremin, and Evan Smith, contributing synthesizer and percussion for the track, are both members of Jack Antonoff's rock project Bleachers.

High Infidelity

Fourth Bonus track on her Tenth Album
Released October 21, 2022
Recorded: Long Pond Studios in Hudson, NY

Did you know?

Taylor premiered "High Infidelity" as the first surprise song in Atlanta on April 29, 2023, during The Eras Tour. Taylor noted during her live performance that she may perform a song again if she messes up; this song may be performed again due to an error in the second verse. Taylor chose the song for the show on April 29th, corresponding to a famous line in the song.

Co-writer Aaron Dessner revealed that "High Infidelity" was crafted in March 2021 during his stay at Taylor's Los Angeles home before the Grammy Awards, where they later won "Album of the Year" for "folklore."

Taylor delves into the complexities of cheating and infidelity, a theme also explored in tracks like "illicit affairs," "august," "betty," "no body, no crime," and "ivy."

Charts & Awards

- Peaked at #33 on the Billboard Hot 100 Charts
- Spent 3 weeks on the chart
- Certified RIAA Gold
- To date, the track has been streamed 131,303,266 times

Glitch

Fifth Bonus track on her Tenth Album
Released October 21, 2022
Recorded: Rough Customer Studios in Brooklyn, NY

Did you know?

"Glitch" contemplates a relationship that initially began as a friendship, casually transitioned into a friends-with-benefits dynamic, and unexpectedly transformed into a genuine romance—so improbable that it seemed like a glitch.

It is speculated that Taylor wrote "Glitch" about her relationship with Joe Alwyn. In the summer of 2016, Swift and Alwyn had their first outing. "Glitch" was likely written in the summer of 2022, exactly 2,190 days, or six years, later.

Swift co-wrote "Glitch" with Jack Antonoff, Sounwave, and Sam Dew during the same studio session that produced "Lavender Haze."

Co-writer and producer, Sounwave, says of the track: ""Not to toot my own horn, but I like the weirdness of 'Glitch'. The breakdown part is everything it was meant to be. This is so amazing to me." Sounwave is best known for his collaborations in production with Kendrick Lamar.

Charts & Awards

- Peaked at #41 on the Billboard Hot 100 Charts
- Spent 2 weeks on the chart
- Certified RIAA Gold
- To date, the track has been streamed 104,546,806 times

Would've Could've Should've

Sixth Bonus track on her Tenth Album
Released October 21, 2022
Recorded: Long Pond Studios in Hudson, NY

Did you know?

Taylor so-produced the song with Aaron Dessner. He says of the song: "I think the best song we've ever written is called 'Would've, Could've, Should've'. We wrote that song together, and recorded it, while we were together in LA for the folklore Grammys. So it goes back that far. And the same goes for 'High Infidelity'. Those songs we actually recorded in her house then. And eventually she obviously made most of Midnights with Jack and it became something different, but we made 'Would've, Could've, Should've', 'High Infidelity', 'The Great War' and 'Hits Different' together. And it was great to be a part of that record in that way. It was really special."

The song is widely speculated to center around Taylor's relationship with John Mayer in 2009 when she was nineteen, and he was 32. Serving as a poignant follow-up to "Dear John," the track explores the heartbreak associated with their connection.

The lyrics, particularly referring to stained glass and other religious imagery in the song, are connected to Mayer's former residence in New York—an apartment that once served as a church, complete with stained glass windows.

Charts & Awards

- Peaked at #20 on the Billboard Hot 100 Charts
- Spent 4 weeks on the chart
- Certified RIAA Platinum
- To date, the track has been streamed 225,333,031 times

Dear Reader

Seventh Bonus track on her Tenth Album
Released October 21, 2022
Recorded: Rough Customer Studios in Brooklyn, NY

Did you know?

The song is presented from the viewpoint of an advice columnist, with Taylor endeavoring to offer life guidance to the listener or reader. She starts the track by giving several pieces of advice, but then quickly advises against following her advice because even she hasn't figured it all out yet. Even further, the lyrics seem to suggest that her advice could directly cause the reader harm.

Taylor notes that "self loathing" is a major theme of the album "Midnights." Although that theme is also explored in songs like "Anti-Hero", this particular track is a more subtle commentary.

Taylor revealed in September 2022, that in writing each of her songs, they fall Into 3 distinct categories: "Fountain Pen", "Quill Pen" or "Glitter Gel Pen". Taylor notes: "I came up with these categories based on what writing tool I imagine having in my hand when I scribbled it down, figuratively." This song Is thought to be categorized as a "Quill Pen" song which include delicate and/or antiquated lyrics with structure inspired by Old English poetry.

Rolling stone notes, "'Reader, I married him' is one of the most famous lines in 19th century novels, from Charlotte Bronte's Jane Eyre, so "Dear Reader" is a suitable flex for Quill Pen Taylor."

Charts & Awards

- Peaked at #45 on the Billboard Hot 100 Charts
- Spent 2 weeks on the chart
- Certified RIAA Platinum
- To date, the track has been streamed 106,344,153 times

Made in United States
Troutdale, OR
03/08/2024

18294113R00117